Long Engagements

Long Engagements

MATURITY IN MODERN JAPAN

David W. Plath

STANFORD UNIVERSITY PRESS
STANFORD, CALIFORNIA

Stanford University Press
Stanford, California
© 1980 by the Board of Trustees of the
Leland Stanford Junior University
Printed in the United States of America
Cloth ISBN 0-8047-1054-6
Paper ISBN 0-8047-1176-3

Original edition 1980
Last figure below indicates year of this printing:
92   91   90   89   88   87   86   85   84   83

Acknowledgments

Seven years have gone into the making of this book. It has been a long engagement with ideas, with materials, and with people who have helped me focus my thinking and curb my mannered writing. Such persons are many in number; all have my gratitude, but I must mention a few who deserve special thanks.

An ethnographer's greatest debt is always to those who have allowed him to peer into their lives. For this I thank 23 people who must remain pseudonymous: the Hanshin men and women who accepted the burden of being interviewed, and who so patiently responded to questions that must often have seemed to them outlandish.

Financial support for my year of study in the Hanshin in 1972–73 came in the form of sabbatical leave from the University of Illinois at Urbana-Champaign, and of a fellowship from the John Simon Guggenheim Memorial Foundation. The University of Illinois Research Board and its Center for Asian Studies supplied me with research expense money during the field year, and have given me funds to hire an assistant twice in the years since.

Professor Masuda Kōkichi and his staff in the Department of Sociology, Kōnan University, Kobe, provided me with a base of operations in the Hanshin. They aided me in numerous ways, not the least being those very crucial personal introductions to the people whom I eventually interviewed. Other colleagues who were particularly helpful during the field phase of the study include Ishige Naomichi, Sugiyama Sadao, Umesao Tadao, Wagatsuma Hiroshi, and Yoneyama Toshinao.

Ikeda Keiko, my chief assistant in the field, was a superlative interviewer; she deserves most of the credit for the quality of the materials from which I put together the life histories that appear in Chapters 3–6.

Portions of this book derive from essays, lectures, and conference papers that I have written during the past six years. I have also discussed some of these materials with an array of classes, seminars, and colloquia in my own and other universities. The result is that so many people have commented upon parts of the work that I could not hope to list them all. However, I want to offer special thanks to four persons who critiqued the entire manuscript in one or another of its several drafts: L. Keith Brown, Philip Lilienthal, Lyn L. Plath, and Thomas Rohlen.

Parts of Chapter 3 first appeared in different form as an essay, "Bourbon in the Tea: Dilemmas of an Aging *Senzenha*," in *The Japan Interpreter* II, 3 (1977), 362–83.

I first offered the gist of section IV of Chapter 4, in "The Last Confucian Sandwich: Becoming Middle-Aged," in the *Journal of Asian and African Studies* 10, 1–2 (1975), 51–63. Versions of the same material were also given at the 1973 annual meeting of the American Anthropological Association and at the May 1974 meeting of the Midwest Japan Seminar.

Most of the ideas in Chapter 5 were first presented in an essay, "Cycles, Circles and Selves: Consociation in the Japanese City," written for the Workshop on the Japanese City, Mt. Kisco, New York, April 1976. The section on *The Makioka Sisters* was also given at colloquia at the University of Illinois at Chicago Circle in May 1977, and at the University of Pittsburgh in April 1979. The section on Goryōhan's life was presented first at the Triangle East Asia Colloquium, Chapel Hill, North Carolina, in April 1978. Goryōhan's narrative also served as the basis for three other papers, given to the Mita Tetsugakkai, Keiō University, November 1976; to the Midwest Conference on Asian Affairs in October 1977; and to the 1977 annual meeting of the American Anthropological Association.

Section I of Chapter 6 derives from an analysis of the book *A Man in Ecstasy*, which appeared as "Cares of Career, and Careers of Caretaking," in *Journal of Nervous and Mental Disease* 157, 5 (1973), 346–57.

Perhaps I should also say a word in behalf of my university's Center for Advanced Study. When I returned from Japan in 1973 I asked for a semester's appointment in the Center, so that I could give full time to the writing of this book at once, while my impressions of the Hanshin and of my interviewees were still fresh. In its wisdom the Center rejected my request. So instead of the six months that I had projected for the task, I ended up needing six years to finish the writing. I have a hunch that the book may have aged and mellowed because of it all.

Contents

Long Engagements

How very extraordinary it was, this being middle-aged, being the person who ran and managed and kept going. . . . It was as if more than ever one was forced back into that place in oneself where one watched; whereas all around the silent watcher were a series of defences, or subsidiary creatures, on guard, always working, engaged with—and this was the point—earlier versions of oneself.

DORIS LESSING, *The Four-Gated City*

CHAPTER I

The Rhetoric of Maturity

The drama of life seems to develop like a dialectical play between the initial one-sided starting position of ego-orientation—that which we find we "are" when we have come to the first awareness of ourselves—and the later opposing claims of the Self which pull in a new direction with the demand that we become what we are "meant to be."

EDWARD WHITMONT, *The Symbolic Quest*

The gift of mass longevity seems as unsettling to people in our day as the gift of mass productivity was to people a century ago. Mass productivity raised hopes that material want might at last be overcome. It also brought fears that many would be forever alienated from the output of their own labors. Mass longevity raises hopes that everyone born human may enjoy a full span of years on this earth. It also brings fears that many will be ultimately alienated from their own experience, barred from employing it in the social marketplace.

The nineteenth century had to ask itself: if most people must work for pay, in an industrial order, what then is the value of human labor? Today we must begin to ask: if most people will live into adulthood, and many into advanced age, in a post-industrial world, what then is the value of human maturity? If the essential cultural nightmare of the nineteenth century was to be in poverty, perhaps ours is to be old and alone or afflicted with terminal disease.

Mass longevity is transforming the social framework of the life course, as mass productivity transformed the social framework of work and property. With work redefined as paid activity, personal maturity comes to be defined in terms of access to "gainful employment." But employment more and more is controlled by the state or by large enterprises, both of which enforce arbitrary, categorical rules for entry into and exit from employment. Youths, older adults, and women in general may find themselves unemployable—shut out not only from the material rewards but also from the moral stature that is conferred upon those who are at paid work. The post-industrial world, as some foresee it, may bring a new era of class struggle—pitting age-class against age-class in disputes over the right to participate in those activities and institutions that validate one's human maturity.

Mass longevity is transforming the arenas of personal life as well as those of public life. The traditional cycle of roles is being stretched out, so to speak, at least two decades longer than was typical for our great-great-grandparents. Customary distinctions between life's stages are attenuated, and what it means to "grow" or to "age" becomes unclear at all points along the way. The meaning of age—of *when* we are at some way station along life's trajectory—comes into question in our everyday activities. It comes into question as well in those moments when we privately reflect upon who we are, where we may be going, and whether we are continuing to grow or are only growing older.

Mass longevity means co-longevity. Not only does the average person live longer, so too do those around him. He and they will travel the life course together a greater distance. Thus nuclear households may be on the increase in post-industrial nations, but so too are four-generation families, whether or not they happen to live under the same roof. A century ago the average person could anticipate that by the time he was old enough to marry, at least one of his parents would have died. Today the chances are great that both parents will live to witness his wedding—and possibly his retirement ceremony as well.

Consider the orphan: much less visible today, but a prominent figure in fact and fiction in the nineteenth-century West. Orphanages, once a flourishing enterprise, are beginning to close their doors—to be replaced by a clamoring, by a few of the childless, for the fewer homeless children. And at the other end of the life course, older age is coming more and more to be a matter of older womanhood, of widowhood. Before the industrial revolution the male/female ratio in older age appears to have been nearly equal; now older women are in a clear and increasing majority.

In short, in post-industrial nations a new pattern of constraints and opportunities is shaping the entire course of life for persons as they go along enacting their allotted span of years. The situation calls for a fresh look at the biographical timelines of human maturation, for the mature person is one of the most remarkable products that any society can bring forth. He or she is a living cathedral, the handiwork of many individuals over many years. No single Rubicon divides those who are mature from those who are not. To know if we are mature we must convince people— ourselves included—that we embody the right history of personal experience. And to gain this history the self must enter into long engagements with the cultural symbols that identify experience, and with others in society who guard the meaning of the symbols. Rhetoric is the social art of such identifications, and in these chapters I explore the rhetoric of maturity as it is carried on in modern Japan.

The Japanese Experience

The mental purchase that we already hold upon the meanings of maturity in post-industrial societies has been gained through the scrutiny of humankind in the West. My own intellectual debt to Western scholars will be obvious to anyone familiar with the work of Erik Erikson, or that of Bernice Neugarten or Robert White, to name only three. Japan, however, has come into its post-industrial era in its own way. The demographic transition has taken place more swiftly there than in the West: it has come within the lifetime of the post-World War II generation. Since 1950 Japan has earned world acclaim for her "miraculous" rate of economic growth. What is less widely known is that in these years Japan's rising rate of longevity has also set a world pace: average life-expectancy at birth is now higher in Japan than in the United States, and rivals that in northern Europe.

So like us in technology, so near in the shape of her major political and social institutions; yet Japan remains culturally distant. The gulf is particularly wide in the arenas of personal conduct. A century of struggle with industrial technics and with democratic institutions has, to be sure, brought change: the Japanese have—depending on your perspective—either "borrowed from" or "converged upon" Western or modern versions of what it is to be most human in our century. But Japanese continue to draw sustenance from a heritage of idioms of the self and social relations that retains its distinct configuration.

Two clusters of idioms are especially relevant. One has to do with the nature of the self and how it is to be cultivated, the other with the properties of social ties. Westerners often take the view that the Japanese are collectivistic whereas we are individualistic, and see the Japanese as peculiarly attuned to hierarchy or seniority in social relations where we are said to favor equality. Like all stereotypes these contain some elements of truth, but they can also drastically distort our understanding of the tempo and tenor of ordinary lives.

Arguing from such stereotypes Western observers have been tempted to conclude that Japanese as persons are able more simply and comfortably than we are to submit to the changes wrought upon them by aging. This might have been true in some era in the peasant past—though I am skeptical. Mass longevity has shaken any such framework of life-cycle security. Furthermore the stereotypes may, however unintentionally, amount to an ethnic snub. For the person who is "dependent," whose self is "submerged," who has "weak and permeable ego boundaries" —phrases applied to the Japanese—is by Western measures immature. He can scarcely be acknowledged to be "his own man," gliding about with Emersonian self-reliance. Such images fail to take account of the expanding awareness of the world and the self, the ripening capacity to care for others in their terms, the increasing ability to apply one's own experience, that are hallmarks of the mature person in Japan as elsewhere.

If I can show how such properties of the mature individual emerge, as Japanese build their biographies, then perhaps we can begin to redress the misleading images. If we can redress the images, then perhaps we can begin to see how widespread the dislocation is between life course and life cycle in *all* post-industrial societies. And if we can grasp the magnitude of that dislocation, then perhaps we will begin to understand why mass longevity seems so unsettling.

Limits to Growth

Growth as a biological event can be described in terms of trends and stages within an organism. But growth as a human event is cultural as well as biological. It must be described in terms of a mutual building of biographies, a collective shaping and self-shaping of lives according to a heritage of values. To comprehend it we must keep the human animal in focus both as an *individual*, a separate center of initiative and integrity, and as a *person*, a moral actor in society's dramas. There is no question that we are marvelously malleable beings. The questions arise over the extent to which we can retain our adaptability in adulthood and can sustain growth humanly despite biological stasis or decline.

In East Asia the heritage of possibilism—the idea that we can go on improving with age—can be found expressed as early in history as Confucius. In the *Analects* the master says, "At 15 I thought only of study; at 30 I began playing my role; at 40 I was sure of myself; at 50 I was conscious of my position in the universe; at 60 I was no longer argumentative; and now at 70 I can follow my heart's desire without violating custom."

Modern students of human development in the West echo this point of view in their own phrasings. Erikson, for example, cites "generativity" and "integrity" as two chief strengths that emerge only during adulthood. Robert White, sketching trends of "natural" growth during early adulthood, refers to a "stabilizing of ego identity," a "freeing of personal relationships," and an "expansion of caring." Bernice Neugarten, in one of her essays on middle age, emphasizes "the central importance of what might be called the executive processes of personality: self-awareness, selectivity, manipulation and control of the environment, mastery, competence, the wide array of cognitive strategies." And in another essay she remarks that conduct in maturity is a matter of "conscious self-utilization rather than the self-consciousness of youth."

Adult Japanese, when I ask them how they have changed since their youth years, often respond with the word *atsukamashisa*, which can be glossed as "boldness" or "nerve." It does not imply bravado: rather that one has established one's ability to judge people and situations, and knows how to deal with them so as to obtain results. One continues to care about what others are thinking, and about the Oughts of morality; but one no longer feels driven by them.

To say this is not to claim that time inevitably brings growth in its train. The processes of human maturation, like all biological and social processes, seem to be legislated by a parliament of prodigals: there can be immense pain and waste; tragedy and future-shock can overcome anybody; growth must always be seen in the context of a discouraging potential for regress. Nevertheless, given time enough and health we do appear to have the potential to continue growing as persons indefinitely.

Like all human phenomena, growth is the child of circumstance, nurtured by opportunity and constraint. Whether there are absolute limits to personal growth—so long as vitality proceeds—remains a mystery. The most that modern social theory is able to do is to indicate orders of constraints that operate upon maturity and aging. Three such orders have had particular attention in twentieth-century thinking: the cultural, the individual, and the social. For each of these orders a vocabulary of analytic concepts has been coined. And as is true of any theory, each of the vocabularies can serve us well by illuminating one aspect of the phenomenon—at the cost of obscuring other aspects. Whether or not there are limits to personal growth, there are limits to what we are able, with our present philosophy, to explain about personal growth.

Culture in one of its anthropological usages can be thought of as a legacy of idioms and values that give point and purpose to living, a collection of recipes for human cultivation. During our early years in this world we become enculturated—infused and informed with the timetables for growth that are standard for our generation and locale. Later, in adulthood, we adjust our unique historical thrust to these normalizing careers that make up the life cycle. There is an open-ended quality to the view: we are presumed capable of continuing to learn new role after new role so long as we are not—to use the current euphemism—developmentally disabled.

But the vocabulary of culture has difficulty accounting for growth that may occur despite, or even in playful opposition to, the standard roles and careers. And it tends to overstate the amount of personal discontinuity from one role to the next, from one stage of life to the next. It does not see how the human life course can be, in Robert Redfield's phrase, "a succession of added comprehensions." People can continue to grow, says the cultural view, but only to the extent that their culture provides forms in which to realize that growth.

The idea of *character* has to do with one's distinctive features as a person, the mark of individuality made by nature and nurture. Often, too, it connotes the kind of moral vigor acquired by self-discipline. Culturally defined roles and timetables are categorical. They offer only general instructions about how to become a certain type of person—a poet or a pensioner, for example. We must interpret their import for our unique situation and course of conduct. We are born with the potential for becoming a hundred different kinds of person, for following a thousand possible careers. But we realize, after all, only one obituary. To become human is to become particular and to know it. In the existentialist phrase, each of us must live the meaning of his own life.

The psychodynamic vocabulary of character sees the individual as propelled through life by inner drives that must be realized in practice or rationalized in fantasy. Character as an organization of these drives is thought to unfold in a more or less regular sequence of stages, at least up through puberty. After that the psychodynamic view is unclear about whether the earlier stages of character can be outgrown.

Classical psychoanalysis held that we grow only to the stage of "genital maturity," and after that are likely to stagnate or decline, playing out the primal scenes of our infancy upon persons encountered in adulthood. Freud is alleged to have said that psychoanalysis would be wasted on anyone over 45. At the very least, significant character change in adulthood was thought improbable. Later theorists—Sullivan, Erikson, Lidz—allow for considerable changes during maturity in patterns of identity, if not, perhaps, in basic personality. People may continue to grow, says the psychodynamic view, but only to the extent that they can be liberated from childhood traumata.

We do not apply the cultural codes to ourselves in isolation; other people interpret them for us as well. Character and growth are shaped by the rest of society. The psychodynamic vocabulary grants other people the power to influence our character but tends, uncertainly, to see that power operating mainly in childhood. The interactionist vocabulary in social psychology, by contrast, regards the human self as always open to major reform. The interactionist self is a kind of blossom that appears in social relations. As reflexive (self-aware) beings we must constantly integrate our subjective and objective sides, reconcile the "I" and the "me." We do not become actualized as persons simply by playing a role or cathecting a drive; what we are doing must be recognized or validated by others. People can continue to grow, says the interactionist view, but only to the extent that others allow or confirm that growth.

Growth then becomes in part a property of others, particularly of those who are one's *consociates*. The term may be an unfamiliar one, but it is apt here. It derives from the work of Alfred Schutz and the phenomenologists. If "associates" are persons you happen to encounter somewhere, sometime, "consociates" are people you relate with across time and in some degree of intimacy. They are friends, lovers, kinsmen, colleagues, classmates. Figuratively speaking, they are empaneled as a special jury to examine and confirm the course of your being and becoming. Your biography would make little sense if it does not mention them. Consociates thus are at once our primary social resource and restraint. We grow on each other.

Culture, character, and consociates weave a complicated fabric of biography. The process is not only lifelong; it is longer than life. Consociates begin to shape our personal course even before we are born, and may continue to renegotiate the meaning of our life long after we are dead. To this extent, a person is a collective product. We all must "author" our own biographies, using the idioms of our heritage, but our biographies must be "authorized" by those who live them with us.

The Problem of Time Depth

In its elementary forms the rhetoric of maturity is much the same as any dynamic of human identification and persuasion. But it works across broad as well as brief intervals of time. And time depth complicates the problems of analysis. In the life-history chapters that make up the bulk of the book (Chapters 3 through 6) we shall watch the rhetoric in its workings across spans of more than a quarter-century—though the rhetoric operates in short compass as well as long.

Analytically we might think of a rhetorical "event" as consisting of three operations. Let us call them identification, justification, and projection. A person has to be timed along his or her life course, identified in terms of one of the standard cultural timetables for maturity and aging. He or she may initiate the claim; others may seek to impose it. Either way, self and consociates must reach an agreement on the matter. In the process of doing so they must justify the identification, offer culturally valid reasons for it. Once they are in agreement on the identification, self and others use it as a basis for projecting their mutual futures.

Grandparenthood, for example, is a very ordinary and expectable part of middle adulthood. But many people greet it with mixed feelings. Grandchildren can be a pleasure, but to be a grandparent is to be placed inexorably among the old of the earth. One of my Japanese interviewees is a woman in her mid-fifties, outgoing and socially active as the wife of the vice-president of a major national business firm. When her first grandchild was born she rejected being categorized as a grandmother. For some days she told friends and family, "Call me anything but that. Call me by my personal name. Call me Elder Sister. But don't you dare call me Granny." Not surprisingly, her consociates refused to comply. Her child had given birth to a child—a compelling enough reason to reclassify her. She had to capitulate, and begin acting as a grandmother ought.

Granny's rhetorical event covered an interval of only a few days; the time dimension was muted. But even in what seem to be momentary events, our actions can be informed by our awareness of the longer engagements between our life cycle and the life cycles of those around us. A second example may make this clearer, an example that not only spans a longer period but also brings out the importance of *time consciousness* in the rhetoric of maturity.

The episode is taken from one of the foremost modern Japanese novels, Tanizaki Jun'ichirō's *Sasameyuki*. The English translation was given the title *The Makioka Sisters*, perhaps to invite comparisons with landmarks of world literature such as *The Brothers Karamazov*. The English title in any case fails to convey the nuances of the original title. To be sure, the book is the story of all four daughters of the Makioka house—we shall meet them again in a later chapter. But the central story line has to do with finding a husband for the third daughter, Yukiko ("Snow"). The phrase *sasameyuki* is old poetic diction for "a delicate snowfall." In order to enjoy the beauty of such a scene, one must refrain from trampling down the delicate Snow.

The Makiokas have been an old-line merchant house of downtown Osaka, but ever since the death of the girls' parents the family wealth and prestige have been slipping. The two oldest daughters, Tsuruko and Sachiko, have been married for more than a decade, as the story opens. The youngest daughter, Taeko, has found a suitor whom she is eager to wed; she even threatens to elope. For Yukiko, however, the outlook remains cloudy. Her 30th birthday has passed and she is in danger of superannuation in the marriage market. The family continues to negotiate with candidates for her; but as each negotiation fails, she and the family must reevaluate her prospects. Early in the novel Tanizaki describes one such incident:

It was nonetheless out of the question to have the younger sister marry first, and since a match for Taeko was as good as arranged, it became more urgent than ever to find a husband for Yukiko. In addition to the complications we have already described, however, yet another fact operated to Yukiko's disadvantage: she had been born in a bad year. In Tokyo the Year of the Horse is sometimes unlucky for women. In Osaka, on the other hand, it is the Year of the Ram that keeps a girl from finding a husband. Especially in the old Osaka merchant class, men fear taking a bride from the Year of the Ram. "Do not let the woman of the Year of the Ram stand in your door," says the Osaka proverb. The superstition is a deep-rooted one in Osaka, so strongly colored by the merchant and his beliefs, and Tsuruko liked to say that the Year of the Ram was really responsible for poor Yukiko's failure to find a husband. Everything considered, then, the people in the main house, too, had concluded that it would be senseless to cling to their high standards. At first they said that, since it was Yukiko's first marriage, it must also be the man's first marriage; presently they concluded that a man who had been married once would be acceptable if he had no children, and then that there should be no more than two children, and even that he might be a year or two older than Teinosuke, Sachiko's husband, provided he looked younger.

Yukiko herself said that she would marry anyone her brothers-in-law and sisters agreed upon. She therefore had no particular objection to these revised standards, although she did say that if the man had children she hoped they would be pretty little girls. She thought she could really become fond of little stepdaughters. She added that if the man were in his forties, the climax of his career would be in sight and there would be little chance that his income would grow. It was quite possible that she would be left a widow, moreover, and, though she did not demand a large estate, she hoped that there would at least be enough to give her security in her old age. The main Osaka house and the Ashiya house agreed that this was most reasonable, and the standards were revised again.

Identification. Without question Yukiko is behind schedule, unmarried at age 30. Not only has she "failed" to live up to the timetable, but the failure falls also upon her seniors in the family, who are responsible in due course for finding her a mate.

Justification. The family hungers for an excuse for the situation, and finds some consolation in an old set of beliefs about the unlucky properties of certain years of birth. The vast majority of Japanese will tell you that such zodiacal notions are only ancient superstition. If we could ask them, the Makiokas themselves might say so in a less anxious moment. Nevertheless, vital statistics in the twentieth century record a sharp decline in the number of female births recorded in Japan during the two years *hinoe-uma* when the sign of the horse has been in conjunction with that of fire—1906 and 1966—as well as a sharp rise in female births registered the year before and the year after.

Yukiko's character also may be partly to blame. On the one hand she is the ideal docile daughter ready to marry anyone chosen by her seniors. On the other hand she is the humble Snow, so silent and unassertive that suitors are soon discouraged. Tanizaki offers only a vague hereditary explanation for her character: she is said to take after her mother, a classic, quiet Kyoto beauty. Be that as it may, as the story unfolds we realize that her consociates treasure Yukiko for her soft charm and are at pains to preserve it. For her greatest talent is to be able to reflect light back into the lives of others, like the gentle snowfall that brightens the interior of a dim room. Such beauty, the family is aware, cannot survive alone; it has value only when it is counterposed. They are reluctant to send Yukiko into marriage, for that may dim their own lives. So they too are to blame for the lag in her life cycle. For though they turn down some suitors out of status pride, they reject others for being unable to appreciate and sustain Yukiko's special charm.

Projection. Nevertheless the family cannot allow Yukiko to continue unwed; her failure is delaying her younger sister's marriage as well. So the family must now identify candidates they would once have refused bluntly, consider men who maritally speaking are second-hand goods. Widowers with children, men several years older—these are acceptable so long as they *look* young enough to provide an impression that seniority has been preserved. Yukiko, for her part, can readily project her course when it is paired to that of such a man, and can foresee him passing into retirement and death. She insists that he have property or wealth enough to secure her in her widowhood and old age. And the family reenters the marriage market with a new set of propensities for investment.

A brief example such as this tends to point up the "forensic" aspects of the rhetoric, but these must not be given undue attention. To do so would be to slip into a soap-opera view of aging and maturity as a serial of performances, a battery of games people play socially. Performances leave their long-term precipitates in the character of each performer and, as well, in the policies or styles that evolve among consociates. In *The Makioka Sisters* we can only guess at the changes in Yukiko's character, since the author does not take us into her mind or narrate the action from her point of view. But as the novel progresses across five years of action-time and several further marriage negotiations we can discern a clear "Yukiko policy" crystallizing in the minds of others in the family.

Time thus enters into the rhetoric of long engagements through the cumulative powers of experience. Usual social-science concepts of the life cycle focus upon the flow of persons through time. But a mature human consciousness is also a compound resultant of the flow of time through persons. Further comprehensions come to us when we revise our views about our cultural heritage, our consociates, and ourselves, as all of these change across the years and seasons. Most often this comes about in little epiphanies of self-realization, only rarely in Pauline flashes of blinding insight. But it normally adds up. By midlife we come to a new awareness of time as it flows through *our* life as well as the lives of people in general. We notice a dislocation between our culture's ideal pathways of life and the actual paths we are traveling. James Baldwin refers to the dislocation as the sense of a baffling geography:

Though we would like to live without regrets, and sometimes proudly insist that we have none, this is not really possible, if only because we are mortal. When more time stretches behind than stretches before one, some assessments, however reluctantly and incompletely, begin to be made. Between what one wished to become and what one *has* become there is a momentous gap, which will now never be closed. And this gap seems to operate as one's final margin, one's last opportunity, for creation. And between the self as it is and the self as one sees it, there is also a distance, even harder to gauge. Some of us are compelled, around the middle of our lives, to make a study of this baffling geography, less in the hope of conquering these distances than in the determination that the distances shall not become any greater.

I have put this book together in a way that will, I hope, bring out these manifold features of lives through adult time, and of time through adult lives. Some day we may have comprehensive case records of the rhetoric of maturity as observed within canons of scientific precision. That someday is not now, nor is it likely to arrive tomorrow. To record the rhetoric in its fullness we would need to enlist a platoon of investigators. And since the animal being observed exists on the same molar timeline as those doing the observing, a study in time-depth would require the collaboration of investigators spanning two or more successive generations.

There are longitudinal case records in the West that begin to approach this ideal of perfection. Studies based on these records have taken us many steps forward in our understanding of adult human development: I think for example of White's *Lives in Progress* or Glen Elder, Jr.'s *Children of the Great Depression*. But no such longitudinal archives exist in Japan. And this means that a lone investigator with limited resources must make do with materials that are already on hand or that can be obtained economically. By criteria of scientific perfection such materials will be full of human contaminations. We must attend to these biases and distortions as best we can, discounting and allowing for them. These exigencies bring our task closer to that of the clinician or art critic than to that of the usual social researcher jealously guarding his accuracies of fact.

My sources for background materials are diverse. I draw upon published items that are popular as well as those that are scholarly, those written by foreigners about Japan as well as those written by Japanese themselves. I make use of my own notes from interviews both formal and casual, draw on personal impressions, extract data from mass surveys. And I bring to bear all the experience I can muster from 25 years of study and teaching about modern Japanese life. But I have built the main exposition around two types of documents. I make use of modern Japanese novels, and of personal narratives drawn up from interviews tape-recorded with people in the Hanshin region (Osaka–Kobe) in 1972–73. Out of some two dozen narratives in my file I selected a set of four that, taken together, illustrate an array of issues and dilemmas of adulthood. Each of the four is paired with a novel that echoes and supplements in "fiction" some of the central themes that appear in "real life" in the personal narrative.

As I explicate these themes in sections of commentary, I shall introduce a number of analytic concepts. I shall sketch each concept at the point where I bring it in, and I shall return to assess the aggregate cluster of concepts in the concluding chapter. For now I simply want to indicate that my intention in offering these concepts is to rewrite the more general and static notions of culture, character, and consociates into a vocabulary of analysis that will point up the time-depth inherent in human maturation.

Thus instead of speaking of cultural values in general, I shall refer to *pathways* as life-course directives for one's self-realization of these values. Instead of consociates in general I shall examine *convoys* as the unique clusters of intimates who sojourn with one through a particular phase of life. Instead of character I shall focus upon *perduring self-images* as major guides by which one steers one's personal course.

Each of my four chapters of exposition takes up one or more of the standard pathways of Japanese culture, as manifested in a personal narrative and in a novel. I begin the chapter with a précis of the novel, as a way of raising key issues and ambiguities that an individual must resolve within himself and with his convoy. I go on to sketch background features of Japanese values, social organization, and modern history. This is information that I believe most American readers will need in order to fully appreciate the particular Japanese ambience surrounding the issues. The shared and more generally human components will be evident without emphasis. Next, the narrative is related in first person in the words of the individual himself or herself, as best I can render them in translation. Finally, I return to the scene and offer some pages interpreting that life from *my* perspectives on the rhetoric of maturity.

I chose novels that I find useful for elucidating themes in the rhetoric. I am not particularly concerned about these novels as works of literary craftsmanship, and do not address them as a critic of the art might do. Cavalier as it will seem to the literatus, I treat the novels as if they were case records. I see no reasonable objection to this so long as the novels are—as these four are—naturalistic in depicting persons and events well within the bounds of ordinary human variation. The operations of rhetoric must be conveyed by symbols and images that hold collective meaning. We can learn these symbols and their allowed permutations through "as if" narratives as well as we might through "as lived" ones.

All four of these novels are widely read, known, and admired by audiences in Japan. The titles of two of the four have, for that matter, been absorbed into the popular vocabulary of notions about maturity and aging. *Resistance at Forty-eight* has become a term for "middle-age crisis," and "ecstasy" (from the title of *A Man in Ecstasy*) a euphemism for the terminal phase of senile decay. Furthermore, three of the four are available in English translation, the exception being *A Man in Ecstasy*. You may judge their literary properties for yourself, if you wish; you can also form your own opinions about whether I am justified in using them as case documents.

Novels and personal narratives are paired for yet another reason. The writer of fiction will take pains to heighten a character's dilemmas and to dramatize turnings in the person's awareness of self. Often the action is condensed into a span of days or even hours. By contrast, the ambiguities in a "real life" narrative tend to be resolved at the speed of a slow-motion film, and without evident progress. Every one of my Hanshin interviewees can relate moments of awareness from the past, memorable times when change became known. But however suddenly the awareness flashed, it was likely only to cap a resolution that had been building for many months, even years.

That is, the elementary operations of the rhetoric may not differ between fictional and real lives. But real lives have rhythms and poetics all their own, which the novelist may not always be able to capture within the forms of his art. I have tried to present each personal narrative in a way that points up the pace and tenor its narrator perceives in his or her own record of experience. If this more ordinary rhythm of maturity does not come across, then I have failed my interviewees and my readers too.

In judging the narratives, you are obliged to rely upon the materials offered in these pages, and you therefore deserve to know how the materials were obtained. One cannot stop random strangers on the street and hope to enlist much cooperation in a venture such as this. Distortions, furthermore, enter at every step of the work—in selecting among those who are willing to be interviewed, in enlisting their enthusiasm, in the actual interview conditions, in transcribing and editing the tapes that result. All these technical operations require comment: that is the burden of Chapter 2.

CHAPTER 2

The Fabrication of Lives

Before coming of age—the formative years when the reservoir of raw material was filling—I had led, or rather been led by, half a dozen separate lives. Each life had its own scene, its own milieu; it frequently appeared to have its own beginning and ending, the only connecting tissue being the narrow thread of my *self*. I had been *there*, but that, indeed, explained nothing. In an effort to come to terms with the experience, I processed it in fragments, collecting pieces of the puzzle. In time, a certain over-all pattern *appeared* to be there. But this appearance was essentially a process —an imaginative act of apprehension—rather than a research into the artifacts of my life.

The realization that I had to create coherence, conjure up my synthesis, rather than find it, came to me . . . disturbingly late. Having sawed out the pieces of my jigsaw puzzle, I was faced with the problem of fitting them together. There is a powerful inclination to leave this chore to someone else.

WRIGHT MORRIS, *The Territory Ahead*

The Hanshin Shelf

Travel folders tout the "million dollar view." On a clear night it can be just that. From the top of the Rokkō mountain range the panorama down the Hanshin shelf, across Osaka bay, on over Osaka city to the Ikoma mountains and the shores of Wakayama can rival the glitter and grandeur of Rio de Janeiro or Hong Kong. By day the view is more often obscured by haze and smoke. And even on the mountaintops you are aware of the sounds, mingled, rising from below, of millions of lives in commotion.

The term "Hanshin" is a modern coinage. It is formed by linking the second graph for Osaka and the first graph for Kobe, and reading the combination with Sinitic rather than native Japanese pronunciation. As the combination of graphs suggests, the word denotes a vaguely defined region between Osaka on the east and Kobe 40 kilometers to the west. In between lies a continuous belt of suburban cities: from east to west, Itami, Takarazuka, Amagasaki, Nishinomiya, and Ashiya. It amounts to a vast metropolitan strand squeezed between the Rokkō range on the north and Osaka bay on the south. At the eastern end the shelf of human habitation widens to a span of about 20 kilometers, but along the western two-thirds it is only about 4 kilometers across. Depending on how much of Osaka and Kobe one chooses to include in it, the area is home to upwards of 4 million Japanese.

Throughout the premodern centuries the Hanshin was a sparsely populated western doorway to the heartland of the Japanese civilization that flourished on the Yamato plain and in the Kyoto basin. Imperial grave mounds were sometimes built in the Hanshin in the early era, but they are few in number when compared with the dozens on the Yamato plain. In medieval times two famous battles were fought in what is now Kobe, at Ichinotani in 1184 and at Minatogawa in 1333. For centuries the spring waters of Nada (now eastern Kobe) have been used in brewing what some regard as the finest sake in all Japan. From the seventeenth century onward, traffic through the Hanshin corridor increased as Osaka became the capital city of Japanese commerce, but the area itself remained undeveloped.

Change came in the 1870's, when Japan opened itself to extensive Western trade for the first time in three centuries and began to build an industrial economy. The minor Inland Sea shipping station at Kobe was designated to be developed as the major international port for Osaka and southwestern Japan. Foreign consuls, traders, engineers, and missionaries were allowed to settle in Kobe, and a few of their Victorian-era colonial houses can still be found near the center of the city. (Even today the Hanshin area has the largest cluster of foreign residents outside the Tokyo metropolitan area.) A chain-reaction process of industrial development was set off, and it continues unabated.

A century ago the Hanshin shelf held little but a string of fishing and farming villages. Today, inshore fishing is depleted, and one has to search to find a farmhouse still standing or a field still under cultivation. Auto ferries and container-cargo superships fill the bay, and transport terminals line its shores. Factories intersperse with warehouses, blanketing virtually the entire shoreline. Inland from the industrial belt a tight tangle of railway lines, highways, and residential districts covers the shelf and rubs against the lower slopes of the mountains. Along the upper rim of the shelf, schools jostle for space amid high-income houses and apartments. Only the steep slopes of the mountains remain relatively tree-clad and free from habitation. For the most part they have been protected as park and forest areas. But here and there one sees company villas, a hotel, or a cluster of houses, and on the very summit a scatter of broadcasting towers and microwave relay stations.

Traffic flows east to Osaka and west to Kobe along a skein of routes. The Hankyū and Hanshin private lines compete with the National Railways for the commuter trade. All three offer high-speed electric service every ten to fifteen minutes during the daytime, more frequently in rush hours. Until 1974 an ancient trolley line also rumbled down the center of the Hanshin national road, but it has since been replaced by a grassy median strip—and ever more tangled auto traffic. When the National Railways extended its new main line—what Americans know as the "bullet train" line—westward from Osaka a few years ago, planners sensibly avoided the Hanshin shelf altogether. Most of the new line from Osaka to Kobe tunnels through the length of the Rokkō range.

Suburbanization came to the area with the construction of the electric railways, and the new lifestyle that evolved around them, early in the twentieth century. Ashiya became to Osaka what Highland Park was to Chicago. Here and there along the upper rim of the shelf one comes across great mansions erected by the industrial new-rich during the prosperous 1920's. The pace of growth was relatively gradual, however, until the economic boom that began in the 1950's. Even a decade ago one could still find swatches of open land; single-family dwellings were the norm. Now the lower and middle reaches of the shelf are dotted with vast apartment complexes put up by public housing agencies. And on higher ground there is an irregular but growing strip of more expensive private townhouses. Their developers shun the pedestrian label of "apartment" (*apāto* in Japanese). These are known as "residence" (*rejidensu*) or "casa" (*kasa*) or "heights" (*haitsu*).

Culturally the area is difficult to categorize in a few phrases. The basic pattern of life is Japanese-suburban with a mixture of elements from the old Osaka bourgeois heritage and a dash of Kobe cosmopolitanism. For a loose American parallel one might try to imagine a blend of Chicago and San Francisco lifestyles. The tempo of daily living is a white-collar suburban one not much different from that of any other industrial nation. Tides of people flow from the houses and apartments to the railway stations in the morning and back at night. Only on Sundays and holidays are there many men around in the daytime, or families walking together, or anybody other than children, housewives and the elderly moving about.

It is not unusual to hear people talking in the streets in the clipped accents of national standard (Tokyo) speech. But most conversations are carried on in the more melodic patois of the Kansai (Western Japan). And from time to time you catch the nasal brogue of downtown Osaka. The people next door may be from an old-line Osaka merchant family that, like the Makiokas, has moved out to suburbia in the last generation. Next to them could be an apartment complex filled with the families of young executives posted to the Hanshin from all over the nation.

Like Southerners in the United States, natives of the Hanshin are often stubbornly attached to Kansai speech patterns and regional cuisine. They like to think of themselves and of the region as being relatively independent of the policy-making and cultural pace-setting powers of The Center (*chūō*), i.e. Tokyo. They cling to a self-image as easygoing and open people, more gentle and humane than the high-strung eastern establishmentarians.

Some boast that the Osaka townsman subculture and its 400-year heritage offer an alternative lifestyle to the upstart Tokyo pattern that has become the nationwide norm. But behind the claim lies a recognition that in Japan as in other industrial nations the once-diverse popular lifeways have been homogenized through mass production and marketing, central control over schools and social policy, centrally edited mass media, and wide social mobility.

The Hanshin region is as open socially as it is compacted geographically. To be sure, a small percentage of the population continues to be blocked from easy participation—and public opinion in general sets barriers in the way of women. The outsiders cluster at the low and high ends of the economic scale. Poor incomes and de facto discrimination are the lot of native Japanese outcasts called *burakumin* and of Asian immigrants (and their Japan-born descendants). Most of the immigrants are Koreans who arrived during the first half of the twentieth century (almost half of the Korean population in Japan lives in the Hanshin). Euro-American residents, a few thousand in total, are also essentially outside the system, but most of them are from executive and professional families who can afford a kind of gilded ghetto existence.

For the majority, however, the way is open. Few will make or lose a fortune in one lifetime. Most will climb or fall only a notch or two from the level occupied by their parents. Parental wealth or power can of course provide obvious advantages to the offspring, not the least being the money needed for advanced schooling. For it is the school system that initially sorts young people into probable career tracks. However, after graduation day your promise must be demonstrated; you must prove that you can continue to learn and to grow on your own initiative as an adult. In the long run, your biography will be written not about inherited wealth or status but about what in your mature years you have done and the kind of person you have become.

Motives for Studying

Early in the summer of 1972 I rented a house in Takarazuka and arranged to spend a sabbatical year looking into human change in adulthood in the Hanshin milieu. Along with my family and our boxes of impedimenta I brought a sheaf of notes and a bundle of mental notions. These had to do with studies I hoped to carry out. Some were modest, some ambitious; some were realized; some remain in dream-work. But my first priority was to enlist the help of Hanshin men and women in verbally reconstructing the course of their adult years.

No one particular event had bent me toward this topic or toward the Hanshin. Four years earlier I had been commissioned to write an essay on old age in Japan. That had set me to reading and thinking about aspects of Japanese culture, and human life generally, that had been on the fringes of my mind. Watching my parents and their age-mates move into retirement afforded a further push. And I found myself contemplating my own approach to that continental divide in the flow of the American life course: my 40th birthday.

For some time I had been studying communes, utopian groups, and movements for social reconstruction. In doing so I became more and more curious about the dynamics of ideological conversion. I was not satisfied with theories that seek to explain why some people convert and others do not by referring either to inner psychological propensities or to outer currents of change in society. Such factors need to be taken into account, of course. But among converts I knew, or read about, as often as not the conversion had been preceded by trauma or pain within the person's micro-milieu of consociates: there had been death, degradation, severe illness. A similar line of reasoning, taken on a broader plane, seems to underlie recent research on stressful life-events and their aftershocks for the individual himself. This sense of problem was in the back of my mind as I turned to consider the more ordinary sorts of long-term human change that take place across the adult years. Could the idea of conversion-process, I began to ask myself, be adapted and used to help account for the long-wave, slow-motion "conversions" of selfhood that emerge in the course of adult experience?

At that point I met an empirical barrier. I could find relatively few documents that were suitable for analyzing as case studies of consocial change in adulthood. Some novels are usable; most biographies and life histories and nonfictional case records are a disappointment. And the novels, for their part, must be selected and used sensibly. Some genres, such as science fiction and historical romance, tend to be so removed from the everyday rhythms of the normal life course that they pose complicated problems analytically. Best are narratives that are naturalistic in the sense of depicting molar persons and events wholly within the bounds of ordinary human variation. Often enough such narratives are modeled upon persons and events from the author's own experience—transformed, to be sure, by the rules of storytelling. Happily, for my purposes, narratives of this quality have been part of Japanese literary tradition ever since that tradition gave the world its very earliest great novel, the eleventh-century *Tale of Genji*.

In nonfiction narrative, however, the biographer tends to deal with his subject's public life and to say little about the relationships and changing self-perceptions that are the heart of the rhetoric of maturity. And although the autobiographer may recall for us his shifting senses of identity he is likely to be close-mouthed about his consociates. Worst of all, the published biographies and life-history documents overwhelmingly depict the lives of the famed or the notorious. This is not much help when one hopes, as I do here, to examine the creativity, will, and wit that are just as evident in the lives of the unsung.

In order to obtain documents of the type I needed—I began to realize—I would have to coach people so that they would discourse for me on topics I consider of moment. My primary goal was to generate materials that I could use for later analysis. But the ethnographer in me also hoped that the narratives would be usable in another way—as in the chapters that follow—to provide an American audience with portraits of ordinary Japanese lives through time. For I take it as part of an ethnographer's duty to report on domains of a way of life that are slighted by the official cultural ambassadors and the mass media. Our understanding of a culture is thin if we fail to see the rainbow of ways in which its heirs turn that heritage into lived lives.

Motives for Being Studied

My interviewees could not be expected to share my purposes or enthusiasms. Sometimes I wondered why they were so good-natured about the whole procedure—arranging to meet with my assistant and me, allowing us to repeatedly invade their living space for hours, submitting to questions that may often have seemed odd, allowing their impromptu responses to be recorded. Perhaps the explanation is that most of us most of the time are pleased to be asked about our own lives. Particularly so when we are encouraged to speak about what experience has taught us. And all the more so when someone has come halfway around the world to do the asking.

The other chief attraction for most interviewees was a chance to converse with an outlander on their home turf, in the security of their mother dialect. Euro-Americans are seen in the Hanshin streets all the time, but few are fluent in Japanese, and most of the fluent ones are Christian proselytizers. Similarly, none of my interviewees is confident of being able to sustain a conversation in English, though all of them know fragments and phrases. Only one claimed that he once *had* been comfortably articulate, during the seven years he worked for a U.S. Army purchasing office in Kobe. But that, he sighed, was 20 years ago. And although he still exchanges casual banter with Euro-Americans who trade at his bread-and-cake shop, his verbal skill has almost vanished from disuse. To my interviewees, then, I could offer a rare opportunity for exotic discourse. I have a tolerable listening comprehension of the Kansai dialect and, more shakily, of the Osaka brogue, though I speak neither. However, I can speak the Tokyo standard idiom well enough to "pass" as Japanese over the telephone—not, of course, face to face.

So I suspect that many people thought of themselves as trading information about their lives in return for opportunities to question a native informant about American life. Their curiosity ranged wide and deep. We would talk of Vietnam and of Nixon, of racial discrimination in the United States, of American stereotypes about Japan. They would ask, of course, about how Americans deal with the issues of maturity and aging that I seemed so eager to ask them to discourse upon. From my selfish point of view it seemed sometimes that they revealed as much about themselves through the questions they asked me as through the answers they gave me. But they, too, probably gained secondary rewards in the form of prestige in their social circles ("This American professor was at my place the other day and he was telling me . . .").

Some interviewees may have felt a modicum of social pressure to cooperate. The invitation to participate in the project had come to them, in every instance, from one or another of my Japanese colleagues who was a consociate of theirs—a neighbor, kinsman, or friend. A few may have thought that by helping me they could repay my colleague for past favors or build goodwill with him for future ones, though I did not sense this to be a major consideration. The only people to comment in this vein were shopkeepers, who said it was difficult to refuse a request from a customer of 20 years' standing. (Two of the shopkeepers participated less than enthusiastically and in fact were "too busy" to complete the full cycle of sessions.)

My introduction from a colleague known personally to them was crucial in establishing my bona fides and in easing propensities to be close-mouthed. I doubt that many of the interviewees ever felt sure about the value of this kind of research. Opinion polls and questionnaire surveys are rampant in Japan, and everybody is used to being queried in those formats. My style of study was unfamiliar. Not once, though, did I catch a hint of doubt that my purposes were legitimate or that my promises of confidentiality were less than solid. My introducer, after all, was near at hand as a living warranty for my conduct. Formally, too, I would have seemed trustworthy, for I held research appointments to the faculties of Kyoto National University and of Kōnan University in Kobe. These were listed on my calling card as institutional sponsors to whom I was officially accountable.

Over time a few people became caught up in the "life review" aspect of the sessions and found it stimulating. They had of course engaged in retrospect many times before but never in such an ordered and verbalized way. (Gail Sheehy was told the same by a number of the Americans she interviewed for her book *Passages*.) For one woman, on the other hand, the process became too threatening, and she politely but pointedly asked us not to continue after the second session. She had known tragedy in her household, and though it had taken place some years earlier, she impressed me as being yet in mourning. She was, in addition, a Tokyo native who after 20 years in the Hanshin still adamantly refused to adopt Kansai speech and lifeways.

For three people there were elements of professional curiosity about the techniques of the interviewing, in addition to the content. One of the three has a position with duties that sometimes involve him in survey research. One is a television producer (Chapter 6) who often must interview prospective participants for her programs. And the third is a housewife who had studied social science in college and who has hopes, once her children are grown, of becoming an essayist on social issues. Diffident at first —she was bothered by the spontaneity of the procedure—she came gradually to welcome my questions. On the tape of the first session, her voice is barely audible. A few days later she wrote me a long letter saying she doubted her ability to continue the series, adding extended notes to supplement the terse oral answers she had offered. Contacted by phone, she agreed to give it another try. By the third session she was speaking loudly and firmly, becoming intrigued by the whole course of the research, and lecturing me on what she took to be my misconceptions about Japanese society.

One motive I am sure did *not* obtain was hope for material reward. No pay was given for the interview sessions, and people probably would have been offended had money been offered. On my first visit I presented each of them with a lacquerware tray. The trays were ordered from a well-known Kobe shop, and were inscribed on the back with my name and a phrase indicating the occasion. They could be kept for their souvenir value, or used practically around the house. Their cash worth was about five dollars. But in every instance—as has always been my experience when doing field research in Japan—the money value of the gift pales by comparison with the cost of the snacks, drinks, and sometimes full meals that the interviewees bestowed upon my assistant and me.

The Context of Discovery

Whatever their by-products might be, the interviews were intended above all to reveal the operations of the rhetoric of maturity among ordinary adults. I tried to hold to this principle as I made decisions about whom to see and how to relate with them.

I had in mind meeting with healthy, functioning people who were well along in their adult lives but not into retirement or senility—people between, say, 35 and 55 years of age. I did not want them to be under duress of poverty, ethnic prejudice, unemployment, or pathology. Though I could offer an outsider's sympathy to the disadvantaged I was in no position to provide them with therapy or welfare aid. More positively, I was at pains to bring out the processes of natural or normal growth. Large parts of our scholarly vocabulary for adult human development were coined in the study of persons clinically or socially afflicted. We are not nearly so well equipped to discuss growth patterns among the less disadvantaged sectors of mankind. Whatever potentials there are for self-realization, for creativity, for maturation in the commonplace settings of Japanese culture today, I wanted to maximize my chances for finding them.

The goal was discovery, not validation. I was not constrained to apply rigorous canons of statistical sampling for my purposes. Even though I might want to, such detailed social mapping would require a corporate research team; for a lone investigator with a few thousand dollars at hand, such a procedure was out of the question. For what the claim may be worth, I could say that my cases "represent" the normal majority of Japanese who are middle-aged and middle class. But we are talking about a segment of the population that includes at least 20 million persons, and two dozen cases can only begin to hint at its many dimensions of internal diversity.

"Sampling" is not the right word for it, but I did want to "explore" some obvious dimensions of adult life-course variation. I wanted some of my male interviewees to be company men and others to be independents—long-term corporate employees on the one hand and self-employed shopkeepers or craftsmen or professionals on the other. I wanted some of the women to have working careers, others to be career homemakers. On grounds that the most significant other of all in a normal adult convoy is one's spouse, I hoped to interview both partners to a marriage. This ruled out the widowed, the divorced, and the never-married. To mute convoy diversity I sought persons from intact families with children. Given the age of the adults, one or more children were likely to be living in the home, and possibly a grandparent or two.

Over the months I eventually held sessions with 23 people (14 women and nine men) who met some combination of my criteria. This included nine married pairs—in five other cases the husbands, all of them executives, pleaded the press of business. In terms of their careers, two of the men interviewed are salaried employees (e.g. Beisuke, Chapter 4), and seven are independents. Of the latter, four operate retail shops along the same street in a residential neighborhood, one is a carpenter, one a research chemist, and one a realtor (Shōji, Chapter 3). Of the women, eight are career homemakers (e.g. Goryōhan, Chapter 5); four run retail shops jointly with their husbands; and two are salaried employees, one in a municipal insurance bureau and one as a television producer (Tomoko, Chapter 6).

With all of these people, my task was a challenge, for discovery interviewing can be exhilarating and exhausting at the same time. Every session brings you new ideas as well as new information, to the point where you struggle against idea-overload, unable to process it all. Then, too, you hold few of the controls over the situation that are in the hands of the clinician or laboratory researcher. You can do some rough-hewing, but often you can only let the interaction run its course. You seek certain types of response from your partner, yet you do not want to dampen spontaneity.

The investigator of human affairs should hold no illusions

about merely observing or recording the motions of the universe. He cannot help influencing the behavior of those he studies, and must therefore be alert to the dangers of solipsism, to the possibility that he is only putting ideas into other people's heads and then deluding himself that he discovered them there. He can never eliminate "investigator effects." But with a little care he can minimize them.

The interview sessions were conducted with this goal in mind. I wanted people to present their lives to me—go through their rhetorics of self-identification and change—in idioms most familiar and meaningful to them. Because doing that involves one's own being in such personal ways, treads upon sensitive areas, this can be a tension-raising activity. But I hoped the tensions would prove to be more creative than defensive.

The need to perform personally for a stranger, and a foreign one at that, seemed to me enough of a challenge to impose upon interviewees. I did not want other features of the situation to compound it. Rather, I wanted the setting to be one where the interviewee felt secure (not wondering where the toilet is, for example). Most of the time our sessions were at the interviewee's home —though this involved minor distractions of its own. Visitors, telephones, children, and elders importuned now and then; people felt obliged to offer snacks and to attend to my comfort as a guest; others in the house might eavesdrop, though in fact I never caught any signs of it. Still, the fact that others were around could be inhibiting. But the interviewees themselves protected the privacy of the situation, except that at times a wife might be in the room during parts of an interview with her husband, on grounds that she was needed to pour tea and serve cakes.

On occasion we might meet at a man's office, borrow an office from one of my colleagues, or meet at my house or the house of a mutual acquaintance. Worst of all, we sometimes met at coffee shops. The Japanese coffee shop is a fine locus for many types of interviewing. It is physically comfortable, and often has background music. You can sit there for hours and not fear being asked to leave. And though the place may be filled with people, it is anonymous, which is to say private. People will talk to you quite openly. But for my purposes there was one terrible drawback: tapes recorded in a coffee shop are so full of noise pollution that they are painful to the ears, often undecipherable.

Sessions also were scheduled for times convenient to the interviewees. For housewives this meant weekday mornings or afternoons when the family was away. For shopkeepers it meant Tuesdays, the one day a week when all shops on that street are shuttered. For those employed outside the home it meant evenings or weekends, though one man seemed to welcome the excuse that we provided him for escaping from his office for an afternoon now and then.

Because of busy and slack periods, any one interviewee was likely to be seen irregularly over the months. Shopkeepers, for example, could spare no time during the rush of year-end business. Some houses were closed to visitors during the early spring while children were cramming for examinations. And no one was keen about holding sessions during the holiday weeks of early January.

Some sessions evolved into conversations that extended for hours, often capped by a meal. In general I asked people to allow for at least two hours per session and for a total of five sessions— though only in half the cases did we meet five separate times. Two hours, I reasoned, would allow time for casual chatter as well as for concentrated exploration of a set of topics. And it was just right for using both sides of a one-hour cassette tape.

All sessions were voice-recorded, to retain as much as possible of the immediacy of the discourse. People were well aware of the tape recorder, and no doubt this was inhibiting at times, though only once or twice was I asked to stop the tape momentarily. But it also freed me from taking notes during the sessions (except once when the machine jammed and once when the din in a coffee shop was deafening), and in any event, note-taking is likely to be even more inhibiting than is taping.

Throughout the sessions I was accompanied by my research assistant, a young Japanese woman who was taking graduate courses in sociology at Kōnan University. A Hanshin native, she could phrase topics and questions with finesse in the local idiom. This helped counteract the tone of discourse that might otherwise have been set by my speech pattern: Tokyo-standard, relatively polite, slightly stilted and distance-putting. People could respond instead to her, with the shorthand ease of co-regionals. A word or two would suffice to indicate Hanshin places or events—or for that matter items any Japanese adult should know as common sense. Toward me people might feel a need to offer explanations, and over a long period of time that would be burdensome.

Most often my assistant steered the conversation, following an outline of topics and questions I had prepared. This left me free to attend to cues that I might then explore with the interviewee. I was also free to claim the privileges of the ignorant alien, and ask for explanations and elaborations. Then, too, this procedure softened the potential—always latent—that the interviewee would respond with a culturally typical presentation-of-self rather than in terms of his or her own ideas and experience. Ethnographers share an occupational hazard with diplomats: the risk of overexposure to an endless series of presentations of the same small set of "cultural performances" that are supposed to edify the outlander.

The fact that my assistant was on the scene may now and then have been a hindrance. I sensed times when men would rather have talked with me alone. On the other hand, women were spared the possible embarrassments of speaking directly to me about "woman talk" topics, and the probable embarrassments of neighborhood gossip had they entertained a strange male alone in the house.

The Context of Presentation

I came home from the Hanshin to face the task that handbooks on social research sometimes glibly refer to as write-up. With my family and our baggage came more than two hundred hours' worth of interview tapes, and a stack of transcriptions and memoranda (also boxes of books, field diaries, questionnaires, and newspaper clippings, all a part of other studies I had been executing). Much of the interview material is yet to be processed, and the four narratives I use in this book are only a small part of it.

The writing has not been done "up" half as easily as I had anticipated. My "archive" is not all that large in size; but even so, much effort is involved in sorting it, sifting it, ordering it so that meanings can be extracted. Most of my working time has been given over to university duties, academic and administrative; some of it to involvements in other projects. But my main difficulty has been that of hammering out a style of presentation. I tested various styles on students in my graduate seminars, but each style drew a mixed audience rating that left me no more sure than before about which to use. I tore up more outlines for potential books than I care to remember. I became a fixture in the family kitchen, hunched over its long counter playing a peculiar kind of solitaire, endlessly shifting pages of notes from one pile to another to a third.

I was wrestling with a dilemma that haunts every ethnographer. On the one hand, he wants to re-present the singularity and dignity of individual lives as he encounters them in alien settings. On the other hand, he also wants to convey the life-ordering powers, even the beauty, of the social institutions and cultural patterns found in those settings. It has been as routine in ethnographic field procedure to collect life histories and personal narratives as it has been to collect information on, say, rules of inheritance or techniques for detoxifying manioc. Back in the context of presentation, however, the most common way to resolve the dilemma has been to compartmentalize it. Personal narratives are tucked into a chapter in the back of a monograph, as a sample of representative lives. Or they are run through in a paragraph or two somewhere in mid-passage, with a lick and a promise. Other times, the life histories are published as a separate book, often with little or no commentary apart from background notes on the cultural setting. A rather considerable number of such life-history volumes have been accumulating on the shelves of social science libraries. But the only ones to win wide popular readership have been those produced by my Illinois colleague, the late Oscar Lewis.

In the chapters that follow I try to hold on to both horns of this dilemma of presentation—and, I hope, hold both horns *in*. I offer each of the narratives as a unit-statement rendered in my English approximation of the person's own speech. I bracket each narrative with sections of commentary intended to provide a bridge between the idiosyncrasies of lives and the generalities of Japanese lifeways. Neither the narratives nor the commentaries are meant to be "complete." The problem is that of how to be selective, of deciding what to omit. I have sacrificed comprehensiveness in an effort to point up connectedness.

As in the interview process, so in processing the raw materials into narrative form I have tried to guard against injecting too much of myself. This has not been easy, since my partner no longer sits across from me ready to offer his or her views on the emerging document. Though I have sought to re-present each life as my partner understands it, I am the one who has ordered, edited, and fabricated these narratives. The result falls somewhere between biography and autobiography. I am author of the text, but it is a montage of spontaneous statements by the author of that life.

All the interview tapes were transcribed into Japanese script by a team of part-time Hanshin assistants. One was a professional secretary, the others were college students. Those with some skill in the language also prepared English summaries of the transcriptions. But the quality of these was so erratic that they are little use except as crude guides for retrieving information from the originals.

In putting together the narratives used in this book I worked with a combination of the interview tapes, the transcriptions, the summaries, and notes I had jotted down during and after the interviews. I listened to the tapes many times, making additional notes, checking them against the transcripts—for often enough a key word might be misunderstood, or a vital inflection or voice tone or hesitation or pause not rendered by the canons of orthography would be overlooked. I drew up rough translations of all the sections I thought I might want to include. This amounted to about half the material in each set of transcripts and tapes. I set aside material on topics that seemed tangential to the themes of this book. This is material gathered with other studies in mind: on memories of the Pacific War period, on genealogies and kinship ties, on various Japanese customs that interest me.

Next I strung the sections of rough translation into a narrative sequence. I chose pseudonyms for persons mentioned in the text, and altered place names, names of schools, and in some instances the occupations of kinsmen, as a means of preserving privacy. With frequent referrals to the tapes and transcripts I wrote out the narrative in clean copy. Since then I have made only minor shifts in sequence, a few improvements in wording, and deletions of a few sections that seemed on later reading redundant or irrelevant.

Each clean copy was back-translated into Japanese by my former field assistant, and sent to that interviewee for comment. I did not encourage the interviewees to edit or rewrite the text so long as they felt it was a fair approximation of their views on their lives. They suggested only a few emendations, and a few rewordings to better preserve privacy. Thus these might be called "authorized" versions of the narratives, though ideally I would like to have been able to work together with my partners to produce versions more "authoritative."

So I have influenced these narratives in many ways. They were collected for my purposes, not for the purposes of my interviewees. I asked the questions, I fed people topics I hoped would reveal aspects of the rhetoric of maturity. I translated and edited the tapes. However, the narratives were completed in the form in which they appear here months before I sat down to prepare my own pages of interpretation. Which is to say that the whole operation has been carried out in ways that would help ensure my narrators of the right to explain their lives as *they* understand them. They are, as I can never be, the truest experts in the meaning of these lives.

Four lives can do no more than suggest the variety of pathways, convoys, and self-images to be found in a post-industrial civilization of 110 million people. These four are middle-class urbanites.

In this respect they share attributes with the majority of the population, since four-fifths of the Japanese reside in metropolitan areas and two-thirds of them consider themselves to be middle class.

The four would be embarrassed if told they were "typical" Japanese; but at the same time they would agree that they are "ordinary." None of them is famous or powerful, none would attract attention walking on the Hanshin streets. During the months that I met with them none was in serious pain, stress, or disease, though some had consociates who were so afflicted. All recounted episodes of trouble in the past, some could see troubles ahead. But each was, at the time, functioning, vital, effective as an adult human experienced in "conscious self-utilization." However Japanese they may appear, they also stand forth as singular. And I have tried hard to convey this extraordinary singularity that I continue to marvel at in human lives.

I am writing for a wide audience and assume of it no detailed knowledge of Japan. I have fought to fend off the virus of scholarly jargon, which keeps invading my vocabulary. And I was obliged to vaccinate myself against the footnote, which otherwise flares and cannot be arrested until it has infested every paragraph. My ideal has been the Japanese literary tenet of *hosomi*, prose like a slender sword, trenchant and supple. But I have to admit that a book of 200-odd pages is no model of terseness.

On one matter I adhere to scholarly convention: the transcribing of Japanese words. When an individual's name appears I first give the patronym and then follow it with the personal name. With a few exceptions all words are romanized in the modified Hepburn system, which indicates long vowels with a superscript bar, or macron. The exceptions are words already absorbed into English, which does not distinguish long from short vowels. Thus I write Osaka rather than Ōsaka, and aikido rather than aikidō, for example. Japanese words are printed in italics when they first appear but after that are given in roman letters. All this attention to orthography may seem wasted on those who are not versed in the Japanese language. But to those who are so versed there is a world of difference between, say, *rōba* ("an old woman") and *roba* ("a donkey"). A man who cannot distinguish a donkey from a granny must have the mentality of a jackass.

In each of the next four chapters—the substance of the book—there are four main sections. We begin each chapter with a look at a modern Japanese novel. We consider the life of the protagonist and what it has to suggest about themes of human growth in the adult years.

In the second section I attempt to set the novel in the context of one or more of the dimensions of the rhetoric of maturity—pathways, convoys, self-images—as these are manifested in Japanese tradition.

In the third section, one of my interviewees comes onto the scene and narrates for us his or her life's story.

And finally I reappear in the fourth section to offer further comments upon patterns that I see as important in the novel and the life history.

Let us begin with *The Buddha Tree*, a novel by the widely read author Niwa Fumio.

CHAPTER 3

A Suicide Cadet

A man of true sincerity will be an example to the world even after
his death. . . . . When an insincere man is spoken well of, he has,
so to speak, got a windfall, but a man of deep sincerity will, even
if he is unknown in his lifetime, have a lasting reward: the esteem
of posterity.

SAIGŌ TAKAMORI, *Sayings*

I. THE HUNGER FOR WHOLENESS

The central story line of *The Buddha Tree* is that of Sōshū's
lonely quest for wholeness. By his own description, Sōshū is a
servant to the Buddha and a slave to lust. Through all the 20 years
that he has been chief priest of the Temple of the Merciful Buddha, Sōshū has sustained an adulterous affair with his wife's
mother. Two decades of duplicity have sapped his spiritual fiber.
Though he longs to cleanse away his guilt by making a public
confession to his parishioners, he cannot marshal the courage to
do so, and in so doing destroy his position and popularity. And
yet, he wonders, does this not make me precisely the sort of person that St. Shinran longs to rescue?

Portions of the story were drawn from author Niwa's own
childhood, for he grew up in just such a neighborhood temple
in a regional town in central Japan. Sōshū and his wife are based
in some measure upon Niwa's own parents; and the young boy
in the novel, Ryo, has episodes that are described in such vivid
particulars that they seem to be taken from eidetic memory. But
the book is also a product of Niwa's return, in the early 50's of his
life, to the view of the human condition that is found in Shin

Buddhism—a pathway to enlightenment that Niwa had turned from when he fled the family temple as a young man.

One cannot go far in understanding the rhetoric of maturity in any society without attending to its pathways to personal growth. A pathway is a patrimony for integrity and wholeness, plus a career guide to conduct. It connects the trivia of the minute with the root powers of the universe. It gives a direction and time-depth to the individual potential that is symbolized in one's own name. It gives effort a purpose, and enables one to face the prospect of continuing to grow older.

We struggle to overcome the social traps sprung upon us, the role-duties that may curb our sense of fullness. We struggle for greater awareness and competence within our complicated array of internal identifications and external involvements. We struggle to enact the poetry of our uniqueness at the same time that we must confess how our life cycle replicates the species pattern.

Japanese can draw upon a rich heritage of pathways. Pathways in the Buddhist tradition are more evidently spiritual in their idioms of enlightenment and salvation. Those in the Shinto tradition are more aesthetic in their idioms of spontaneity and pure action. But every pathway includes both aspects. It provides for spiritual engagement by placing an overarching frame of meaning upon mundane activities. It provides for aesthetic engagement by conducing toward climax or fulfillment—perhaps not toward perfecting the self as separable monad, as suggested in Western phrasings of individual self-realization, but toward an ever-tougher tempering of the self-as-instrument ultimately capable of perfect expression.

Niwa's novel introduces us to the Buddhist version of this quest; in the life of Shōji the realtor, later in the chapter, we shall see a Shinto version. And in succeeding chapters we shall find still others.

"Temple" Buddhism

The Shin sect and its sister denominations attract little interest in the West, though these are the forms of Buddhism practiced by the majority of Japanese. Perhaps these sects lack the exotic aura that the Westerner finds in Zen and its spiritual gymnastics. Shin has its unfamiliar idioms, to be sure, but many of its concepts—of guilt and grace, of helplessness and compassion—seem not far distant from Christian notions of sin and salvation or of Christ's love.

The tree in the title of Niwa's novel is the bo tree under which Gautama achieved his final enlightenment, a symbol of every man's struggle for wholeness. And though *The Buddha Tree* relates a spiritual pilgrimage, it is not one in which Sōshū implodes as his inner eyes see the glory. Rather he slowly, painfully, works to free himself from attachments that have warped and narrowed his growth, to slough off the shell of a lesser selfhood and risk the promise of a greater one.

To understand Sōshū's situation we must take note of certain features of the organization and functioning of the hereditary Buddhist temples found in Japanese villages and neighborhoods. Japanese like to carp that the local temple is little more than a glorified mortuary business. This is unfair to the spiritual heritage of Buddhism, but it does indicate the temple's major practical activity and source of revenue. For each temple is sustained by a relatively fixed clientele of hereditary parish families. And the temples in any locale agree not to proselytize, thus restraining competition for each other's clients.

The temple priest offers religious instruction and pastoral counseling. In addition he usually offers as well to teach one or more of the traditional Japanese arts of calligraphy or flower arranging or the aesthetics of Tea. His personality and skill may attract some outsiders into his sphere, but his primary obligation is to the parish families. He must maintain their temple and its cycle of holy days, maintain its cemetery, officiate at funerals, and go into the neighborhood to conduct the periodic death-day memorial services for the departed who are enshrined in each family's home altar.

The temple establishment is inherited like any family farm or business. The office of priest, together with the worship halls, dwellings, cemetery, and clientele, pass from father to son, with the heir first having been sent for professional training and ordination at the sect's national headquarters. (Author Niwa's father, for example, was sixteenth in the line of hereditary priests of the family's temple in Yokkaichi.) If there is no blood heir the usual practice, as in any hereditary trade in Japan, is to adopt one—to adopt not an infant but a young man whose talent and character already are fairly evident.

The adoptee takes on the family name as well as the office of priest. If the family has an unwed daughter, she is likely to become his wife. And this is the situation in the novel. Twenty years ago, while he still was a divinity-school student, Sōshū was adopted by the Getsudōs, the family line of the Temple of the Merciful Buddha. (Though scion of a priestly family, Sōshū was its second-born son and thus not in line to succeed his father.) Popular Japanese sayings counsel against becoming an adopted heir, but the practice is far from unusual. It can offer a step up the social ladder for an able and ambitious junior son, or the son of a poor family. One finds many adoptees among the leaders in all sectors of Japanese society. The greatest drawback is that in his early years an adoptee is a sort of "male bride," an outsider and newcomer who may easily be dominated by the blood-line members of the family.

For purposes of drama the priest can be good material; he can be made to embody in extreme form the panhuman tensions between passion and purity, attachment and aspiration. Sōshū has become caught in a very ordinary web of human bondage; he must break from it if he is to pursue his true calling. In order to show how his pathway shapes his struggle to escape, I must outline his bondage. But I feel obliged to warn that Niwa has produced a richly realistic novel in *The Buddha Tree* and not, as may seem from my analytic précis, a dryly didactic tale of the sort common in "religious" fiction.

The Trap of Passion

Sōshū is a mild and gentle sort. Admirable as these qualities may be, however, they leave him at a double disadvantage in the face of the temple's dependence upon its clientele and in the situation of an adopted heir. The conditions of his adoption add further complications. The previous chief priest of the temple had died at an early age, leaving a young widow, Mineyo, 34, and daughter, Renko, 9. To Mineyo fell the duty of finding a successor. Rebounding in grief, she was overwhelmed with passion for the handsome student Sōshū, and soon seduced him. Outwardly, however, she arranged to pay for his tuition, to install him as the next priest of the temple, and to promise that Renko would in time become his wife.

In the symbolic logic of the story Mineyo is physical attachment incarnate and tyrannical, counterfoil to Sōshū's spiritual striving. Mineyo, for example, refuses to allow anyone, even members of the family, to glimpse her face in the morning until she has beautified it. She wears tight, bright kimonos unsuited to her age. In her efforts to remain attractive physically she has disfigured herself behaviorally.

Her strategy over the years has been to maintain an appearance of normality in the daytime—a prosaic temple-household routine that alerts no concern—but to let passion rule after the gates are closed at night. She has taken advantage of position, using her power as the senior member of the family line to neutralize her opponents.

First Shōjū, younger brother of her dead husband, is silenced. Shōjū had been ordained but never was called to a priestly position, and he never married. We are left wondering if he may actually be mildly retarded. In any event he has slipped the surly bonds of the flesh that lead to sorrow. He has served the family temple unselfishly as a factotum. But his own spirituality plus his silent witness to Mineyo's passion make him anathema to her. So at night she buries him symbolically, sending him to sleep in a shed in the temple cemetery outside the town.

Daughter Renko is more difficult to control. Several years junior to Sōshū, she grew up to be more a younger sister than a lover to him. Even after they were married Renko continued to sleep in a distant wing of the rambling temple compound. In time their union gave birth to a son, but it was unable to give birth to conjugal affection. Arguing that a son needs to sleep between his parents—a common practice in Japan—Renko moved into Sōshū's room. Mineyo, however, continued to find pretexts for luring Sōshū away during the dark hours. Certain of her control over Sōshū as his de facto wife, Mineyo began to covet the role of mother to his son. Assuring herself that Renko was not competent to rear the future priest and heir, Mineyo made her daughter's life miserable. Sōshū saw what was happening and drew away from Mineyo, but could not effectively sustain his wife. Even though it means leaving her son behind, Renko runs away to live with an actor.

Mineyo glows in triumph. In practice if not in public recognition she once again has the "young" roles of wife and mother in the household. Her grandson sleeps with her and is becoming her pet. When Sōshū returns from his daily parish rounds she greets him as a wife would, at the door. She lavishes money on renovating a room for herself. And she nags Sōshū to exert himself professionally so that he—and the temple—will be promoted above their present position on the lowest rung of the ecclesiastical hierarchy.

Renko's departure is a stain on the family's honor. But the parishioners, covertly well aware of conditions inside the family, are inclined to blame Mineyo. They are willing to overlook the situation; if necessary they will even drive Mineyo out of the house—if only Sōshū will remarry and continue to serve his flock as before.

The Trap of Position

Though he temporizes, Sōshū for the first time is able to resist Mineyo's nocturnal advances. He pushes her from his bed, and gropes his way to sanctuary in the Great Hall, there reading sutras before the statue of Amida. It is successful as a tactic, but Sōshū soon realizes that he is merely hiding behind his official role. He questions the quality of his faith. "He was a coward, then—using his position as a priest, merely, seeking peace cheaply in an atmosphere where repentance, penance, strength of will came ready-made. And the scriptures did give peace of a kind. To an observer, Sōshū's 'penance' would probably have seemed exaggerated, too dramatic to be genuine. Just like a priest! he might have said—just like a priest!"

Sōshū recalls how St. Shinran 700 years before fought to liberate priests from the rule of chastity, to encourage a more honest recognition of human weakness. New disgust surges in him for having misused this freedom. One must not merely avoid temptation, one must overcome it.

For Mineyo, by contrast, religion is little more than a lifestyle habit and a repertoire of business patter. Every morning she reads scripture before the family altar, rapidly and without ever seeming to care what the words mean. "It was enough if she could finish each morning's duty in good time. The fact that she had never once missed a morning seemed to her proof of the depth of her faith; and being convinced of her saintliness, she convinced others of it, too." Sōshū is astonished by her knack for copying mannerisms from him and from other priests, when he overhears her quoting scripture and expounding karma to the parish women. Mineyo on her part cannot tolerate his doubts. She scolds him for failing his duty as a priest, a duty to display confidence and assuage the doubts of others even though he may be lost amid his own. Sōshū answers that the patina of professionalism is precisely what St. Shinran warned against. And he becomes aware for the first time that Mineyo cannot understand how professional duty may actually serve to block one's quest for personal enlightenment.

Mineyo's tone was accusing; like a creditor demanding payment of a debt. Sōshū saw her in a new light, realizing that she understood nothing of what he was thinking. Shinran had come to the point where he felt himself to be so hardened and steeped in sin that he was beyond even the hope of being saved—but it was this very despair of self that proved to be the beginning of his salvation. Sōshū wanted to say that he had realized how far from complete his own self-despair had been.

Had Mineyo been able to accept his deepening sense of guilt, his longing to leap beyond the ruts of role-routine, Sōshū might have found an accommodation with her. But she is able only to cling in noisy desperation to signs of physical vitality, family continuity, and professional fidelity. Sōshū will not allow her to be sacrificed simply to preserve his own position, for he acknowledges his share of responsibility for their adulterous affair. The very fact that she has now become repulsive to him personally makes her that much more a test of his capacity for compassion. Sōshū must come to accept and forgive her feelings, measure for measure as she truculently refuses to accept his.

The Trap of Self

Because any drastic move on his part will affect Mineyo, affect the future of his son, affect the entire parish, affect even the generations of dead parishioners whose souls are entrusted to his care, Sōshū knows that as a responsible man he must move with due deliberation. Nevertheless, in his own mind he is ready to shake off his position and profession. Though he continues his rounds as a priest, inwardly he is rehearsing the scene in which he will confess before his congregation and surrender his office to them. And yet, he admits, there is an even greater barrier to action; and that is his personal debility. "He merely lacked the courage—not only the courage to face the world, but the courage to confront the reality of his own situation, the need to gouge out of his own nature the weakness that made him so easy-going and willing to compromise."

But by listlessly remaining in his professional orbit he allows himself to be drawn into a deeper entanglement. As he goes to offer monthly prayers for the soul of her deceased husband, Sōshū finds that affection is blossoming between himself and a young widow. The two even dream of a new future together, though in this Sōshū recognizes a new bondage, being possessed by love. In his pilgrimage to the Buddha tree he has come upon yet another paradox: that if suffering originates from self-centered desire, so too does joy. The immediate price, however, is that he must practice a new pattern of deception, attempting to conceal his affair from family and parishioners.

Through further struggles Sōshū eventually comes to new insights into his lifelong imitation of St. Shinran. His agony of self-questioning has been a mistake, he realizes, for his own feeble strength would never be enough to carry him beyond the imprisoning bounds of self. Talking about it with a parishioner, Sōshū explain's Shinran's view as follows, contrasting it with the view of Shinran's own teacher, Hōnen.

Hōnen longed to give up every thought of trying to save himself, so that he could have absolute faith in the grace of Amida's Holy Vow. But is it really possible for a man to give up all self-striving? Theorizing apart, none of us could live a day without this activity of the self. We feel we ought to give it up, get rid of it altogether, but in practice we can't. Shinran insisted we couldn't save ourselves, just as Hōnen did. We may not be able to get rid of the selves working inside of us, but we can and do know how powerless they are. Shinran believed the attempt to get rid of self was itself as much an activity of the self as any of its more obvious manifestations—in which he was certainly correct. Then the real meaning of salvation by faith struck him. It means a man must take this struggling self, this ego so divisive, so conscious of its own identity, and surrender it just as it is—surrender his whole personality, in other words —to the mercy of the Holy Vow. That was something even Hōnen had never been able to do. Shinran's great achievement was to show that there needn't be any inconsistency between the ideas of self-salvation and salvation by grace.

... It means waking up to the truth that our lives as we actually live them, our ordinary day-to-day lives, are in fact lived under Amida's direction all the time. It means realizing that each of us is one with his Buddha-spirit. It's true that this realization is still an act of the self; but it does enable a man to avoid the big pitfalls in life. It gives him security, a feeling that life itself is trustworthy. All this is easy to talk about, of course. The mind has to take a big leap to get that far, though, and I find it terribly difficult.

Sōshū cannot yet shed self-attachment in that final leap of faith, but he has come to the point where he can shed his other attachments. Summoning his parishioners to an emergency meeting, he confesses before them and before the portrait of St. Shinran, and takes his leave from the Temple of the Merciful Buddha.

II. PATHWAYS TO PURE ACTION

To sketch in a few lines the Japanese heritage of pathways to personal growth is to court exaggeration and perhaps to do a disservice to centuries of spiritual and philosophical endeavor. My concern here, however, is not with the details of these recipes for liberation as doctrinal texts; I am looking to how they are applied in the contexts of maturation in ordinary lives.

If any single idiom can be taken as central to the many Japanese vocabularies of growth it is the notion of reaching out for "sincerity" (*makoto*), of striving to act from motives that are totally pure. Pure action may take many forms. One finds an array of different prescriptions for it in Japanese religion, ethics, politics, and art. Pure action might come as the opening of the inner eye in Zen satori, as the self-explosion of a kamikaze pilot striking his target, as the outpouring of creative impulse when a master calligrapher moves the microscopic tip of his brush across paper. Or it might come in the form that Sōshū seeks, as a total abandonment of the self in faith in the saving grace of Amida.

Whatever its form, however it be labeled, pure action is totally absorbing. It is human "peak experience" in its Japanese guise. In such moments you no longer are hampered by awareness. No longer are "you" acting; "it" or the "universe" is doing so. You are not "communing" with nature but *are* nature, moving with it in bursts of spontaneity that express the greatest truth of human nature. Only in such moments can you be certain that your actions spring from primal motives unsullied by attachments to self or to social position, by calculations of pain or gain.

These moments of truth—or moments when truth, beauty, and purity are one—are likely to be brief. They may be terminal. But try to force them to stay, à la Faust; try to stop the flow of change and impermanence; and you will slide back into temporizing, into expedients. You will once more be trapped into weighing good and evil, clinging again to those mundane illusions from which only pure action can deliver you. Indeed you may, like Sōshū, be drawn ever deeper into the worldly quicksand.

You cannot plan or schedule moments of pure action any more than you can plan moments of inspiration. Instead you must cultivate a readiness for them, even a passionate readiness. "The regard of the Japanese seems to be a kind of tense listening," writes Kurt Singer, "waiting for the sound that calls for action." This is the heart of the haiku spirit, of the *zuihitsu* "following the brush" or "stream of awareness" mentality in Japanese diary-keeping and other verbal arts. It is the goal of "one-pointedness" and the centering of being in Buddhist meditation or the aesthetics of Tea or the disciplines of traditional Japanese martial arts.

Though it is by no means limited to artistic pursuits, this might be considered a predominantly aesthetic view of the human potential. Moral and intellectual and technical components are included but are secondary. One could liken it to Keats's notion of "negative capability," the poet's openness to the world and readiness to respond to it.

Readiness can be gained only through persistent effort and self-discipline. And to give self-discipline a direction you must willingly suspend disobedience and channel your energies along a pathway that will lead to "expertness." Lacking a pathway, or taking a wrong one, you are likely to stop short. Your actions will end in "selfishness" (*wagamama*), in "arbitrariness" (*muri*), in "blockages" (*ikizumari*). Internally you may suffer psychological warping of the sorts that Freudian psychiatry attributes more narrowly to blocked sexuality. Externally you may only go through the motions of your role, and fail to merge with those around you in a creative flow of teamwork.

Japanese attention to the long-term cultivation of feeling-capacity or spirit stands out even against the general this-worldly or human-centered focus found in East Asian traditions. In a carefully executed questionnaire study, Takie Lebra has investigated attitudes toward justice and reward on the part of Japanese, Koreans, and (Hong Kong) Chinese. One of her conclusions, backed by several lines of evidence in the questionnaire responses, is that:

Japanese are concerned with the "human" implications of moral action, as seen in their preoccupation with building up a morally or emotionally strong, mature personality. Japanese goal orientation, then, appears to be directed toward a human "means" as well as toward an end result, while Chinese are much more exclusively biased for the latter and Koreans pay least attention to cultivation of the human means. . . . Japanese may be as success-oriented as Chinese, but constrained by the priority of the inner quality of man over an external successful outcome and by a long-ranged view of a human career.

It is not as if all Japanese in their adult years are occupied with formal training for pure action, though the concern for self-discipline can be found in some measure in most institutions and behavior settings. On their own initiative, relatively few Japanese would take religious orders; even Sōshū came to his Shin pathway by family tradition. Of my two dozen Hanshin interviewees, only one is taking religious instruction: Shōji's wife Haruko, who is caught up in Esoteric Buddhism (*Mikkyō*).

But secular forms of "spiritual education" (*seishin kyōiku*) are commonly offered as part of training programs for new employees in Japanese corporations and government agencies. The programs are mainly for younger adults, but more senior employees may also be sent for periodic refresher sessions. Cynics like to dismiss such programs as cow sociology, an attempt to produce docile and contented workers. But the programs tap that most widely taken of all Japanese stances toward liberation: that it can be more readily achieved *in* one's everyday roles—by learning to perform them "wholly"—than by seeking an other-worldly release *from* them. In his study of spiritual education in a banking corporation in western Japan, Thomas Rohlen puts it this way:

Stated simply, devotion to duty, perfected through greater self-discipline, in time leads to a reduction of the disturbance caused by conflicting demands. The result is an improved state of personal spiritual freedom and a sense of joy focused on fulfillment in one's work. This is a solution to man's problems in society based on a preoccupation with or absorption in socially prescribed activity. Devotion to duty, long esteemed in Japan, is the road to spiritual growth or fulfillment.

Avocations, arts, even a dedicated cultivation of taste: these also can provide pathways to wholeness. About half of my Hanshin interviewees currently take lessons in one or another of the traditional arts, such as flower-arranging, calligraphy, or the reciting of Nō-drama texts. Most of them readily pointed out to me that in these pursuits they were gaining not merely the satisfactions of skill but also those of discipline and self-composure. Some added that in their younger years they had often taken such lessons mainly because they ought to. A competent executive should be able to write with a clean and firm script; a competent housewife should be able to arrange flowers well. Now, however, they have taken up or returned to such lessons because they *want* to—they have become aware of the plane of "expertness" that can lie beyond mere skill.

Pathways vary in their appeal for different persons or for the same person at different phases of life. They also shift in popularity with the shifting slopes of history. Events may discredit an institution and thereby bring into disrepute the pathway it embodies. Adults may find that the pathway instilled in them early in life is now out of joint with the times. And this is the human situation of Japanese today in their middle and senior decades, the dilemma of the "prewar generation," the *senzenha*.

Buddhism already had begun to compromise itself in the seventeenth century when it accepted official sponsorship from the Tokugawa regime (1603–1868). From then until late in the nineteenth century local Buddhist temples were ordered to maintain census records, provide primary schooling, and ferret out subversive Christians. When these functions were abolished in the 1870's there arose a wave of popular revulsion toward the temples, some even being put to the torch. Hence the popular sneer that temple Buddhism survives only as a funeral business. In the postwar decades a few sects have been able to revitalize the Buddhist pathway. Sects such as Nichiren Shōshū—best known in the West as the Sōka Gakkai—claim several million members. But temple Buddhism has thus far been unable to rekindle this enthusiasm.

Shinto was thrust forward in the 1870's as the moral base for the modern nation. Officially sponsored and propagated, Bushido, a blend of Shinto and neo-Confucian and Zen concepts that had been the ethos of the Tokugawa ruling class, came to be widely absorbed throughout the population in the years of modern nation-building and military expansion. When Imperial Japan went down in defeat in the Pacific War, however, and the Allied Powers came in to reorder the nation, the Shinto pathway also became soiled. And this has been the nub of the dilemma for the prewar generation.

In the flippant phrase of the Japanese mass media, the senzenha are the Last Confucians. They are the last cohort born and raised in the prewar era, with its ethos of dedication to family, community, and emperor. They were thrust into their adult roles just at the moment when Imperial Japan was thrust into defeat and devastation. Without ever leaving home they became Displaced Persons, because all that they had been trained to revere and to strive for was now in public disrepute.

The dilemma affects men one way, women another. Both were given much the same indoctrination, but for women the pathway to pure action led through private rather than public roles. They could best realize their peak sincerity by becoming "good wives and wise mothers." During the war some women were trained with bamboo spears as a civil guard to repel an expected invasion army. But they were offered only the possibility of home-front heroism. Women were mobilized in large numbers for war-materiel factories, and were mustered into air-raid fire-fighting teams. But even during the darkest days of the war, Japan's leaders did not seriously consider allowing women into the armed forces, not even in the auxiliary roles open to them in the Western military. Whenever the policy was mooted the standard rebuttal was that to do so would be to abandon the very ideals the war was being fought to preserve.

The postwar years, however, have brought a turning. Public roles are open to women as never before in Japanese history. They even may enlist in the armed forces. Anyone who scorns "working women" risks being branded as unregenerate. And for women—as we shall see in Chapters 5 and 6—the plane of greatest friction is that between the pathways of "work" and "family" careers.

For senzenha men the problem is instead one of finding a more suitable kind of work. In interview after interview they elaborated a theme that I shall call aesthetic unemployment. Some men say flatly, "I died on August 15, 1945." They go on to explain that of course they have married, raised children, supported their families, pursued ordinary occupations. But they have had to struggle to find an outlet for the idioms of pure action and sincerity instilled by their earlier training. That pathway had been embedded in the institutions of the state and the military, but defeat stained those institutions and left the idioms in limbo. And the chief postwar alternatives—pathways of entrepreneurship and of enjoyment—are what Shōji the realtor and his age-mates had been taught were the very cause of industrial Japan's human malaise.

Such materialism, said the famed author Mishima Yukio, is a green snake gnawing inside the Japanese bosom. Mishima's own suicide at the age of 45 dramatized flamboyantly the sense of aesthetic unemployment that he shared with his generation. Few of his contemporaries might emulate his resolve, but most of them found it easy to admire the total dedication he summoned in 1970 when he took his life in classic seppuku, calling upon the Ground Self-Defense Force to rise up and lead the nation to a moral rearmament. Shōji is one such man; permit me to introduce him to you.

III. SHŌJI

Words are Shōji's favorite tools. He chooses them thoughtfully, uses them easily. At times he will pause to order his phrases but almost never will he edit or amend in mid-utterance. The tone is sober but not somber, dappled with a self-accepting humor as he reviews his life. No question draws a look of annoyance, much less of shock. His words seem to comfort him like a many-layered self-defense force.

As we sit in his furniture-filled little living room his wife is in and out, punctuating the conversation with snacks and verbal footnotes. Shōji leans back slightly in an overstuffed chair, in a posture of relaxed alertness. To his right against the wall stands a light teakwood secretary of a Scandinavian design, perhaps even imported. In front of it is an ordinary gray-steel office chair. The glass-front shelves of the secretary reveal a dozen or more books on real estate law plus a few others on Japanese politics. The shelves also offer an assortment of drinking glasses and bottles of whiskey of varying brands, sizes, and qualities. On one shelf there are several two-ounce bottles; on another are quarts and fifths, including one of Jack Daniels with a miniature apron—probably wife-made—draped across its midriff.

Traffic noises can be heard in the distance, from the arterial highway and the suburban railway line. But closer to hand, in the gardens of this tract of cramped single-family dwellings, the voices of songbirds dominate.

Shōji frequently, though not compulsively, lights cigarettes as he talks. An almost imperceptible twitch appears on the left side of his face —a mild tic that seems to belie his apparent ease.

On my last visit to his house, as I stood up to leave, Shōji stopped me. He groped under the sofa and eventually pulled out a cardboard carton. It contained about two dozen stereo recordings, all alike, in covers that were pure white with a modest blue-and-gold nautical emblem. Diffidently, he offered me one. The title read simply:

CADETS OF THE SEAGOING SPECIAL FORCES
Remembering Our Youth

A passerby glancing at the scene might have wondered if Shōji were a closet militarist secretly touting the old Imperial Japanese Army. Or he might have seen Shōji as one of those middle-aged men who never outgrow an adolescent enthusiasm for playing soldier. But to me the gift had little to do with militarism. I accepted it as a powerful symbol of what Shōji had been trying to convey to me in words for many weeks —the meaning of his quarter-century of struggle to find an outlet for his ideals of pure action.

I don't believe a middle-age crisis is in store for me. Mine came ten years early. I am in what the world regards as middle age, but in my case the crisis passed a decade ago when I opened my real estate agency.

You have to realize that most men in my generation have been tossed around by society, though not, perhaps, as much as I have. When we graduated from college there was a job shortage. Even my friends who did find jobs often had to change or were pushed out in corporate mergers. Now that social conditions finally have stabilized we are settling down and breathing easier. But also we have reached the age where you don't go taking big risks anymore.

Perhaps we would feel differently if things had been more stable, but we've been buffeted by storms and have acquired a powerful hunger for security. In us you find a distaste for uncertainty. Now we have families, and kids are expensive to raise. In Japan it's difficult for older men to find good jobs; nobody is seeking us out. We aren't technicians, we have no special skills to offer an employer, so there aren't any opportunities for us to take a new plunge. We aren't marketable.

This has been a transition period for Japan. In the old days if you graduated from college your salary would be pegged to your education. Now with the spread of the "mass media" school system a college degree doesn't have much value. And my age group has been in the middle of it all. But if the turmoil is over I'm not sorry. Actually it's been more fun for me than for a lot of other men—at least I try to draw some consolation from that—and I think I have had more experience than the guy who has plodded along steadily in the same single line of work.

My powers of reasoning continue to grow, but I feel as if somewhere along the line my development as a full human being was halted. I have not been in an environment, past or present, that brings out the best of my abilities and talents. In that sense I have been madly accumulating years without getting any benefit from them. I reckon that even as a young man I was capable of doing the work I am doing now. When I think about it I suppose I have been maturing as a person, but my abilities haven't grown.

I'm aware that I am not making the most of my talents. I'm not at the age when a man should be taking it easy: I wish I were in more stimulating circumstances. I would like to bring in a few people and expand the size of the agency: take advantage of the alter ego that makes my mind so complex. But realtors are in short supply now. So nothing comes of the idea. I earn enough to feed my family so I coast along on inertia.

I look upon myself as fundamentally honest, a good sort of guy who has a strong sense of justice. Basically I am not a businessman. After ten years in this line of work I find that people in general do not regard realtors as honest. No man wants to betray his conscience. I mean, in this business you have to lie and deceive as a matter of course, and since I am getting so I do that very naturally, I suppose I am changing. If a client seems to doubt my honesty I'm able to make him believe in me—that's new. But at heart I am not the realtor type, I think. Other people tell me that, too. As a matter of fact, there is a plus factor in the gap between the professional me and the real me. Customers seem to accept the idea that although I am a realtor I do not have the usual realtor faults.

When I first found out about how much you have to lie as a routine part of the work, I doubted that I could make a go of it. You have to make statements that are ethically wrong even though they are not contrary to commercial law. Still, you know it's not right. For example, I am now buying up plots of land and putting together a large tract for a development corporation. Some people are cooperative and good-natured about it all, and will sell their land to you at any reasonable price; others refuse to cooperate and stubbornly hold you up for more money. The terms of the contract are the same in both cases, but one man gets a higher price—and you have to conceal that from the other fellow. That seems contrary to common honesty, but if you did just what the ethics textbooks say you should, you'd be a flop in this business.

Sometimes I feel sorry for a customer—but you can't make a living by being totally honest. So I go and have a couple of drinks at a music bar, sing a few songs, and tell myself what's a man to do? I am able to slough off the humiliation that way. I don't carry my discontent home and dump it on the family.

It used to be that real estate, and the securities trades, were looked down on by the public. When I first opened my agency, people said my work would make it difficult to find a husband for our daughter. I don't hear that kind of thing lately. In the old days a man might not be accepted by a private college because his grandfather had been a stockbroker. But you know the wife and I found out that just this past year the local colleges decided that applicants no longer have to fill in the blank that asks "Father's Occupation."

In my experience the very best line of work is teaching. In business there are times when you are obliged to lie. But a teacher, now, he can operate in the open, live an honest life. Of course an educator may have to deal with messy human relations, but he does not need to betray himself with professional cunning and trickery. No need to beat his head against the wall every day. No need to stop for a drink on the way home so he can make a mental 180-degree turn. A small turn, maybe, but his work need not subvert his values. My boyhood dream of being a soldier was snuffed out by the war, and after the war my career in politics never got off the ground. But I served as an educator for a short time and I know what it's like.

Lately I find myself wondering, though, if I may not have something of a businessman's personality after all. Maybe this *is* the right profession for me. I've learned to manipulate clients. I find the step-by-step process of bringing off a deal downright fascinating. The moment when an agreement is reached, know-ing the transaction will take place the next day, is for me a mo-ment of pure pleasure.

I seem to be too busy for hobbies. Does it sound affected to say that my work is my hobby? There is nothing in life I like as much as conferring with people. The only part of it that I dislike is having to cater to them for the sake of business. To flatter people, appease their vanity—that's *not* me.

I admit that I have regrets. To understand why, you have to know that after the war I burned with political ambition. Had I been able to follow a career in politics, regardless of how far I might or might not have gone, I am sure that I would not feel any regrets. Sometimes I tell myself I wasn't born right. Or that if I hadn't got married I could have done what I really wanted to. Under the marital yoke it became impossible.

Childhood and Dedication

I should make it clear that the regrets cover my more recent years, not my earlier ones. I have no regrets about my childhood or about the army. Young people today probably can't under-stand that. But when I was in the army, I gave my life to it. To be a young man was to be a soldier, so far as I was concerned, and the feeling was terrific. I don't envy the freedom that young men have today, but probably it's a mistake to force comparisons between youth now and youth in my day. If anything I feel sorry for young people today because they have so much in material goods that they have difficulty controlling their desires. All you need today is money, and the less you have the more miserable you are. I believe that when I was young things were more equal, and that made life easier.

If I think back to when I first began to be aware of the world, my memories are full of seeing young men off to join the army and welcoming them home again. One of our primary school textbooks began with the lines:

> Blossoming, blossoming, the cherry trees are blossoming;
> Advancing, advancing, the soldiers are advancing.

Everybody admired a soldier in those days. In the village where I lived in Shikoku you weren't a real man until you had served your two-year hitch. From what I could see, young men who returned from the army really did have a new dignity in the way they carried themselves, and that must have come from the training they had been given.

My family was among the village elite, and I was treated with more respect than most kids. I would take part in the festivals and the Bon dances and such, but I never was a regular member of the village youth group. I also was one of the few in that primary school who went on to middle school. Our little school had about two hundred students altogether; and maybe one per year, some years none, would enroll in middle school.

Our family line was the hereditary line of priests for the Shinto guardian shrine of the village. In the Tokugawa period, we were given permission to take a family name and were treated the same as samurai. My grandfather, country priest that he was, gained a reputation as a scholar, and every year he was invited to Tokyo to serve as a special lecturer at the College of National Studies. His first son succeeded him as chief priest of the village shrine, and *his* son—my cousin—is now the fifteenth generation in office.

As second son, my father had to establish a branch family, although he too was qualified to serve as a priest. So he ran a general store and served as a priest part-time. It was a typical rural store, with all sorts of everyday items. Dad took care of the purchasing and stocking but it was my mother who transacted most of the daily trade.

I was in second grade in 1936 when the China war began. I entered middle school in 1940, which the teachers reminded us was the year 2600 of the Japanese calendar. "You've come here in a memorable year," they told us. "Prove yourselves worthy of it." Actually, middle school wasn't much different from what it is today, except that we took military training. And of course there weren't any sports to speak of. Baseball was forbidden, as an enemy game. Judo and kendo were required as part of physical education, but we had nothing else.

In September 1944, the fall term of my fifth year in middle school, I volunteered for military service. I was sent to Shōdoshima for training in an outfit that was part of the army's Seagoing Special Forces. By that stage in the war the army and navy were at odds, and the army was creating its own maritime units. I was in the second battalion, which was made up of some fifteen hundred volunteers recruited from all over the country. Hardly anybody from my outfit died in action, though almost everybody from the first battalion did.

More than half of us were trained to be so-called *marurei*—riders on human torpedoes. When I think about it now it makes me shudder, but at the time on Shōdoshima we had no doubts about what we were doing. We had volunteered, we wanted to fight. The highest goal of life was to die in action. I gave myself to it totally. Life on Shōdoshima was pure joy for me, and I can be very nostalgic for it. It was my second home village. When I go to a bar now to sing, I go to a place where they sing army songs. I know them all by heart. About the only recordings I buy are ones of army songs.

Much as I like to sing I can only sing army songs. Even though I know quite a few popular tunes, I don't try to sing them—other than a few sentimental ones. The army songs have a different rhythm. The verses all link up. There is continuity from beginning to end, and I like that. Some of them are mighty long, but I can sing them all the way through. Whereas in today's songs I don't understand the words at all. It could be that I learned the army songs at a time when my ability to memorize was better, and I can recall every verse of "Wheat and Soldiers" or "Katō Hayabusa's Combat Squad." I don't sing in the car or in the bath, usually—just at parties, and at bars where customers can request numbers. I know that some men have bitter memories of army life, and that to them the songs bring sadness. To me the army was a direct extension of my boyhood years, and when I sing army songs my whole heart goes into them.

I don't care much for being hemmed in by rules. I wouldn't make a good salary man, because an organization that is loose enough to allow room for complaints will let out a vigorous spirit of opposition in me. But I have no difficulty submitting to an absolute order like that in the army.

We've organized a veterans association and have met in alternate years in Tokyo and on Shōdoshima. We get a turnout of a hundred to a hundred and fifty men from all over the country each time. We keep alive the memory of what we had then. We've also talked about erecting a memorial to those of our outfit who died in action.

At the time the war ended I could not readily comprehend what had happened. After a while I gradually came to the relaxing sense that I actually was going home again. My outfit remained on active duty, but I was mustered out on September 4, 1945, exactly one year to the day after I had enlisted.

Political Ambition

In November of that year I moved in with my elder sister and her husband in their house here in Takarazuka. I lived there while attending Kwansei Gakuin College. I had to take an entrance examination, but it was an easy one compared to what you have today. Also, because of the war, many of the departments had low enrollments; some weren't even filling their quotas. I went into the College of Law, majoring in political science, since by then my ambitions had turned to politics. Actually, I didn't spend as much time on studies as I did on the student movement. By senior year I was president of the student council.

In those days the main goals of the student movement were to fight against tuition hikes and to demand that campus facilities be improved. There was rampant inflation, and the tuition was being raised every semester. So our struggles were almost all confined to campus issues. Although the Zengakuren had already been organized, we didn't join it; instead, we organized a separate private-college league of students from Kandai, Dōshisha, and Ritsumeikan.

My class, the class of 1950, was the first to graduate under the new system. But you have to remember that in 1950 the allied occupation army was still here. Leftists were often suppressed and under suspicion. Economic conditions were unfavorable, and jobs were not easy to come by. But this was one college student who hadn't paid much attention to the job situation. I didn't go to school with the idea that it would be a stepping-stone to a comfy job. By the time I had finished my term of office as student council president, most corporations already had held their examinations for new employees. I failed the examinations that I did take, since the attitude of most corporations was that anybody with leadership talent would, if hired, be likely to try to organize a union, and who needs that?

Since none of the corporations wanted me, I stayed on and entered the graduate college, but also accepted an offer to teach in a middle school. My students from that year are grown up now, but some of them still come to visit me and still call me *sensei* ("teacher" or "master").

Not long after that, a friend invited me to work with him in a nylon-processing business he had organized in Osaka. So after a year I resigned from teaching and from graduate college and joined him. All in all I was with the company nine years. At first we printed nylon cloth. Then we began manufacturing nylon badminton-racquet strings. The old-type strings were of silk that went through a gelatinizing process, but our company with a burst of effort developed a much better nylon type. And small as we were—really a tiny operation—we controlled 80 percent of national sales during the badminton boom of the 1950's.

But working in a little business was not, after all, my life's ambition. So although I was with the company for some nine years, in 1958 I took leave to run for the city council in Takarazuka. Many friends who had been with me in the student movement were by then in local political circles and were encouraging me to run.

I wanted mine to be a completely honest campaign, with no entanglements. Some of my former students came to work for me, even though they were still not old enough to vote themselves. So in part I was inspired by the idea of proving to them that you can win with an honest campaign. Their enthusiasm was so pure that I would not have dared to let myself be bought, even if I had wanted to.

I made a point of not canvassing for votes before the official campaign period opened. We put up posters, of course, to announce when and where I would make appearances. But I drew most of them myself the night before. My father took charge of campaign headquarters—I should explain that by then he was sickly, and he, mother, and my three younger sisters all had moved here to live with us.

We calculated that I needed 1,200 votes. That meant persuading one hundred people a day during the twelve-day electioneering period. If you figure you may be able to win four or five votes per appearance, it added up to 25 appearances—speaking and shaking hands—a day. We gave it all we had, but in the end we lost.

I tried not to be downcast about the defeat, knowing that in Japanese politics you need a lot of money or a lot of luck. Since then I've tried to console myself that I probably would not have accomplished anything in politics on my own anyway. You can't buck the system and hope to get anything done. But it really cut me to see how the students cried the night of the election. I felt I had let them down, and I told myself I could never run for office again. In return for their pure flow of enthusiasm I had brought them only the bitter taste of hopelessness. That election was the biggest turning point in my life. When I gave up my political ambitions it really changed me.

Work and the Self

Not that it happened all at once. You're probably wondering how I came to be in real estate. Well, I stayed with the nylon company for about three years after the election. During that time I began studying for the test for a realtor's license. I intended to run for office again, and I reasoned that I needed a job that would keep me in town during the daytime, so that people could get to know me. After all, I had been leaving Takarazuka in the morning to go to work in Osaka and not coming home until evening. I wasn't around town where I could be seen. Becoming a realtor seemed like a good way to accomplish that. So I wanted to get my license even though at the time I was not sure that I actually would practice the trade.

But I never ran for office again, and don't expect to be asked to do so. It didn't work out, and that's that. I believe I have come to accept it.

Over the years I have gained self-confidence in my work and am even finding some enthusiasm for it. I consider myself a full-fledged professional, especially now that I have this commission to buy up land for a development corporation. It involves more than a hundred parcels of farmland owned by some forty different families. The corporation is investing 1,500 million yen in the enterprise.

This is not like purchasing land that has been held on spec: it's land that has been handed down in farm families from generation to generation, so the process gets complicated. It's not just a simple cash-and-carry transaction. You have to get the owners to consider what the future holds for them. They know their village is on the edge of the urban area and will soon be part of it. They know that there is no future for their families in farming even if they hang on for one more generation. But they also know that land prices are certain to keep on going up, and so they are reluctant to sell. It's like being a consultant on taxes and financial management. Land buying is your business, of course, but you can't take too short-range a view. You need only a few parcels of land from them for the current project. But if it's a success the tract will be enlarged and you'll be going back to the farmers again. You hurt yourself over the long run if you leave them with the feeling that "He sure talked a good line—and it was all a pack of lies!"

But the sums involved are enormous, the human relationships intricate, and it can be a challenge. There are drawbacks to this line of work, naturally. There is never a time when you are really off duty—not that I find myself hungry for time off anyway. When somebody asks you to call on them you don't dare refuse. These farmers work year-round and don't take vacations. So even when I do set aside a block of time now and then for a short vacation, I may be called out in the middle of it, even called back from a trip. And if I enjoy the negotiating, being an intermediary, I sure don't enjoy the paperwork or the dealings with the tax office. You see, my transactions are all a matter of public record, out in the open. Not a chance for any kind of secret maneuvering; and that makes the record-keeping very cumbersome.

I have started smoking again because of the work. In the army I used to have a smoke once in a while. But I only started smoking regularly after the war. I was a heavy smoker for about fifteen years, then quit for about eight years. One day my daughter complained about the smell and I just quit cold. Lately I'll go at it for two or three months and then quit again for a while. I know it isn't good for your health. But there are times when that cigarette tastes mighty fine. The one I like is in the morning when I go out to let the car engine run for a while to get it warmed up, and I sit there waiting for breakfast.

And you know there are times when you are calling on a customer, and for every three things you tell him he hardly says word one. Some people just sit there mute. If they'll just say *something*, you can take it from there and lead them around to the purpose of the visit. At times like that when you have to do tricks to create an opening you can say to them, "How about a cigarette?" and offer a light.

So it's a business tool. The fact that he needs such a tool may be a sign that there is something lacking in a man. But at times I get restless, anxious, determined to get my hands on a certain piece of property. That's when a cigarette is perfect for soothing the nerves. A man with a load of faults has to resort to little tricks.

I have also gotten to drinking these last few years as part of the business—never used to be much of a drinker at all. A few drops of sake compensate for a lot of weaknesses. And many of my clients like their liquor. Talk to them cold sober and there is no chance to open channels of communication. Gradually I have developed a tolerance and can hold my own now. Not that I like the taste of it so much, but I like the atmosphere it creates.

Years Passing

There's an optical illusion that goes with this business. What I mean is that you handle enormous sums of other people's money and you get to fantasizing. Lately, with the rapid rise in land prices, the amounts of money I handle are larger and larger every year. But it's also true that I ought to be earning more money for myself soon. I'm not getting any younger. Not that I hanker after more money than we need to live on. Just that when you pass 40 you begin to stare at the end. You are more conscious of your health even though you don't talk about it. You sense the coming of age in the deaths of your friends, and know that you need to set aside savings for old age. Who wants to be a seedy old man?

For about ten years I have noticed that when I walk a ways I get to hobbling. The first time was when I once had to climb to the top of a hill to look at a tract of land. Made it to the top all right, but not with any speed. At first I thought I must be just over-tired. Since then, well, it's annoying. I have been taking pills for strength and stamina. With Haruko's interest in Esoteric Buddhism, the family has been using Chinese herb medicines and garlic purgative pills daily. I am mildly diabetic. And my eyes are getting a little funny, probably far-sighted. I don't wear glasses yet, but I've noticed that some of the print on forms is incredibly tiny these days.

Mentally, of course, I'm young. Aren't we all that way: at 25 we think we're 18, and at 45 we think we're 25. I went to my 25th class reunion a while ago and noticed that you can recognize some people at a glance, but others you just don't recognize at all, they have changed so much. Everybody recognized me at once. I am more conscious of age nowadays, but I think that the salary men are the ones who are really concerned about it. Their incomes are pegged to age. They have to think about retiring in a few years. Those who are section chiefs or department heads deal regularly with younger men under them, so naturally they are going to be more attentive to age differences. In my profession you can continue to work as long as your health holds up, so naturally I pay more attention to health. Ask me what it's like to be in your 40's and I'll tell you—the period when you start feasting your eyes on the medical-advice columns the minute you think nobody is watching. There is no pleasure in wearing an old body.

I try to get plenty of rest—sleep late in the morning when I've been out late with a client. There can be a stupendous racket in the house and I'll sleep through it. And I can nap anytime, anywhere. Haruko teases me about catnapping even during the time between going into a coffee shop and ordering a cup of coffee, and the time the waitress brings it to the table.

I've been cutting down on food consciously. Sometimes I don't eat a meal. My tastes haven't changed noticeably—all my life I have preferred plain dishes. Haruko likes to make elaborate ones every so often. When she does, I eat what she puts in front of me. But she knows my preferences—and she never uses Worcestershire sauce, for example.

I know I should exercise, but I don't. I keep wanting to go for long walks, but I feel funny walking around the park in the daytime when all the salary men are at their offices. I've even considered getting a dog.

If I find myself with time to spare, I just loaf around the house, napping or watching the tube. Out on the job if I need to kill time I go to a music bar. My hours are so irregular that I can't watch the same TV program from week to week. When I feel really run down I knock off for three or four days. But it's hard to arrange for a regular day off. Some people can see you only on Sundays. The family tries to take a short vacation trip about once a year, but even that poses problems. A while ago we had made reservations to go to the Japan Sea coast. We wanted to taste the crab there. But because of business I had to back out at the last minute, so Haruko and Yoko went without me. For us it's a matter of packing up and leaving the moment we have decided to take a trip.

We eat dinner out fairly often as a family, usually in Kobe. Places where the food's good and the cost reasonable, like the Itō Grill or the Chiyozushi. With only the three of us it's easy to come to an agreement about where we'll go. Now and then we go bowling, too. Otherwise there's not much time to do things as a family.

Marriage and Family

I don't sense that Haruko has changed as much as I have over the years. I'm healthier and I think I look younger, even though I'm two years older. But she's a sturdy sort and fights back. We laugh about how I used to say, "Look at the mother before you marry—and see what *I* got!" Her mother was a classic example of the obedient Japanese wife.

We first met when we were in college, though she was in a different school. We knew each other for seven years before we married, part of a group of a half dozen who hung around together. It was a very pure relationship. Her father kept hoping she would marry a man who would take over his family business. And I just plain didn't think much about marriage at that time, it wasn't in my life plans.

I don't see that we are much different from any ordinary married couple. Just that comparatively speaking we have more in common. Sure, I had expected her to be more tractable—but we share all sorts of topics of conversation, and we've known each other's friends since college days. We have also had friends in common all these years. On that score it's different for us than for others in our college group. Each of them married somebody outside the group.

The worst time for us as a family was in the late 1950's. I had lost the election and was taking up real estate. My parents and the three younger sisters had come here to live. As the only son, I had to see that they were married off. Then my parents died, and so did Haruko's mother. For five years after Yoko was born, Haruko had a severe skin rash. Finally she went to a *seimei handan* specialist—one of those who advises you on whether your name and the characters you write it with are favorable or not. He devised new names for all three of us in the family. We changed simultaneously to three names that he had calculated would be good not only for each of us individually but for the family as a whole. Not that anything happened suddenly. But over a couple of years Haruko began to be more easygoing, and we finally took care of the sisters. And I started to take a drink now and then.

At times we were strapped financially. The agency didn't do well at first. Even now our income is not all that predictable from year to year, although at least we are up to an ordinary Japanese standard of living. Hard up as we were, however, I never had to put Haruko to work. I have not had to lean on her financially, and that's true emotionally as well. I have never worried myself into such a state that everything had to be left to her. Same's true in reverse. She is stable, and has not had to cling to me. Twenty years seems like a long time to be married, but you look back on it and it's very short.

I have to acknowledge the fact that I am becoming more conservative in the way I act. How I argue with people, how I state my views. Compared to the way I was when I was young, I hold back now. I was full of fire when I was younger—took what I was thinking and went right into action. Not now. On political issues I am still a reformer, but I suppose you could say that I go about it in a more mature way now.

When I look at my daughter, Yoko, she seems too grown up and reticent for her age. She ought to be more radical. Having expectations put on you can be a heavy burden, so I haven't loaded her with any. I just want her to develop along the lines *she* wants. Since she's a girl, to put it abstractly, I'd like her to grow up to be a gentle woman. But I do not believe it is good to make demands on a girl. If we had had a son I would want him to develop socially, to take up some of the projects I couldn't.

Futures

When Yoko marries, I suppose it will mean a change in our life-style, but I don't expect that to make a change in me. I'll just go on being conservative. Can't very well drop what I'm doing as long as there's the wife to support.

I used to be active socially, but there's not enough time for it now. For a while I was in the environment movement. When Yoko was in primary school Haruko hated being in the PTA, so I went instead. After all, it's mostly a mamma's organization, so if a man shows up they like to put him to work. Not that I asked to take on offices, but they probably knew that I enjoy helping out and running things. The year I was president was also the year of the school's 80th anniversary, so there was more to do than usual. It was mostly a matter of mediating between the P and the T. I'd been an educator myself and could appreciate the teachers' sense of position as well as the self-centeredness of the parents. Not that a major flap ever erupted, but the arguments could get interesting. There's nothing like grabbing hold of a messy tangle and straightening it out. However, all that ended when Yoko graduated. Besides, these days I'm not around the house so much any more.

I almost never vote now. Used to be I did so regularly, but not in the last few years. Partly it's that nobody ever comes to campaign in this neighborhood, so you don't pick up the election fever. But it's hard to stir up interest in elections: the favorite always carries the district. And no matter who wins it's the same old politics.

When I'm old I want to do something that will benefit society. Maybe I could build an old people's home and run it, and meet my end there. I don't expect Yoko to look after me when I'm old. That's an imposition on your child. I want to manage things on my own. I can get along with all kinds of people. When you go to a class reunion the athletic types will be sitting at one table and the studious types at another. I'm invited to both tables. Last time I ended up at the head table, as a sort of emcee leading the singing. After all, I trained my voice for debate in college, and it still comes out strong.

With my luck, I know better than to go chasing rainbows again. I'm aware of my age, which is the same as saying that I have become utterly commonsensical. I really couldn't care less if my agency never gets to be very large. But I do think I should expand it beyond a lone-wolf operation, take in some younger people. That requires more capital than I can put together yet, however. I don't mind now, but once a man has gray hairs on his head he should not have to go from house to house humbling himself and begging people to sell their land. That's a miserable sight to see. In that sense there is an age limit to this business after all.

One thing I will have to decide about while I'm still alive is re- ligion—whether I want my funeral to be Shinto or Buddhist. Lately I have been feeling strongly that I should drop Shinto and change over to Buddhism. I might seem to be Shinto by heredity, but I don't put much store in it. As I see it, Shinto was supported and protected by the state in the war years. You might call it a patriotic self-discipline. When you go to war you offer prayers; if you return safely you give thanks. And while you are away the family prays for victory in battle. It's all based on sacred myths. At any rate that's what I was taught.

Buddhism is more profound. I'm more at ease thinking about my parents as Buddhist souls than as Shinto gods. It amounts to the same thing, I know, but the Buddhist view sits better with me. Basically I am not religious, but what faith I have is probably Buddhist.

My mother was Buddhist, so the relatives on her side hold Buddhist anniversary services for the deceased. My father's kin, of course, are mainly Shinto and follow Shinto services. For my parents we have had fifth- and tenth-anniversary Shinto services. But this year happens to be Dad's thirteenth and Mother's seventh anniversary. The fact that both fall in the same year is especial- ly significant in Buddhism, so this year we will hold Buddhist services.

I am not one to think much about either the past or the future, and I have never put myself out to hang onto mementos or souvenirs. We do have some essays and samples of calligraphy of mine that my parents saved from my primary school days. Like all foolish parents, they probably were hoarding them for the day when I became famous. Out in the villages, people show off such things. But I'm different as a parent. Of course we have snapshots, and a few drawings that Yoko made. But our attitude toward them is not like my parents' attitude. When I take out those old writings and look at them I realize that life has turned out very differently from what I had hoped in those days—it's a bittersweet feeling, let me tell you. I guess I was a romantic then.

IV. PATHWAYS AND THE INDIVIDUAL

If a pathway provides direction and depth for one's character, to abandon a pathway is to risk succumbing to confusion, to assail integrity. Since 1945 this has been a key dilemma for Shōji and for other men of the prewar generation. Their "starting position of ego-orientation" was a certainty that the pathway of the soldier-patriot offered the most secure career of aesthetic employment. After 1945 they could perhaps accept national defeat and devastation as evidence that the pathway was ruinous in its social consequences. But they have been vastly more reluctant to accept the idea that the pathway may be a poor guide to *personal* conduct.

The dilemma became compounded in two ways. First, within the patriot pathway itself, stress on immediate action made more troublesome the prospect of surviving and growing older in a peaceful postwar milieu. As Thomas Rohlen has put it, the official code allowed that "violent impatience with the world's problems . . . was justified in terms of personal sacrifice. The goals of quietude and wisdom were subordinated to action, and youthful impetuousness was equated with purity of motive. . . . The sense of biographical growth was subordinated to that of instant moral achievement."

Second, the official postwar code has not offered a new pathway that is as personally compelling. The democratic ethos offers social ideals, plus techniques for determining the collective will;

and this can evoke personal sacrifice and dedication. But so far, at least, it has been difficult to translate democracy into a new career of lifetime aesthetic employment. New images have been created, of the person as "citizen" (*shimin*) or as "member of society" (*shakaijin*), but they seem shallow in terms of biographical growth. The pathways of entrepreneurship and enjoyment, long available in the Japanese heritage as alternatives, now seem to rival patriotism and citizenship in the time-depth they offer. And it is no longer so certain—as once claimed in the orthodoxy—that entrepreneurship and enjoyment will eventuate in societal ruin.

Sōshū's situation is uncomplicated by this kind of pathway dilemma. Early and late he commits his course toward Buddhist enlightenment. His task is to renew his determination, to shed the illusions and attachments that stand in his way. Sōshū can also draw on tradition for career models, finding his chief model in the life of St. Shinran 700 years earlier.

Shōji's situation is more diffuse, more that of an ordinary man trying to muddle through. I once asked him if there were any particular person he had sought to emulate in his own life. "No," he replied, and thought for a minute. There was a time in middle school, he said, when he had been inordinately fascinated by the life of Yoshida Shōin. Yoshida (1831–59) was born of humble village samurai ancestry. In that respect he was similar to Shōji. He was martyred in his campaign to rid the country of what he regarded as corrupt shogunal leadership. In subsequent generations many Japanese have taken him as an exemplar; his life even drew paragraphs of praise from Robert Louis Stevenson. Yoshida was executed in 1859 on the 25th of November, the month and day that Mishima Yukio chose for his own suicide of self-martyrdom more than a century later.

After 1945 Shōji purged the military element from within himself, as the occupying forces purged military leaders from the government. Shōdoshima became sanctified for Shōji as the milieu of his seventeenth year, the time when he was able to vibrate in a pure outpouring of his whole being. The military manifestations of it became incidental. Shōdoshima, he told me, had become his utopia.

For more than a decade afterward he sought to actualize that utopia and to preserve the pathway it symbolizes, by attempting a career of pure patriotism in the Yoshida image. The idea that Shōji was destined to be a leader had been fostered already in his childhood. He was the son of a local elite family. Generations earlier they had been allowed to take a family name and had been treated like samurai. He was one of the very few students in his village to advance to middle school. The idea gained strength when he was accepted into the Special Forces; it was reinforced when he was accepted into a university. His election as student council president gave the idea validation in a more adult setting. The capstone came when friends asked him to run for election to the city council. Marriage was not even in his life plans then, and his courtship was protracted for seven years. He took a position as a manager in a small factory, but that was a concession to practicality—just as his father before him had opened a general store in order to support a career as a rural Shinto priest.

During the military years the career of politician had been suspect. It might lead one into a morass of intrigue and payola. Perhaps, though, in the new democratic era the political life could be purified. In thrusting himself into an impetuous campaign of honest electioneering, Shōji was holding to his patrimonial pathway and its hope of "instant moral achievement." The loss of that campaign precipitated the most severe crisis of his life. He was forced to admit that society may have no place for his style of integrity and fulfillment. Perhaps the soldier-patriot pathway was as ruinous for him personally as for society generally. For the defeat fell not only upon him but upon those dear to him—father, wife, former pupils—who also had campaigned so honestly.

Names and Continuities

The loss of the election plunged the whole family into a period of inner unrest. There were parental deaths, and difficulties in marrying off the younger sisters. His wife Haruko had a persisting skin rash. Conditions began to take a turn for the better only after Shōji, Haruko, and his daughter Yoko all took new names.

In some societies—Bali, for example—one's personal name

may be composed of nonsense syllables. It imputes no individual qualities or properties; it confers only society's irreducible minimum of recognition to the person as a unique source of action and center of sentience. But in Japan, as in the West, personal names ordinarily indicate gender, may indicate birth-order, and often suggest qualities of character. Males, for example, are given names such as Makoto ("sincerity") or Shigeru ("to flourish"), females names such as Yukiko ("Snow") or Yuriko ("Lily"). To change one's name is to symbolically bury certain qualities and give birth to others.

Not only do names carry meanings when spoken, but in the literate East Asian heritage, names are written with Chinese graphs, and each graph may convey additional layers of meaning. Fortune and misfortune are widely, if uncertainly, thought to be linked with these graphics. One of my Japanese colleagues, for example, uses the graph for "light" as part of his personal name. Some years ago, when he was hospitalized with an eye disease, friends warned him that the "light" in his name was dangerous to his eyes and should be replaced. He rejected the suggestion, wrote a newspaper article denouncing "superstitious onomancy"—and found himself on the receiving end of a number of letters of protest.

On their way to adulthood most Japanese pick up rudiments of this name-graph lore as part of their standard equipment for living. My Hanshin interviewees all know that in choosing the graphs for a name one must count the number of strokes used in writing each graph. Certain combinations of strokes, and certain totals of them, are favorable, others not. Several interviewees added, though, that when the time came to name a child of their own they found their knowledge of the system inadequate, and they turned for help to senior relatives or to experts.

Which graphs you select is a matter of relatively free variation, a domain of Japanese symbolics open to idiosyncrasy. The only legal restriction is that in recording your name officially you must use graphs that are in the national standard list. This affords choice from among some 1,900 signs: approximately 1,870 graphs that comprise the basic literacy list, plus another score of graphs that may be used only for personal names. However, there are no restrictions on how you *pronounce* a graph when used in a name. Most of the time most people will use the graphs in standard pronunciation. But one can never be certain, short of asking the person, just how the graphs of his or her name are meant to be read.

Furthermore, you can retain the spoken form of your name but change its written form, as a symbolic shift in identification: the written name is different; the spoken name continues as before. Several of my interviewees had done so at some point in life, and virtually all of them knew kinsmen or friends who had done so.

In Shōji's case there was a further complication. During the family's period of difficulties his wife Haruko became intrigued with the naming system, and for two years she took lessons on it from an expert in a neighboring city. During one of my visits she brought out her copy-books, made while she was taking the lessons. She wanted to show me some of the many ways that the system may be used not only to forecast individual fates but also to gauge whether two individuals are likely to be compatible. In most instances, she said, when she does not "hit it off" (*aishō mo nai*) with somebody, a study of their name graphs will reveal an incompatibility with hers. Likewise when Shōji complains about a tough customer, the client's graph-personality usually will not match his. Nevertheless, Haruko added, she did not have the new graphs for her name entered into the family register—as Shōji and Yoko did—since she almost never has occasion to write her legal name. So she let the previous form stand.

Change and Growth

Shōji himself is more diffident when he talks about the name change. But whatever it meant to him at the time, in retrospect it marked his turning toward a commercial career. And it has since led him to ask himself if he might not have been mistaken in some of his deepest convictions about who he is and where his life may be leading.

Shōji took up the realtor's trade for extraneous reasons at first, intending to use it as a bridge to a political career. Even after he abandoned his ambitions for elective office he was slow to generate enthusiasm for his trade. Haruko remarked to me that in those days he often spent more time on PTA activities than he did on his work. Over the years, however, his craft has come to occupy most of his waking hours. It has become, he says, his avocation as well as his vocation.

"A man's work," writes Everett Hughes, "is as good a clue as any to the course of his life, and to his social being and identity." There is a no-nonsense type of sociologist who likes to cast work in what are known as "instrumental" terms. Work for him becomes synonymous with income-producing activity. "Expressive" dimensions of work—styles of self-realization, Veblenian instincts of workmanship, and the like—fade from his analytic screen or are relegated to the art historian. The tensions that may arise between economic and aesthetic careers, between differing pathways to growth, are likely to be overlooked.

The no-nonsense sociologist might find in Shōji's career as a realtor a straightforward case of role-assimilation. But to see only that is to miss the tension generated between his initial pathway of patriotism and the later claims of his entrepreneurial one: tensions between what he believed was his "real me" and his newly discovered "realtor me." At age 45, Shōji's life course exhibits none of the fearful symmetry that burned so bright during his seventeenth year on Shōdoshima. His utopia, and the pathway it represents, have been set aside but not abandoned. His current situation may not trigger his full capacities for leadership or for pure action, but army songs retain their purifying powers. They are his personal hymns to a hope that his utopia may yet be actualized one fine day. They reassure him that he is more honest than the ordinary realtor, that deep inside him is a pure heart unstained by commercial needs to calculate gain and loss.

Perhaps—Shōji toys with the vision—his chance will come later in life. His mercenary trade does not, he must admit, seem to be for the greater good of society. And it engages only a portion of his leadership talents, his "alter ego." But the wealth he is earning might be used some years hence to build a home for the aged. He himself will be the home's director, for after all a man with silver hair should not have to bow before farmers and beg them

to sell their land to him. Thus he will conclude his life in a scenario of senior statesmanship.

Shōji is no mindless keeper of a sacred flame. Some of the tensions between his new entrepreneurial self and his Shōdoshima
ideal leave him dismayed. Some he can expel in self-denigrating
humor. Some he can turn into growth material. Perhaps he will
never discover a new pathway of the realtor. But his mourning
for his lost career in politics appears to have run its course. His
trade has come to absorb him, much to his surprise. He is not sure
that he has developed very much as a person since he entered this
profession. But he has discovered in it moments of sheer pleasure,
when a transaction is about to be concluded; nothing in life seems
so satisfying as the chance to grab hold of a complicated human
tangle and unravel it. Professional prevarication comes to his lips
easily, so much so that he seems almost ready to embrace the
"later opposing claims of the Self that pull in a new direction."

The work brings on personal pollution: Shōji has learned to
drink bourbon as a business tool even though he is not especially
fond of the taste; he must exert himself to segregate his home life
from the taint of trade. But people praise him for remaining honest amid the muck of materialism. He is not just a land-broker but
a family financial *consultant*—he used the English word. And
this, perhaps, is what he really was meant to be.

It was late in the morning when Shōji and I sat down in his
sunny living room the last time I called on him. Haruko brought
us tea. Then, in what seemed a spontaneous gesture, he ordered
her to uncap his best bourbon and give our cups a double dose.

CHAPTER 4

A Team Captain

It is, I agree, pointless merely to count off on your fingers the years you have spent on this earth, and to pine for your lost youth. Nevertheless, by looking back over your life and reviewing all its various events in turn, you should be able to recall those times when, with heart aflame, you lost yourself in pure happiness. If you cannot do this, then you have nothing left to live for.

NATSUME SŌSEKI, *Kusamakura*

I. THIS BAFFLING GEOGRAPHY

From time to time the mass media in Japan, as in the West, take up the topic of middle-age crisis. When I ask people in the Han-shin area to explain what the idea means to them they hesitate, unsure if there is one crisis peculiar to the middle years. Perhaps for men—some suggest with a wry smile—it means "resistance at forty-eight."

Resistance at Forty-eight is a popular novel by Ishikawa Tat-suzō. First published serially in the national newspaper *Yomiuri* from November 1955 to April 1956, it remains available in book-stores today, having gone through more than twenty reprintings. The story revolves around a pattern of hungers that I shall call the last-chance syndrome. Nishimura Kōtarō, minor executive for two dozen years in a Tokyo insurance company, aches to escape from his routinized life. Just once he wants to fulfill his vision of *kaishō*, of virility, by having an affair with a young woman. "Or if my youthful vigor is gone," he says, "then I must know the extent of my senile decay."

The theme is a common one in world fiction, the classic version being Goethe's *Faust*. People everywhere need ways to express the inexorable decline of bodily vitality, to symbolize it in order to come to terms with it. But the body's timetable is a difficult one to decipher, it is so caught up in the person's capacity to function in society.

For upwards of three decades during normal adulthood, the body and its activities alter only gradually, almost imperceptibly. With exercise and diet one can control weight gain. Gray hair and wrinkles can be dismissed comically or disguised cosmetically. The American detergent ads taunt the housewife: Are you young enough to lie about your hands? But by the fifth decade of life no longer can biological wounds be easily dissembled. They attract comment and affect conduct. Loss and decline may come slowly. The Japanese folk-timetable for men specifies no speed, only a sequence. Decline, it says, occurs in three alliterative stages: *me*, *mimi*, *mara*—eyes, ears, penis. But slow or fast, decline cannot be ignored. And with that recognition rises a sense of unfinished business.

One's strategies for combating the decline depend upon one's investments in different pathways. Shōji, for example, notes that his consciousness of calendar years is not the same as that of a salaried employee. For Shōji, his income depends upon his sales volume, and he has no fixed retirement age. For the typical salary man, by contrast, there are annual longevity increases in base pay. By age 40, though, he may find that he has reached his peak position in the hierarchy, and will not likely be promoted further before he is obliged to retire at age 55. For purposes of fiction, 48 is a good symbolic midpoint.

Shōji is sensitive to health and to the marks of physical aging, but seems much less fixed upon them than is the typical salary man. Leg and eye troubles can impair his work when he must survey land tracts or fill out official papers. He ought to exercise more. But he is not forced every day to contrast himself with younger men in the office, as a salary man must. His main concern is to be able to retire in due season: it is demeaning for a man with silver hair to kowtow to farmers as a salesman.

Furthermore, Shōji has relatively little interest in the pathways of the pleasures. His is more the typical samurai pattern of indifference to worldly enjoyments. Cigarettes and sake are business tools; something lacks in the man who must resort to them. Shōji goes to bars and sings army songs, to pass the time or else to perform the 180-degree turn that cleanses him of the taint of trade. He is no spartan, but he has none of the enthusiasm for the bourgeois good life that has been central to the "townsman" pathway in Japan ever since it evolved in the "floating world" of seventeenth-century Osaka and Edo. Decline in physical vitality can be a special insult when one has cultivated the physical pleasures. Here too, 48 is a good symbolic Rubicon. "The man who is a pessimist before 48 knows too much," wrote Mark Twain, but "the man who is an optimist after 48 knows too little."

Kaishō Gone

By borrowing blatantly from Goethe, Ishikawa has drawn the ire of the literary establishment. The bored protagonist Nishimura happens to reread *Faust*, and at times after that his adventures border upon Goethean burlesque. The critics also grumble that Nishimura too timidly accepts his fate, that a great novel is one that depicts a heroic battle for liberation. But whatever the book's artistic merit, it has contributed a phrase to the modern Japanese vernacular vocabulary of aging. It continues to attract readers. And for our purposes it offers, in condensed episodes, an account of the dilemmas an ordinary salary man confronts when he acknowledges career stagnation and corporeal decline.

Unlike Doctor Faustus, who had studied "Philosophy and Jurisprudence, Medicine and even, alas! Theology from end to end," Nishimura Kōtarō is a common man. Twenty years of working for the Shōwa Fire and Marine Insurance Corporation have carried him to the post of deputy manager for fire insurance. But he knows that he will not be promoted further, never be named to the Board of Directors. He will remain a deputy manager until the day comes when he must draw his severance pay.

And his body is weakening. In the opening scene of the novel he lingers in bed pondering a stiffness in his hips. A mild neuralgia, he wonders. Later we learn that he is troubled with hypertension. No longer can he play mah-jongg all night with the younger men, or match drink for drink with them, without suffering for it the next day:

If he got too little sleep his blood pressure soon went up. His head grew heavy and his shoulders ached. . . . He couldn't keep his mind on his work. His patience flagged. After everybody else had gone out to lunch he would stay at his desk dawdling. His mind was busy with plans but his body would not pick up on them. Maybe it was a sign of getting on in years. When the body won't do what you want it to, the mind becomes flustered. Probably that's why old men are so crabby.

And as he sits in the barber's chair Nishimura cannot believe how large his bald spot has become: "Physical decline is like a bald spot on the back of your head. While you aren't aware of it, in places you don't notice, secretly and inexorably it spreads over you. And there is not a thing you can do about it."

Nishimura resists with an armament of pills. One nostrum is said to reduce blood pressure, another to prevent the formation of fat in the liver while at the same time to protect against hangover. He takes hormones and vitamin pills to build stamina and potency.

He also goes for a walk every Sunday. A senior colleague had told him that walking is the key to vigor, that a man can always compensate for failing teeth or eyes but not for failing legs. And he wishes he could quit smoking, since that might cure the lingering dryness in his mouth. "There was an ancient Chinese sage," he mutters to himself, "who said that to stay sound in mind and body a person should swallow three gallons of saliva a day. Profuse saliva is proof of health."

He has been a dedicated and diligent employee. The socialist views of his student years have yielded to a recognition that insurance is a business and not an act of social welfare. His work habits have become part of his very being. Even as they attempt to relax in the bath at a spa, Nishimura and his section chief cannot help mentally calculating the worth of the building and its fixtures, and the cost of insurance premiums for them. "They were seriously worrying about how to preserve the profits of the stockholders and board of directors. To worry about such matters was their main occupation. They had been doing it for years. Years of work had made it habitual and had warped their ways of thinking. Like a boxer's broken nose or a jockey's bowed legs, their minds were bent."

But the work no longer holds its challenge. And Nishimura no longer can sustain the illusion that some day he will blossom as a great financial wizard. So is he to be chained to seven more years of slavery?

Family Ties

Nor can Nishimura draw excitement from his future in his family. His wife looks young for her years, her teeth and complexion remain good. But she is putting on weight, her fertility is gone, and her sexuality is fading. Biologically she is a hollow shell. Perhaps as a sort of apology for it all she has become a better cook. But if she remains faithful to him she also is becoming extravagant, defiant, more jealous about his expense-account evenings on the town. She nags him to take his medicines and quit trying to carouse with the younger men.

Nishimura's daughter has a lover whom she insists she will marry despite parental disapproval. She attacks Nishimura's views on arranged marriage as being hopelessly antiquated. And this signals the end of another stage in his family career: "So long as they remain grateful to their parents, they're still in childhood. Once parents get to be in the way it shows that growth is over and the age of independence has arrived. His time as a parent was ending."

And yet . . . a young woman at the office remarks that she could easily fall for a mature man like him. A masseuse admires his "romance gray" hair and tells him it indicates that he is in his virile prime. With his daughter leaving, why should he stay with his wife when they have so little to talk about anymore? A wife should be an ally in a man's resistance. But his wife compares Nishimura to his future son-in-law and snorts, "You haven't got that kind of fight left in you any more, have you." These thoughts continue: "The enviable thing about Doctor Faustus"—Nishimura muses to himself—"is that he seems to have been single. An old man without a wife or kids. So he could afford to abandon his house if he wanted to, and rush off anywhere adventuring with the Devil." Nishimura tries to imagine bachelorhood but knows he could not tolerate the inconveniences and the loneliness.

Retirement will be upon him in seven years, a silver wedding anniversary in two. He can expect to live twenty years more. Adding it all up, Nishimura can conclude only that he is poised at the top of the slope that speeds downhill into senility. I am too old for debauchery, he says to himself, but not too old for desire. What I need is a way to disappear—even if only temporarily— into another life that nobody will know about or even suspect.

The Old Adam

Into these sessions of silent desperation comes Nishimura's tempter, a man known as Sōga Hōsuke. Sōga is a mysterious junior executive in the fire insurance division of the corporation. But he may be—and the author sustains this ambiguity through-out the book—no more than an imaginary alter ego. The graphs for the name Sōga Hōsuke make up a plausible personal name and family name, but they can also be read as "one's former self as guide." Or to translate it with a fundamentalist flourish, "led by the Old Adam." Young, handsome, utterly manly, Sōga is worldly-wise and unattached. He seems able to read Nishimura's every thought, and is fond of quoting *Faust* at every turn of the plot.

Sōga opens new doors to pleasure. He brings pills to restore Nishimura's vitality, and coaxes him into eating grilled pig's-heart and other "hormone broil" dishes that are said to provide stamina. Even in amusement districts that Nishimura thought he knew well, Sōga steers him into new bars and cabarets. And in time Sōga takes him to meet his Marguerite, a winsome young hostess who seems to be untainted by the corrupt cabaret world in which she works.

Nishimura believes that he can marshal his wits and win her love. After all, he tells himself, he has the advantages of experi-ence. And yet he hesitates: "If he were at least ten years younger, people might forgive him; but they are not going to forgive a man who falls in love with a girl younger than his own daughter. Even though ours is the age of many freedoms, freedom has its limits; and at some point Nishimura Kōtarō's realm of options had faded away."

It could be his last chance to keep a woman. But that requires money. Sōga shows him how to pad expense accounts and assures him that all the smart executives in the corporation are doing it anyway. Even so, padded accounts will not yield the amount Nishimura calculates that he needs. There is a family nest egg, but that is in his wife's custody and has, after all, been earmarked to pay for his daughter's wedding. Nishimura decides that he is not bold enough to steal any large sum. Eventually he opts for blackmail. He will travel to Atami to extort from a hotel owner who, Nishimura feels certain, deliberately set fire to his building in order to collect the insurance.

Ashamed that he will be committing a crime, Nishimura argues that his motives are of the purest. He is extorting money to sustain an unsullied love for an innocent woman—a theme that has echoed through "townsman" fiction in Japan ever since the seventeenth-century dramas of Chikamatsu.

But fate saves him. Or perhaps he was the sort who would fail anyway. When Nishimura goes to threaten the hotel owner he finds the man bedridden with a paralytic shock that had been brought on by the fire, incapable even of talking with him. His hostess had accompanied him on the trip, but had elected to sleep in a separate room and was gone by the time Nishimura woke up the next morning. Sitting there, Nishimura looks ahead to see uneventful years, probably lonely ones. Still, part of him feels relief that the episode is safely behind.

The excitement of it all brings on a severe attack of pneumonia. In his weeks of quiet recuperation Nishimura reconciles himself to the idea that he has crossed the threshold. He has learned the extent of his senile decay. His wife turns out to be, after all, an ally in his resistance—though it irks him to see her being so downright cheerful as she fusses over his food, bedding, and medicines. And it dismays him to think that in a few months his daughter will be giving birth, for that means he will be called

"Grandpa" even before he retires from the corporation. "No-body knew how unpleasant the word was to him. He wanted to run away from it. But he would have to come to terms with it. Every man gets to be a grandfather some day. He was coming around to the idea of waiting calmly and serenely for the word to be visited upon him. Perhaps that shows how enervated he had grown."

Nishimura has seen his fate, and acceded to it. After all, he muses, Confucius himself was not able to submit to Heaven's Will until he was 50.

II. PATHWAYS TO PLEASURE

Japanese can draw upon a heritage of idioms of enjoyment that seems every bit as rich as does the heritage of idioms of sincerity. Already a thousand years ago peasant and aristocrat versions of the pathway to pleasure were well codified, and elements from them have carried through into the present. But the mainstream lifestyle of post-industrial Japan is an extension of the "towns-man" pattern that evolved in the booming merchant cities of the seventeenth century.

Being in tune with the moods of passing moments, being un-able to respond to them openly and creatively—these have been central themes in the wider Japanese tradition of aesthetics and even ethics since the dawn of history. The Tokugawa townsmen took these themes and attached them to the material fads and physical pleasures of a world of rapid social mobility. That world had its limits: townsmen could not become samurai or farmers, nor vice versa; open displays of opulence were forbidden. But within these boundaries families might quickly rise and fall, for-tunes might be made and lost overnight. In any such system the symbols of social distinction tend to wear out rapidly. Fads, fashions, and forms of pecuniary emulation come into play. And the townsman or woman of savoir faire must be keenly sensitive to trends, whether manifested in the skirt lengths of today or in the length of kimono sleeves two centuries ago.

The "floating world" was originally a Buddhist idiom. It saw all of human existence as a foamy illusion and a fraud to be out-grown. With typical irreverence, the townsmen took the term and applied it to the passing pleasures of this life, but with the emphasis now upon fickleness *and* excitement. The idea best fits the entertainment districts, where a man could most freely display his taste and panache—and where the samurai guardians of morality were forbidden to interfere. But taste could be expressed as well in the confines of one's home, in elegant furnishings or imported European clocks, in food and decor and dress. So the psychic mobility of the floating world came to characterize much of urban living, influencing as well the wives and children, who were barred from full participation in the entertainment areas.

The variety of temptations available can be sensed readily from the writings of Ihara Saikaku, chief novelist for the seventeenth-century Osaka townsmen. For example, a character in one of his stories, sermonizing on how to make money, offers the following catalog of ways to go astray.

1. Expensive food and women; silk kimono every day
2. Private carrying-chairs for wives; music or card lessons for marriageable daughters
3. Drum lessons for sons of the house
4. Football, miniature archery, incense-appreciation, poetry contests
5. Renovations to the house, addiction to the Tea ceremony
6. Cherry-blossom viewing, boat trips, daily baths
7. Spending nights on the town, gambling parties, playing indoor games
8. Lessons in sword-drawing and dueling
9. Temple visits, and preoccupation with the next world
10. Becoming involved in the troubles of others, and serving as their guarantor
11. Litigation over reclaimed land, and participation in mining projects
12. Sake with the evening meal, excessive pipe smoking, unnecessary trips to Kyoto
13. Sponsoring charity wrestling; excessive contributions to temples
14. Carving small articles during working hours; collecting gold sword-fittings
15. Familiarity with actors and pleasure districts
16. Borrowing money at more than 8 percent per month

All of these, warns the consultant, are "more deadly than cantharides or arsenic."

The townsman lifestyle has played an important role in Japan's transformation into an urban-industrial society in this century. Political leaders might need to urge their countrymen to study foreign science and technology for the good of the nation. But the townsmen already had a built-in hunger for anything foreign that might expand the scope of the urban good life. They needed little or no prodding after 1870, when the doors were opened to a tide of Western popular culture. They took voraciously to baseball, beefsteaks, social dancing, soda pop, and Stephen Foster songs. Figuratively speaking, the townsman lifestyle has been a national "digestive system" that has taken foreign items in great draughts and transmuted them into forms that the rest of the population could readily absorb. Some of my Hanshin interviewees say, with muffled pride, that if anything the contemporary townsman lifestyle goes its Western bourgeois counterpart one better. For in many arenas of enjoyment it offers both Japanese and Western options: sashimi as well as beefsteak, sake as well as bourbon, sumo as well as baseball. One can double the fun.

From time to time the twentieth-century state and its guardians of morality make their sorties against the townsman style. They accuse it of materialism, selfishness, decadence. During the military years they assailed it as unpatriotic, and attempted to purge enemy words from the vocabulary and enemy sports from the schools. Cadres of teen-age girls stood in the railway stations barking at women wearing powdered faces and permed hair. But my Hanshin interviewees recall, too, how they welcomed the return of foreign items after 1945. And in the years since, the basic policing pattern has differed little from that of the Tokugawa era, which pursued a curbing of certain excesses but otherwise cared only that the pleasures be kept in their place.

Narcotics codes, for example, are enforced zealously, but there are few restrictions on other forms of stimulation. Organized prostitution (brothels, pandering, public soliciting) was banned in 1958. But the law makes no objections to the private sale of sexual services between consenting adults—of whatever tastes or preferences. The entertainment areas thrive. And Japan, as visitor after visitor goes home to report, is the drinking man's paradise.

The contours of the townsman pathway are difficult to pin down in a phrase, much less a single word. The townsman strives to embody a combination of elegance, wit, worldly wisdom, and amorousness. By cultivating these sensibilities to the utmost, one may even raise them to spiritual planes of pure action. This goal is particularly to be sought in romantic love, which when pursued "totally" can become transcendent, as in the love-suicide dramas of Chikamatsu (or as it does for that matter, with German accents, in *Faust*). But for the ordinary townsman the pathway is a part-time pursuit, more an avocation than a calling. It allows him to show and to savor his human capacities for feeling and expression. But at the same time he must demonstrate his strength of character by *managing* his pleasures: to abstain from them is to throw away opportunities to be most fully human; but to indulge too fully is to fail in his obligations to family and society. His challenge is to reconcile spontaneity with security.

The samurai too was enjoined by Confucian morality and Japanese custom to sustain his family. But in extremes he was expected to sacrifice even his family in order to fulfill his call to Honor. For the townsman these priorities are reversed. He should indeed cultivate his tastes, but only so long as he can assure support to elders, wife, and children.

Trends in demography and social organization that are familiar to all industrial nations have added to the townsman's dilemma. In Saikaku's Osaka the typical townsman ran a household enterprise, and the demands of family and occupation were almost indistinguishable, as can be seen in the list of paths to ruin, above. But today the typical townsman is, like Nishimura Kōtarō, an employee. Demands from company and vocation add new dimensions to his competing pulls from family and avocation. And his whole adult life course has come to be paced and curved by company policy.

The pattern encompasses much variability, from one occupational line to the next, from small shop to vast multinational corporation. Only about one out of three men employed in Japan today has a career as orderly and as predictable as Nishimura's. But the "company man" (*shain*) or "salary man" (*sarariiman*) is the social cynosure of the era, admired and aspired to for his conditions of employment: long-term job security, fringe benefits, annual seniority raises, and the like. With an income that is predictable even if not plentiful over three decades, one can draft a timetable for family obligations. And then one can, at least in theory, attend to his avocations.

Figure 1 shows how this might work for an ordinary man who has a wife and two children to support. The chart is part of an advertisement for a savings-and-loan institution, and it appeared in daily newspapers and weekly magazines for several months during the latter part of 1972. The headline reads, "For an Unhurried Life Plan." And the subheading explains, "Life brings different times when you will need much more money than you might expect. The key to casual living is to choose a savings plan that fits your needs." The chart does not indicate day-to-day expenses, but it does show the average amounts spent for various life-events at the current average dates along the life cycle: marriage, childbirth, purchase of a house, children's tuitions and wedding expenses, and retirement.

His late 50's are a crunch period for the Japanese company man, both emotionally and economically. Here we can see vividly the modern dislocation between life history and life cycle. Retirement at 55 is the norm, though in some workshops it may be postponed a few years. The fortunate company man will draw severance pay equivalent to two or three years' wages. But aside from that, pension systems are likely to furnish little more than pocket money. At retirement age, about one company man in three still has a child or two at home; he must be prepared to meet tuition bills and wedding costs. (Our average man in the chart spends $3,400 on his daughter's wedding the year after he retires.) Another one in three—not necessarily the same one—has an aged parent or parents to support (a further complication not shown in the chart or in the Ishikawa novel). Small wonder, then,

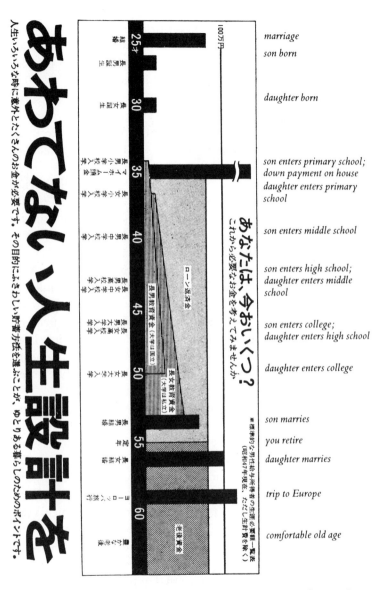

FIGURE I. This life-course chart appeared in newspapers and magazines for several months in 1972 as part of an advertisement for a savings and loan institution. The chart shows, for a typical family of four (father, mother, son, and daughter), the average amounts of expense money needed at key transition points along the domestic cycle: marriage, childbirth, college tuition, etc.

that after "retirement" the vast majority of men seek out "re-hirement," even though for most of them it will mean unchalleng-ing work at entry-level rates of pay. And small wonder that the majority try to set aside savings for their later years.

Seen in the aggregate the myriad individual choices that resolve these conflicting demands add up to clear trends in awareness and commitment across a man's adult years. We can gauge these trends by drawing upon some of the mass surveys that abound in present-day Japan.

For men as a whole, irrespective of line of work, consider Fig-ure 2, which is taken from a nationwide survey that asked people about their sense of *ikigai*. The concept has nuances difficult to translate, but the question asked can be roughly glossed as "What is it that most makes you feel life is worth living?" Up until about age 25, men answer in terms of work, leisure, and lifestyle. Only about one man in five in his early 20's gives priority to family or children—not too surprising, since the average age of marriage for Japanese men is 25. But after age 25, family and children rise rapidly in men's ikigai (as in women's, as we shall see in a later chapter). And from age 35 onward, they preponderate. Concur-rently, work and leisure decline markedly, and lifestyle drops moderately.

Aggregate survey data need to be taken with a dash of skepti-cism. The way a question is asked can strongly shape the answers that are given. But a broadly similar shift in commitments can also be seen in another set of surveys, these taken specifically among company men. Figure 3 is based upon studies done by the Asahi Newspaper Corporation. Samples were drawn from large business and industrial corporations, covering 1,000 men aged 45–55 in 1972 and an unspecified number of men aged 20–30 in 1970. Asked in these studies to choose the three things most im-portant to them, the men, whether junior or senior, overwhelm-ingly pick health as their top concern. For the senior men, family and company rank second and third, but for the junior men they are two notches lower. Historical influences cannot be ruled out, but if we assume that the pattern of concerns of the senior men of 20 years ago was the same as that of their juniors of today, then

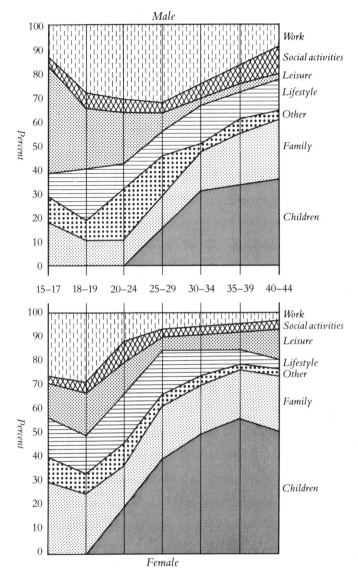

FIGURE 2. Respondents were asked: "What is it that most makes life worth living for you?" The shaded area for each item (e.g. "Children") shows the percentage of persons (in each of seven age ranges) who named that item; thus, 50 percent of women 40–44 years old cite "Children." Data taken from Mita Munesuke, 1970.

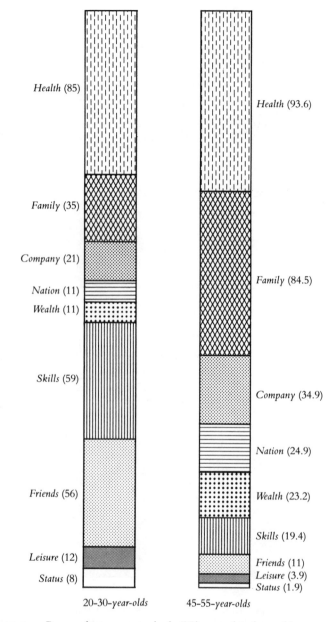

Health (85)

Family (35)

Company (21)

Nation (11)

Wealth (11)

Skills (59)

Friends (56)

Leisure (12)

Status (8)

Health (93.6)

Family (84.5)

Company (34.9)

Nation (24.9)

Wealth (23.2)

Skills (19.4)

Friends (11)

Leisure (3.9)

Status (1.9)

20–30-year-olds   45–55-year-olds

FIGURE 3. Respondents were asked: "Choose the three things most important to you." Figures show, for each item (e.g. "Wealth") the percentage of persons, in each of two age ranges, who chose that item. Based on surveys made by the Asahi Newspaper Corporation in 1970 and 1972.

across their adult years company men tend to give growing significance to health, family, company, nation, and wealth, but to be less and less concerned about skills, friendships, leisure, or status.

Middle-aged company men have mixed feelings about their employment. Two out of three in the Asahi study say they are satisfied with their rate of advancement in the company, but an equal number say that if they could start over again they would not choose the same line of work. Almost as many say that they still think about changing jobs. A small percentage are living in rental housing, but two-thirds own their own home. The remainder are in company housing—though the rule in some corporations is that men must move out of company housing in their late 40's. Two out of three men have set aside savings of at least $3,400.

The company man's typical management strategy is to yield control over family finances to his wife. The usual figure turned up in studies of the topic is that eight out of ten employed men hand over the monthly pay envelope to the wife—after first deducting their personal spending money. By law a Japanese employee can insist upon being paid in cash, should he or she wish to conceal the exact amount from the spouse. Some Hanshin wives tell me that they make a point of not inquiring closely about their husband's take-home pay. They have a fairly good idea, of course, and if a man works for a large corporation or a government bureau the salary scale is a matter of common knowledge. But as Nishimura grumbles, a man cannot get at the family nest egg without approaching his wife. And as Shōji, Beisuke, and other Hanshin men said to me, they would be very reluctant to risk the family savings on a business venture, much less spend it on their own pleasures. In townsman fiction from Chikamatsu onward, one mark of a heroic wife is that she will draw upon family savings, even pawn her jewelry and kimonos, in order to pay off the debts of a husband who has drifted too far into the floating world.

The ordinary salary man, then, has to pursue his enjoyments on modest capital. A 1973 survey of 400 executives in Kobe, aged

38–48, found that nine out of ten spend less than $100 a month on their enjoyments, four out of ten less than $50. Hanshin interviewees said that this is the typical level for them and their friends. The *hyaku-yen sarariiman*, the "hundred-yen salary man" who can afford only one beer after work, may be a comic-strip exaggeration. But half the men in the Kobe executive survey say that they almost always go straight home from the job, and once there they usually sit down and read the papers or watch television.

Familiarity with the floating world is a life-art that can be acquired only with effort. One needs knowledge, skill, and an ability to manage his feelings as well as his finances. Beisuke and Shōji mark the extremes. Shōji is indifferent toward avocations and the townsman lifestyle, Beisuke is an enthusiast. Few men cultivate savoir faire with Beisuke's zest, but most would respect the energy he has expended in mastering the idioms of enjoyment.

III. BEISUKE

Beisuke is a small man but a compact one, a man who inhabits every fiber of his body. "The go-betweens swore that he was tall," his wife said to me, "but he's even shorter than I am." He moves with ease, poise—and with a faintly perceptible reserve.

I always found him dressed in clothes that were neat and well cut. Business suits usually, but with a personal flair showing in his choice of shirts and ties. Some days he wore a turtleneck and a sport jacket.

We met in the evenings, after his day's work, in the house of a mutual friend who had introduced us. Beisuke never invited me to his home, and I called upon him there only once, two years later, after he had built a new house at the lower edge of the Ashiya foothills. I suspect that he might have preferred being interviewed at one of his favorite bars: he hinted once or twice that we should go out drinking together. So perhaps the friend's parlor was a compromise, neither home nor bar but a familiar setting where Beisuke was at ease. A setting, too, where we sometimes were served dinner and always were offered snacks and drinks. The stated reason for meeting there, however, was convenience. It was near Beisuke's route home from the office, and it meant less travel for me than going to his home would have.

Our sessions extended well beyond the appointed two hours. Beisuke was more than ready to talk about his own life—and about a score of other topics, as well. Others say that with them he can often be reticent. With me he tried to strike a suitable tone of deference toward "the professor." And at times he seemed constrained by the thought that I might be viewing him as a specimen, a type-case of the male Japanese creature. But more than most men he sought to draw me out, to nurse an atmosphere of mutuality and a climate in which confidences could be exchanged.

This colored the conversations we had. Connoisseur of enjoyments, he could be expected to talk of them at length. But I have the idea that he also liked to steer us into topics of sex and sensuality in hopes that here there might be grounds for rapport, that here there could be a sharing between two men whose vocations and backgrounds were otherwise so radically different. A good raconteur, he is not above stretching a point if doing so will make a story better. But I know from interviews with his wife Yoshiko that he was forthright, at times brutally honest, in telling me about his own life.

Beisuke spreads out his words in a casual, colorful Osaka townsman's brogue. I can only apologize for not being able to do it justice in translation.

People would call me the townsman type. I'm the sort of man you are likely to find anywhere. I'd describe my personality as unassertive, that of a guy who looks for happiness in the little things of life. In other words, a man filled with the feeling that mine may only be a tiny castle, but inside it I do as I damned well please. A man with a quick temper, but also good natured—and greedy at the same time. That's a very common type of personality, but it's the type of personality I have.

As you grow older you're always thinking to yourself, some day—*some* day—I am going to make it big. There are men who hit success early and men who don't. But little by little as the years go by, you begin to notice something. Although all of us supposedly took off from the same starting line, you get the idea that everybody else is going great guns and the only one left behind is you. When things don't turn out very well a man can say, "I've been had!" and blame the breaks. But life just works that way, as

I see it. Human life never goes by the book; sometimes you fail no matter how hard you've tried. That's what makes it all so complicated.

A salary man's life never goes the way he wants it to. You have an employer and you are a unit, a cell, operating under his orders and directives. So you must do exactly what you're told. Refuse and you are all washed up. That's why you can't do what you'd like to, can't say what you'd like to, but just eagerly wear yourself out for his sake. And that's why I am mighty anxious to slip out of the harness and try to make a go of it on my own.

There are businesses and businesses—I want to try the water trades. A restaurant or a small bar. I groove on looking after customers. When it becomes your job, it can have its nasty moments, of course. But if you're doing it because you like it, I doubt it could be all that much of a pain. By and large I dislike having others working for me. So I wouldn't care if my place was small, I just want a cozy little shop that I can run in my own way. Always make the other fellow feel at home, you know.

After all, I sing a lot. The sentimental oldies most of the time, yes. But you know, the words and music in those old songs have something to them. They hit you right here.

What I sing depends on where I am. Supposing it's a mat-floored room. [Note: a traditional place of entertainment—what the West refers to as a tea house or geisha house.] Then I sing old townsman songs. "Yarisabi" or "Plum Blossoms in Spring." Samisen songs. I mean, when I was in school I used to go there, played around in the houses. I sing songs I learned already as a young boy. Nobody writes new songs in that style anymore, but the oldies are still sung today.

When I was in school, knowing those songs got you a reputation as a playboy. It marked you as a real man about town. I made quite an impression on the other students. Talk about student competitiveness! I competed as a singer. After all, you just don't learn "Plum Blossoms" or "Yarisabi" in one easy lesson. So I'd buy recordings, buy songs recorded by the old geisha, and practice them on my own. Practice them at home and then go out to the houses and perform them. I was playing around a lot in those days. I'd call for a woman. She'd pick up the samisen. I'd say to her, "Play anything, *I* can sing it." That way I made points with the women, too. Two birds with one stone.

Or take popular ballads. Now, they are faithful expressions of the common man's feelings, and that's why we Japanese love popular ballads the best of all. There are huge numbers of them. In the old days a songwriter would stand under a street lamp playing a violin. He would perform for the public, singing his tunes and selling sheet music.

But if you're at a bar, you don't sing townsman songs or even the old pop ballads. And that makes it tough. Because what men my age know best are certain to be songs that date from before about 1955: those are the ones most deeply etched in our minds. However, the bar hostesses—they are only 22 or 23 years old, at most 30. If you don't go and learn some of the current hits, you're from nowhere with the girls.

It depends on the woman, naturally. If she happens to know a few oldies, she'll get together with you on them—you're the customer after all. But these days the girls are darned chintzy. Seems as if most of them have the idea that they are not there to serve a customer so much as to have a good time for themselves in his company. And meanwhile get paid well for doing it. Compared with women in the old days they don't show consideration for the customers, not today.

So it seems insane to pay good money for a hostess, just to drink with her instead of drinking at an ordinary tavern. If you are on an expense account and are wooing a client, then forget the cost and make sure that he enjoys the evening. You'll get it back from him as part of the cost of the contract later. Then a hostess bar is okay. But when you are on the town for the evening on your own money, you don't want to go where the service is shabby and the drinks are pricey. It means you have to search. I explore on my own, and I have a lot of friends who tell me when they have found a good spot. That's when you get some satisfaction out of going drinking. Even if it wasn't cheap, if you can say to yourself, "That was superb!" . . . then a night on the town is worth it.

Childhood and Masculinity

There have been three times in my life when I have most felt like myself. My student days, when I was so keen on sports. My 30's, when for ten years I threw everything I had into my work. And just recently—the feeling is still with me—when I began to sense real gratitude toward the ancestors because whatever I am today I owe to them. I am finding it easy to bless the name of Buddha—wonderful phrase. In that sense too, though I may seem to be harping on the point, I think of myself as an average Japanese.

I'll be frank with you. When I was young I didn't have any particular ambitions, and I'm ashamed to admit it.

I mean that I didn't care about success in the usual sense because I wanted to be a great athlete. When I look back over my school years, all I see is sports and more sports. For seven years, three in high school and four in college, I was sports-crazy. After I was discharged from the army I thought about going back to college so I could play baseball again. That was it: no other ambitions.

Oh, I once thought about becoming a priest. In my last year of primary school, just before the entrance examinations for middle school, I came down with a fever. My mother was a religious sort, and she took me to Kojima to have prayers offered for me. The priestess there said, "When he grows up, if he becomes a priest or restaurant operator he will do well at it." I don't know why she said it, but when you're young, things like that make an impression on you. Anyway, after that I began to take an interest in the joys and the sorrows of human life, in death. I became curious about Buddhism. The pathos—like it says in the opening lines of the *Heike Tales*, "The prosperous inevitably meet their downfall." I didn't object when my mother wanted me to go with her to Buddhist affairs; ever since I was a boy I've enjoyed traveling to Mt. Koya or to the Eihei temple. I suppose that was where I learned to quote those kinds of phrases.

But the other side of it was becoming familiar with worldly pleasures, what you'd call a man of lust. In college I did an about-face and ended up being gross. I really do have a lot of the priest

in me, a tendency to tears; there is that facet in my personality.
But I just can't shake off a fondness for women. And a sex-hungry
priest is going to cut a poor figure. I suppose that must make me
the most average man in Japan.

My father's name was Senji ("thousand, number two"). That's
how they named sons in the olden days. His elder brother was
called Sen'ichi ("thousand, number one") and his younger brother Senzaburō ("thousand, number three"). If you reckon that
their parents were *mizunomi byakushō* ("water-drinker peasants," i.e. too poor even to buy tea), well, they didn't have anything to call their own except their kids. If you named your sons
"thousand," it's because that was fabulous wealth.

I don't know much about my parents in their earlier years. My
father was still young—58—when he died in 1941; Mother's in
her 80's now and going senile. Both of them came to Osaka from
villages in Okayama. She worked as a maid and he was a live-in
apprentice to a toolmaker. Their marriage was arranged by their
masters, who had business dealings with each other.

They had eight children, and I'm the youngest, the fifth and
youngest of the sons. Two siblings died before I was born—in
1923—and my second eldest brother died a year ago.

Eventually, my old man went into business for himself, in the
same trade, having got permission to use his master's shop-name.
By the 1930's he had a branch factory in Shanghai, and would go
there once every three months or so. It was the period of Japan's
great leap, you know, the age of overseas expansion. His business
grew steadily, and he was a man who thrived on hard work. He
just got fatter and fatter.

As far as the family was concerned, we had a posh life, economically speaking. But that old man of mine—he thought it was
enough if he provided for us financially. A homey atmosphere?
He wasn't one to have father-and-son chats. Your feudalistic
man of the Meiji era: he fits the figure to a T. Not terrifying, just
uncommunicative.

He had his mind set on making money. And to see that the
family never lacked for money, that was his idea of *kaishō*. My
father and mother did not get along very well as a couple. I mean

that in a Japanese man's ideal of *kaishō* there is an element of pride in being known for having money and for keeping a mistress or two. You project it openly in the way you behave. You set up a mistress, and if you take sick or are about to die you want it to happen in her house. That's the kind of man he was.

The other side of it was that nobody had the right to say so much as one word about what he did. A kind of pure dictator, a very Japanese sort of one-man boss.

I don't recall that he ever talked with me, much less that he took me to the zoo or out to play. Not even when mother suggested it. But after all, there were so many of us kids. Nobody cared what I did, I was the runt. Already in middle school I could stay out at night until eleven or twelve, even roll in at one a.m. and not hear a word about it. Nobody told me I'd better study, better do this, do that. I was always on the edge of flunking out, and the teachers would coax my parents to try to make me study. But neither of them had gone beyond fourth grade, and they just didn't care much about schooling.

It was my two eldest brothers who took care of me. But partly they were using me as a front, taking me as a cover when they went drinking and womanizing. I can remember very clearly being taken where the girls were while I was still in primary school. I became precocious in that course of studies.

When the old man died, my eldest brother Kanetarō took charge of running the business and providing for the family. The business was already big enough by then that eventually all the sons found places in it. Kanetarō grew with the job, and while I don't feel especially close to him I really admire him and feel a tremendous obligation toward him. He's been more like a father to me than my real father was. He's the kind of man who will say what's on his mind. And he will have things done his way, forcing them through even when he may be a little wrongheaded about them. He tends to be critical of what others say, and he doesn't pay much attention to status. In short, he's the go-get-'em type: if it will be to his benefit, he'll make trouble for other people. He is critical in the negative sense of the word; that's how sure he is of himself. Just the opposite of me, I am more likely to hold back.

Stardom

If I could go back again, it would be to my 20's. The past decade has been a subdued one, so naturally I'd rather go back to a
livelier period. More than any other reason because I was so popular with the girls then. After all, it's love that makes this world go
round. . . .

They took me into college as an athlete, not because I had
passed any written exam. I was a baseball star for those years—
team captain in 1942—even had visions of turning pro. The college years were far and away my best ones. No need to worry
about supporting a family, I did as I pleased. When I get to remi-
niscing, it is always about those days, never about the army, because nothing good happened while I was in the army.

But I am not able to take any pride in the fact that I went to
college. I never really *studied* anything, though it's true I read a
lot of novels—Kobayashi Takiji, Kawabata Yasunari—and
books on the philosophy of life. I still read books almost every
day. But in college all I was really doing was playing ball. In the
army, too, all they ever praised me for was baseball.

Once in a while I go see a game or watch the team practice. But
we were champions so many years ago that not many people
recognize me any more. Once a year there's a reunion, and we ex-
captains wear a ribbon; I always turn out for that. Most of the others show up, too, though a lot of them were killed in the war.
Seems as if it was the best ones who were most likely to get killed.

I bragged all over the place about my sex life. You could have
fun with a geisha from five to eleven p.m. for 5 yen—at the time,
80 yen a month was base pay for a college graduate in his first job.
Nowadays, you're hit for 2,000 yen just for the "flower fee" a
geisha gets merely to show her face for ten minutes. But then a
geisha has to shell out plenty for clothes and accessories; her income isn't all that good, either. And there are fewer and fewer
places with geisha. In Osaka all that's left is one part of Soemon-
chō, and it's so expensive I couldn't afford it. In the old days the
girls were coy as well as sexy, but you have to be a romantic to
believe them now. Now it's money, not affection.

But I never drank until I was 18, and didn't smoke until I was 24. I only took up drinking when I went to college. There was a party to celebrate matriculation, and some upperclassmen from the high school I had attended brought booze. That was the first time I really drank. Of course I had snitched a taste now and then before that at home, but I don't count that as regular drinking.

In high school we simply did not touch the stuff. I myself was a sort of sobersides at the time, and people were very strict about it. Guardians of morality. The police had a vigilance league, spying for delinquent behavior among students. It was a powerful outfit. We all knew about it, and my parents warned me not to tangle with it. If they caught you with sake, you'd be hauled to the station for questioning. That in itself was enough to get you branded as a delinquent. Sake and cigarettes were the number one signs of corruption. Of course the result was that we were constantly making eyes at the girl students. Chasing them. You didn't care if she was all that good-looking, any girl was okay, because you wanted something from her—wanted to get close. That wasn't considered a crime.

It wasn't because I was an athlete that I stayed away from cigarettes, it was because I honestly thought it wrong. But in the army they issued you ration after ration of the stuff. Free. I gave mine away, but even my friends couldn't manage to use them up. And after I became an officer the cigarette rations came in piles. I told everybody, "Smoke them! Smoke them!" but nobody smoked *that* much. So eventually I began to use them myself.

We were drafted into the army right after graduation. From then on, all I could think about was going home again. Some guys were so homesick they talked about deserting. But if you were court-martialed for desertion, people would heckle your family as traitors; so you learned to put up with the situation.

They would test us on things like the Imperial Rescript for Servicemen. We had to memorize every word of it—more than three hundred words, mind you—and be able to repeat it without missing a phrase. That was to develop the "unique fighting spirit of the Japanese soldier." For example, "Bear in mind that duty is weightier than a mountain, while death is lighter than a feather. Never by failing in moral principle fall into disgrace and bring dishonor upon your name." In other words, before you can be captured, commit suicide. After basic training, they sent us by submarine from Shimonoseki to China. My outfit saw action ten times, the longest being six hours and the shortest ten minutes. But it wasn't the battles that got to you, it was the goddam everlasting marching.

However, money talks, even in the service. Kanetarō paid to get me a promotion, and after that life was easier.

As far as I was concerned, it was all for the sake of the Emperor. And yet when I heard the Emperor's surrender broadcast on August 15th, all that was on my mind was that now I could go home. I was not ashamed that in the moment of defeat my mood was one of wanting to get back as quickly as I could. You've got to realize that we were draftees, not gung-ho volunteers like Sergeant Yokoi, who held out alone on Guam for 25 years. Much as I hated it, I never shirked my duty, always did as I was ordered. But whenever we younger men got together the talk inevitably turned to how soon the war would be over. If everybody who went into the service had had the spirit of Sergeant Yokoi, maybe Japan would have won.

The army threw me together with men from different social classes, and it taught me leadership. I learned how to live with others and set aside my selfish interests. Before I joined the corps, I hadn't known much about the wider world. When my outfit was demobilized and I was sent home, that was the first big turning point in my life. Up until that time I had been under the parental wing. But when I returned to Osaka I found that all my friends were setting out on their careers and that I would have to find one of my own.

Working

After I came out of the army, all I did at first was play around. I had no plans for the future, forgot everything I'd learned in the service, and fell into a habit of going out every night. Even now, all I tend to think about is how to have a good time. I was 35 before I realized that I should have been stashing money away as I went along. By then it was too late.

Japanese society is stacked everywhere in favor of public-college men. A guy like me from a private college can only climb so far and then he hits a wall. For him the big corporations are hopeless. After the war, starting salary was 90 yen a month for a public-college man but only 75 for those from private schools. And in those days it wasn't easy to find a position even if you were a college graduate.

In my 30's I really worked hard, and I got a kick out of it. I had thought of myself as pretty much a grown-up man when I was in the army, but I especially had that feeling after my brother put me in charge of one of the factories and gave me the responsibility for dozens of employees. Hard work doesn't faze me. Once the company sent me on an assignment in Korea. I worked round the clock and finished the job in three days, and came right on home without stopping to rest. I've always made it a rule that no matter how late I am out the night before, come morning I report to work on time. The company's feeding and keeping me, after all; it's the least I can do in return.

I'm weak-willed, and because of it I'm left with some painful memories. But when I gave my all to the work, and my men did the same, everything would turn out better than we'd expected. The gods help those who help themselves.

I like physical activity and never mind working with my body. That's just as true today as it was in my 30's. Which is why I can't understand it when a young man shrinks away from a tough job. I feel like saying to him, "Look, get all the experience you can while you're young, even if you have to beg for it." I have other gripes about young people, but frankly I can't get my point of view across to my own son, much less anybody else. Young people today want to grab the brass ring without a struggle. It shows up in the way they amuse themselves. If you set limits and stick to them, you can have your fun and still keep things in proportion. The younger guys don't seem to have that kind of discipline. I didn't take a back seat to any man when it came to living it up, in my younger years. But I believe I have got to where I am today because I have been a responsible human being.

Marriage

Mine was an arranged marriage. Yoshiko and I were brought together by people from the home village of my eldest brother's wife. It was the usual kind of viewing, the prospective mates and three people from each side. We all went to see a play, a family drama. Nobody said a word about marriage; and as I recall Yoshiko and I didn't even sit together. But during the intermission the two of us were told to make ourselves scarce. Even then we didn't talk. But I thought to myself, this is one good-looking woman. We went and had tea at the Daimaru department store, and made a date to go out together another time.

When I came home they asked me, was I willing to proceed. "Uhhh," I said, "I don't mind." For some reason I was shy about the whole thing. "Well, suppose we take her," was all I could say. But Yoshiko appealed to me from the first glance—more than any girl friend I'd ever had—and from the start I had made up my mind to marry her.

We went together for half a year, dated often. I was managing the Okayama factory in those days, so I would phone her from there, come back on Saturday and take her out. On Sunday my buddies and I would have a ball, and then I'd head straight for Okayama to be on the job Monday morning. I hardly ever even stopped in at home unless I needed money—once a month, maybe.

I really was a shit. My buddies and I weren't just having a few drinks, we would take girls with us and go for an overnight at a hot springs resort. I know I don't amount to much as a man, but my conduct in those days was the worst it's ever been. On any test of good faith, my score comes out zero.

But oh man, could I put on a good front. If the police hauled away one of the girls, I tagged along and could persuade them to release her. Even when they charged her with soliciting, I could put on this terribly sincere face, and they usually would release her. Or if one of the girls took sick I might visit her, run errands for her. And all the time I cut such a correct figure as I dated my future bride. How rotten can a man get?

Smooth talk, slick image—I was shrewd, like a con man. Sneaking along in the shadows and doing wrong on the sly. All the time convincing myself that it was all right. Meanwhile people were saying, "For a rich man's kid, he's turning out okay after all." Degenerate? At least not much as a decent man. When I think about it now I feel disgusted.

I need to tell you about Yoshiko's background. Her parents came from farm families in Wakayama. They didn't do well in Osaka, and had about decided to go back. A man who knew her father, a man from Matsushima—that was one of the pleasure quarters in Osaka before the war—he said, "Why not take a crack at managing a house here in the quarter. If you'll be manager, I'll put up the money." So her father took a loan from the guy. I hear that the interest was steep, 10 percent a month. But before long he had paid off the whole thing, and made a real success of the house.

He was a sincere sort, Yoshiko's father. He said, "Damned if I'm going to stay in this dirty business forever." So during the war he sold the house and bought a little farm on the edge of Kyoto. Planned to raise a few crops for the family's own consumption, and live off the interest on the money he had from the sale of the house. However, they hadn't been on the farm more than a year when the war ended. With the postwar turmoil and the revaluation of the yen, what with one thing and another, they found themselves strapped for cash.

Their cropland was about as big as a cat's brow: not enough to produce food for cash sale. But their eldest son had come back from the army and was determined to finish college. They needed money for his tuition. The three of them talked it over—Yoshiko and her parents. Since there was only one business they really had experience in, Yoshiko said, "Buy another house and *I'll* manage it." She's gutsy, my wife. They sold the farm, bought a house in one of the Kyoto quarters, and Yoshiko helped them run it until we were married.

Parenting

The day my son Tatsuo was born was another turning point for me. You realize that you had better settle down, not diddle any more. Also—to tell the truth—when Yoshiko said she was pregnant my first reaction was, "Whose kid is it?" You see, a doctor once had told me that I would never be able to have children; I took that for granted when I got married. Her pregnancy set me back a couple of steps more than it would the average guy. Our daughter Hiroko was born the next year. Later Yoshiko and I talked about having a third, but that never worked out. It's actually a little lonesome with only two.

Not that I'm the type who dotes on children—or who thinks other people's kids are more lovable. What I felt at the time our kids were born was responsibility more than affection. Kids are a lot of trouble. Mine seem to sense that in me, they've attached themselves to their mother and don't have much to say to me. I don't mind it all that much. Some fathers and sons like to drink together, but I'm no good at it. So I hope Tatsuo will be satisfied by my fulfilling my parental duty and making sure he has no worries moneywise. That I'll do even if I have to go out and beg.

When Tatsuo started school, my main concern was that he apply himself to his studies, more than whether or not he made good grades. I hoped he would learn sportsmanship and develop a powerful sense of right and wrong. I want him to be a man who will be of use to society. That's all I really want of him, although if he works hard and rises in the world I'll be pleased. If he's a success. Your garden-variety father's wishes for his son.

I'd wanted Tatsuo to become a doctor, but he has a will of his own and he chose commerce. The medical trade is a neat one, because you can work for the good of society and at the same time be paid well for doing it. I suggested maybe he should go into banking or into government administration, but he has signed on to join the Mitsubishi Trading Corporation after he graduates from college this spring.

Hiroko is in art school. All I really want for her is to find a good husband. I care about both of my kids, but I also have a strong dose of the traditional Japanese attitude that men lead and women follow. So from the beginning I have expected more from Tatsuo. The kids tell me I'm old-fashioned, but until they are fully on their own they ought to at least respect the old man's views. Actually, it was much worse while they were in high school. If they were irked they might not speak a word for two or three days at a time. The rebellious phase.

I just want them to do their duty and do it faithfully. That—and here I don't speak from personal experience—and not drink on other people's money. I've warned them about that. Because from what I know, when somebody treats you to a spree you start feeling sad and lonely even as you toss the stuff down.

I tell my children they should do just the opposite of what I did. I tell them, "Speak out, say what you're thinking. And if you make a mistake, apologize sincerely." If people do that, they keep on growing. I've had serious setbacks because I failed to say what I was thinking.

Marks of Aging

As you get older, much of what happens to you is unpleasant. You concoct fewer and fewer grand schemes. You aim for goals that are more within reach. I don't talk about my dreams the way I could when I was younger. To be specific, my goal these days is to do everything I can for my family—and maybe a little bit more. Give them a comfortable life in good surroundings. That is what I think about most.

Human beings in general tend to become more realistic as they age. Add to that the salary man philosophy, and it follows that you are certain to be realistic. A salary man isn't like a scholar who can pursue a research project. A salary man's whole purpose in life is to make money. To my way of thinking, money is what can give this world a rosy hue. Maybe I say that because I never have gotten much of it. When I talk to my kids, I wish I could tell them the hard realities, and yet I hear myself coming out with lovely spiritual platitudes about how money isn't everything.

When you reach 60 or 70 and look back, what will sustain your self-respect will be knowing that you did all you could. If you look back and see nothing, you are going to be very empty. I can look back fondly now to the decade of my 30's. And though I don't know how many more years are left for me, during those years I am determined to accomplish even more than I did in my 30's. Then I can look back at 70, say "Ahhhh . . ." and put a period to my life. I can't predict *what* I might accomplish. But I want the satisfaction of knowing that I tried.

We all die sooner or later. I'm not especially bothered by the idea. When they tell me they don't need me around this world I'll cash in my chips. Callous? Cold-blooded? Not me. Just that I believe I'm ready to die at any time.

And yet—the other day I noticed some sort of bump on my eyelid—here. I realized since the day before that that the eye had been twitching. When I went to bed it felt funny. I wondered if I was upset about something. Lately without bifocals I'm blind as a bat. "Are you getting senile?" I asked myself. "Never!" I said. But I did decide to have a doctor check it for me. There I am, bravely saying I don't care when I die—when in fact I do. I am constantly aware of how precious life is.

I don't like having medical checkups. I think I'm healthy, though my stomach hasn't been right for a long long time. The time it takes for a medical exam can better be spent playing *pachinko* (Japanese pinball). My philosophy is to enjoy life all you can. The Japanese as a people have far too few amusements, in my view. Pachinko's fun. I'll go at it for five days in a row, then lose interest and not play again for a month. Mah-jongg I've played ever since college and I'm not bad at it; we used to cut classes to play. I like gambling but am not confident at it. I take in the Big Five races, bet a thousand yen on a horse. All told I spend about 30,000 yen a month on amusements.

I exercise for a few minutes almost every day, usually by the morning radio. But I'll be damned if I will take vitamins or geriatric pills. I still can outrun most younger men and beat them getting on board the train. Also, I never nap on public transportation; my eyes are bright when everyone else's head is nodding. I'm not sure I still could, but in my 30's I was able to work all night and still put in a full day the next day. In recent years I have been cutting down on the alcohol, though; I feel it too much the day after.

I look young for my years. Other people tell me that, too. Mentally I *am* young—meaning I don't have a good head for details. Simple-minded. I recognize my immaturities, that I've a ways to go yet. I have to admit that I still lack experience in human relations. I didn't reach out for experience when I was younger, didn't wrestle with all sorts of problems. On that score I am still an infant. I know now how important it is to seek out different kinds of people and hear what they have to say. I don't really like talking with old people. Maybe I haven't the patience, I get mentally uneasy. But I talk all the time with people my age or younger, take in what they have experienced and try to reflect on it. When I am with somebody who has had rich experience in life, it makes me aware of my immaturities. And you'd better believe it leaves me feeling empty. But if I am not fully grown I know that I'm at least halfway there.

People need to share their experiences in order to make progress, don't you think? It takes joint effort. And yet as we grow older we have fewer and fewer such conversations. I mean you establish your security base, and after that your conversation gets shallower and shallower, like teenagers. For the kind of discussion I'm talking about, the 40's are the hollowest years of all. Every year you have fewer and fewer stimulating talks. Maybe that's why once people are secure they start to show signs of senility.

Security

Yoshiko controls the family treasury, does the shopping and pays the bills. In 15 years I haven't bought a thing, except balls for pachinko. I take my pocket money out of my pay envelope and give the rest to her. Not that I take much for myself, 20 to 25 thousand yen. Plus I deduct 100,000 yen from the mid-year and year-end bonuses.

If the family wants to buy anything, I simply tell them to go ahead. That's the way a man should handle it. It's absolutely old-fashioned for a man to tell his family no. My dad never refused. After all, the family knows how much money there is, and they should know better than to try to coax you into buying what you can't afford. Why should you have to act tight-fisted?

I try to maintain a small savings account. Money is the only thing you can depend on, after all. Some people can be tough about their income, set aside so much for this and so much for that. It doesn't work for me. These days it's all I can do to feed a little kitty and keep it alive. In any case, savings plan or no savings plan, when it's time for the kids to be married there naturally are going to be bills to pay. I won't have any colossal sum on hand, but I have to be ready to provide for them at the going rate. So I keep one eye on what the rates are. That makes for a dilemma. Because when I think about how Yoshiko and I are getting old, I know I not only need to hold on to what we've already saved, I should be adding to it. And money for wedding bills should be over and above that.

I won't be trying anything adventurous, not so long as my base isn't secure. If I could build a solid foundation for Yoshiko and the family, then I might take a flier. That's the townsman's way of thinking. I couldn't imagine abandoning my wife and kids in order to shoot for the big money. But I would if the foundation was firm. After all, I'm a businessman's son, I know what to do. Probably I'd trade on the stock market. I have a lot of contacts. But I can't afford it now.

A few years ago the agents pestered me so much that I finally took out a life insurance policy. Just a nose-blow's worth. Enough to cover my funeral expenses and not burden the kids with them. However, at my age it's still to early to be concerned about your grave, unless you're a rich man. Japan's a narrow country, and cemetery plots are expensive. I know it's a serious matter. But as I see it, what's the difference whether you have a gravestone or not. When I think about my relatives, father's father, grandparents on both sides, shoot, I never really knew them at all. Your children remember you, but the next generation down the line may not. As far as I'm concerned, once I'm dead it's enough if my kids will remember the kind of man I was. In our country, the rule is that your children should erect a tombstone for you, but I don't want mine to be burdened with the cost. If they'll just keep one of my bones in the family altar, they can put the rest of them in a temple, where eternal prayers will be said for me.

Aging with Friends

I have a handful of friends I've known for more than two decades. Most of them date from the army and college years. Afterward, it becomes difficult to build true friendships, because you want something from most of the people you meet. Friendship won't last on that basis; you drift apart. With true friends you don't need to fake the affection by sending presents at midsummer and the new year.

Each of them has a different background, and each has had a different set of experiences—one man's a schoolteacher, but the rest are in business—so we don't see eye to eye on everything. But when you are fully aware of the other guy's personality and his past, you can see things from his point of view. Then you can talk frankly and openly. A genuine friend never really changes, basically, does he?

In the days after we were married, we would talk about our wives, but when you get to your 50's all you talk about is your health and your children's futures. But we never talk about retirement. That makes you feel old. Until into our 40's we caroused; now we would rather sit in a quiet bar and talk.

Now and then two or three of us take a short trip. Usually just for one or two nights at a time—the older you get the harder it is to find time off. We most often go to Mt. Koya or places like that. Over the years we've been to most of the hot springs resorts in these parts, and once you've seen one the rest are pretty much the same. You find yourself wanting a less commercial atmosphere—a temple deep in the mountains that doubles as an inn, with priests cooking and serving.

Mt. Koya has more than a hundred temples—and no women. It's completely set apart from the everyday world. I must have gone there at least ten times. There must be ten thousand tombs of old feudal lords on that mountain. Not that I care so much for famous old sites, but nearby in Nightingale Valley there's an entertainment district. With both extremes present, it gives a bite to the experience.

But these days—I suppose it's my years—a night on the town can wear me out. The desire to stay home and watch TV usually wins out. To sleep late on Sunday. Or if I go out on Sunday, to do a little shopping. I mean I don't want to fall behind the times in everything. I want to keep up with how the young people are dressing. So Yoshiko and I go shopping, and I try to master "young fashion."

An Aging Couple

You're aware of Yoshiko's background. I admire her for what she made of it. But her life has been spent at home since we married, and she has grown to be a garden-variety hausfrau. She has forgotten how she used to be. She talks all the time about opening a rooming house or managing a boutique or something of the sort. But I don't approve, even though I'm from a business family myself. She has knocked herself out taking care of our home, and I've worked hard to support the family; when we're old we ought to take life easy.

I often think I'd like to take a long, leisurely trip with her. Doesn't matter where we go, it wouldn't have to be overseas. Why rush off overseas when you don't even know your own country? There's a lot to Japan, from Hokkaido all the way down to Kyushu; and Yoshiko has hardly seen any of it. Once we have time for it, once the kids are independent, I'd really like to take her traveling.

She's a good wife and I depend on her, trust her to look after everything at home. If we had been taking advantage of each other selfishly, only doing what each of us wanted to do, I doubt that things would have gone as well for us as they have. Nine-tenths of a marriage is a good sex life, and ours has been good from the beginning.

We used to snap at each other all the time. Now we show more consideration, think about the other's feelings before speaking out. We have drawn much closer. After 20 or 30 years, you pretty well know what the other one is feeling. That's a great thing to have.

We're a small-time city couple like those you can find anywhere. We don't have much money and don't dare be extravagant. But when you don't have it, you make do without it, learn how to enjoy life within your means. Yoshiko and I are well matched in that area. It's hard to say whether we've matured, but we definitely are much more sophisticated socially. In adjusting to the changing times we've lost our naiveté. Grown a shell of years, like a tortoise shell around us—each year grown more skilled about how to get along in the world.

There's one issue on which I goofed badly, as far as the family is concerned. I didn't get us a house of our own soon enough, and kept them living at my father's place much too long. I still feel edgy toward them on that one; it isn't completely resolved yet. But aside from that I've done what I could to build a good home life for us. I have never bellowed or barked at them. And I don't lean back and act as if I'm king of the hill—pull the petty-tyrant husband role.

And yet—you know your attitude toward your wife changes year by year. She's acting more and more like an old granny. I tell her not to dress that way. In my 30's there was a time when I figured it had been a mistake: I wished I had married somebody younger. On the other hand, when you think about the kind of man I am, what more did I have a right to expect? I'm such a confirmed Casanova. There are ways in which you resign yourself to being married. I haven't had a middle-age crisis. I've kept myself in good condition physically. And I have never seriously thought of running out on her.

But you wish your wife would stay attractive. I mean—so you won't misunderstand me—in the old days if a wife was on the plain side, or even unattractive, the problem didn't arise. She was a woman whose job it was to take care of you. You could be satisfied if she did that well, and scratched where you itch. You pursued love elsewhere.

These days that's out of the question. Since the war. Stockings and women have gotten stronger, as the saying goes. We're in an age where women refuse to go along with the idea any more. Until the war you could, so long's you had money, even a little money, manage to keep a woman. Cheaply. It's just impossible now. I'm not talking about if it's for love, that's different. But if you want a financial arrangement you've got to have plenty of dough. And plenty means—by my calculations—four or five hundred thousand yen a month. First you see to it that your family is secure, and around two hundred thousand a month would just barely take care of that. In addition you need to make the other woman happy, and that means another two hundred thou. So your monthly income has got to be at least four hundred and probably more.

Not many guys pull in that kind of money. None of my friends, even the ones who might be able to afford it, is keeping a woman. They're all *mai hōmu* ("my home") types. It shows you the power of education, at least that's how I look at it. Women have had their sense of self and sense of independence stirred up. Japan's made a lot of progress in educating women as well as men. In the old days it was enough to go to primary school, and if you could afford a mistress or two you were a wealthy man.

For me, life is good first of all when my work goes well. Next, when I look at my children's faces. They come home only once every few months now. "How they're growing," I'll think to myself. And then—maybe this doesn't quite fit in—life is good when Yoshiko and I talk about the future. I may not say it out loud, but as I listen to her I'll be saying to myself, "Hell yes, that's what we'll do!" And I feel alive and full of fight. After all, I want to make life better for her; I haven't done all that much for her yet. With the kids moving out on their own, it's just the two of us, and I want to take good care of her.

My one great hope is that I die before Yoshiko does. An old woman can make herself welcome around the house; she'll get along. An old man is sure to feel miserable.

Yoshiko is growing conservative. She used to be more easygoing than me, but that is changing. Sometimes she seems sort

of neurotic. But of course I'm getting more and more conservative too, at least in the way I think. However, when it comes to
expressing myself, putting my thoughts into words, I try to
phrase them in a trendy way. Advertise that this is one aging man
who remains up to date. Maybe it's a weakness in me. But if you
come out sounding old-fashioned, nobody will take any interest
in you.

IV. THE RHETORIC OF GENERATIONS

We live out our course of years in a milieu that includes three
or more different generations of contemporaries. What happens
to them as they move across their stages of life will powerfully
shape our own sense of place, aging, and being. This is true most
immediately as regards the lives of our kinsmen and friends. We
see examples of it in Nishimura Kōtarō's annoyance over becoming a grandfather even before he has been retired from his
executive post, or in Beisuke's fuss over Yoshiko's acting too
grannyish for her age. But we are also influenced, if more imper-
sonally, by what happens to social generations in the wider sense,
as they cycle severally along the timeline of collective history.
Beisuke is much more sensitive to this than are most of my Hanshin interviewees, exerting himself to stay in tune with "young
fashion" (*yangu fuashiyon*) and to master recent hit tunes so that
bar hostesses will be able to sing along with him.

In Chapters 5 and 6, I shall take up in more detail the topic of
how kin and friends influence one's own sense of maturity. Here I
want to look mainly at the influence of social generations: what
the sociologist in his technical vocabulary calls *cohorts*.

The Senzenha Dilemma

The currents of generational history swirl together in the everyday, and are not easy to sort out. Popular wisdom in Japan, as
elsewhere, provides categories for thinking about generations
and their differences, but the categories are far from watertight.
By one Japanese system of reckoning, Beisuke and Shōji both
belong to the senzenha, the prewar generation. Both were born
and schooled in the nationalist era with its ethos of loyalty, obedi-

ence, and piety. Both saw military service. Both were young during the years of national turmoil that lasted from 1936 to 1951; years of mobilization, emergencies, defeat, shortages, and occupation by conquering armies. Both therefore had a "deprived" youth and young manhood. And yet Shōji, with his rural and priestly background, took this as a call to glory. Beisuke the urbanite and businessman's son proved himself the loyal soldier, but through it all he remained a lover, not a fighter, somewhat skeptically reciting the Imperial writ in the chapel of the holy war.

By another line of popular reckoning, however, Beisuke and Shōji belong to different generations, though only seven years separate them. They were born in different Imperial reign periods, Beisuke late in Taisho (1912–25) and Shōji early in Showa (1925 onward, the reign of the present Emperor, Hirohito). Today's mass media often attack the Early Showa type with barbed wit, but soften stereotypes of the Taisho generation.

Thus in media image-work the Early Showa types are not quite normal. They did not enjoy a normal adolescence, but were robbed of it by years of wartime turmoil. Youth should be a time of greening. The usual word for youth, *seinen*, is in fact a compound of graphs for "green" and "years." It should be a time for romance, recklessness, long, long thoughts. A time when—in Sōseki's words, given in this chapter's motto—with heart aflame you lose yourself in pure happiness.

The media stereotype is partly corroborated in an intriguing study by Mita Munesuke of popular attitudes toward modern history. Mita asked a sample of adults of all ages to choose one era as the best, and one as the worst, for Japan in modern times. Almost everyone, regardless of his or her age, chose the wartime and postwar periods as Japan's worst. (Fewer than 1 percent said that wartime had been Japan's finest hour, and most of those who did so were men who had been of combat age during the war.) Votes for the best era, however, reveal a clear generation difference. For all generations, the present (since 1955) is the finest era of modern Japanese history. But when one looks at second best, at the era given the second largest number of votes, each gen-

eration favors the era when it was in its own youth—each generation, that is, except the Early Showa generation.

If today's youth are the "now" generation (Japan's mass media
also use that term), then the Early Showa types are the "no" generation. They are blunted by comparison either with their parents
or their children, who had a more normal opportunity to learn
how to enjoy life while in their impressionable years. Mr. Early
Showa, jibes one magazine article, is "homo tasteless." He is
maladept at sports and games, clumsy at relating to the opposite
gender, tongue-tied in English, cramped by an inferiority complex toward Euro-Americans. Above all, he is parsimonious. Not
necessarily a string-saver, but a man cramped by a depression-era
mentality in an age of affluence.

If the Early Showa type has one positive talent, it is a capacity
for rate-busting heroics at work. He is the consummate *mōretsu
shain*, translatable as "passionate company man," or more loosely
as workaholic. His wife has the same kind of single-minded dedication, but toward home and family. She is the *kyōiku mama*, the
"education mother": a sort of Japanese Mrs. Portnoy who coaxes
and shames her offspring into producing a good record in the
school entrance examinations.

All of these traits are explained, in mass-media exaggeration, as
having been brought on by social conditions during the decade
of the "dark valley." The upper schools, for example, were sex-
segregated. Dating was frowned upon, even considered unpatriotic. So there were few opportunities to learn to express affection
for the opposite gender openly.

Few women went to high school, fewer to college, and they
want now to recoup their educational deprivation vicariously
through their children.

Most schools ceased the teaching of English, and national campaigns tried to extirpate the several hundred words of the "enemy language" that by then were common coinage in everyday
speech. So the Early Showa types were caught mute when the
GIs arrived, and have been ashamed ever since.

Many sports, games, and amusements were forbidden for the
duration, though physical conditioning was prescribed. By late

in the war, few balls or implements were available anyway. Secondary-school courses were accelerated or canceled, and students mobilized for work in war-materiel factories. Thus, the only thing the Early Showa types learned to do well was to work hard. Above all, throughout the period the nation suffered severe and growing shortages of clothing, housing, food, of anything material. Some people knew malnutrition firsthand, most knew what it was to go hungry. Small wonder, then, that they insist even today that one must eat every grain of rice set before him.

My interviewees, most of whom are of the Early Showa generation, say that with due allowances for hyperbole the stereotype does reflect elements of their own experience. They *are* confident of their capacity for hard work and for survival in times of scarcity —and wonder if the postwar generations are not soft on that score. No one would admit to being a kyōiku mama herself: it's other wives who are that way. But all are deeply concerned about the credential inflation in the postwar job market. They feel sorry that their children must go through an "examination hell" not dreamed of in their own youth years.

On the other hand, my interviewees *do* envy today's youth for fluency in English and for ease in meeting foreigners. And some particularly wish that they could be as free about holding hands or embracing in public as today's young people are. "Too bashful" (*terekusai*) was the usual response when I asked a Hanshin adult if he or she ever held hands with a spouse in public. Even Beisuke said the same, although one time he announced that a few days earlier he and Yoshiko had walked home arm in arm—in the dark, after a shrine festival.

But in the Taisho era Japan had a much more freewheeling atmosphere, above all in the cities. No doubt this was less the case for the lower economic strata, who suffered from inflation and from fluctuations in employment. But for at least the middle and upper strata it was a period of expansion and of bourgeois comfort. Historians, conscious of political considerations, label the period as that of Taisho Democracy. Voting rights, for example, were extended to almost all men (though not to women until 20 years later). Popularly elected national leaders replaced the oligarchs who had ruled during the Meiji era. Labor unions and other movements for social welfare and reform acquired considerable momentum.

Another kind of democratization was also evident, that of lifestyles. It was during the Taisho period that a *modern* townsman lifestyle crystallized, fusing older patterns from the floating world with industrial technology and with elements drawn from Western popular culture. Thanks to economic prosperity the broad mass of the population could now take on this style as their own —in contrast to conditions in the Tokugawa cities, where the masses had been too poor to have much of any part in the life of the floating world.

Thus the mass culture of twentieth-century Japan by and large has evolved in the style put together in the mass-transit, mass-media, suburbanizing cities of the Taisho period. Workers became commuters. "Terminal culture" sprouted in the new department stores, specialty shops, and entertainment districts that were built near the railway stations. People not only moved out of the cities to live, they rode out of the cities to play—to the new amusement parks, racetracks, professional baseball stadiums, and recreation areas in the suburbs. It should come as no surprise that Japanese social scientists first undertook field research into recreation as a social problem in Taisho-era Osaka.

Beisuke himself was only 3 years old when the Taisho emperor died. His exposure to the Taisho atmosphere was indirect, filtered through his family, and it would be a mistake, in attempting to explain his life, to accord much influence to the era of his birth. Nevertheless, his parents and siblings—the eldest being more than 20 years his senior—were steeped in the new townsman lifestyle and could afford to luxuriate in it. His brothers lost no time in initiating him into its more glorious forms. And the commercially aggressive father and eldest brother sustained the family at very comfortable levels of living during the early Showa years, when much of Japan suffered. Yoshiko, for example, tells of how in the postwar years of shortages and rationing she, like many Japanese, had to travel into the countryside to plead with farmers to sell or barter food. Beisuke's family had had servants who could be sent on this unpleasant—and nominally illegal—trade.

For Beisuke, Japan's defeat marked no great discontinuity in lifestyle or in projected pathways, as it did for Shōji. Beisuke did not "die" in August 1945; he went home and resumed his playboy routines. Only reluctantly, unassertively, pressured by mother and siblings, did he begin to launch a working career and a family of his own.

So now, at 50, reflecting back over his adult decades, Beisuke sees a strong line of continuity: he has been in a marathon race with others in his generation. Along the way he has known bright and dull periods. His baseball stardom and his young-adult enthusiasm for his work shine against the dim and uninspiring middle-management tasks of recent years. But by every measure he can apply, he finds that he has been falling behind or barely holding his own. His peers are outrunning him financially. Changing fashions make his talents for enjoyment, his connoisseurship, seem more and more dated. And his body is beginning to be undependable. To use James Baldwin's phrase, he is approaching his "final margin," his "last opportunity for creation." And he is pondering how to muster his forces of resistance.

Resistance and Regeneration

If young adulthood is a time for settling down, middle adulthood is a time for settling up. In the earlier years we are reluctant to forgo alternatives in binding ourselves to career courses in family, vocation, avocations. Shōji clung to his utopia of pure action, but prolonged his courtship for seven years. Beisuke clung to bodily prowess, to baseball and womanizing, and only carried out his work and family duties in pro forma fashion until he was into his 30's. He lacked the usual businessman ambitions, he says. And for several years his wife and children were cared for in his parental family's mansion.

But by the middle years, the results of earlier commitments are there to be seen—by others as well as ourselves. Performance must be reckoned, failure confessed. Old self-images must be buried and mourned if no longer viable, or else revitalized, or neutralized in fantasy. *Resistance at Forty-eight* simplifies the process for dramatic impact. Nishimura Kōtarō's former selves are embodied in the person of Sōga the young executive, the Old Adam whose name could—in yet another play upon its graphs—be rendered also as "many-layered desire." Nishimura-Sōga is a textbook illustration of the clinical explanation: that mid-career crisis results from an eruption of unresolved adolescent identity conflicts. Nishimura spins through a youthful whirl of testing various identifications, fails to sustain them, and only then is able to firmly dispatch his Sōga self.

We are not told what Nishimura's youthful years were like but we know from Beisuke that his were memorable. More than many men, Beisuke at age 50 still mourns a former self. Life today is blunted by comparison. In his green years he was at a peak in most domains of action. He was a star athlete and a team captain, won praise both for bodily prowess and for leadership. He was popular with women. He could gamble all night, drink, pursue amours unhampered either by family obligations or by parental carping—on the contrary, since he was encouraged to take his father and elder brothers as models. And the songs and jokes he knew were on the crest of pop-culture fashion.

That configuration came unhinged in his 30's. All its parts have since faded, and he can sustain them only at lower tempo and with greater effort. Pieces of a new configuration have been emerging, but are not yet consolidated.

Bodily vigor has been such a main line of defense and main tool for success that Beisuke strongly resists the idea that his body can no longer meet his demands upon it. He exercises regularly and still can outrun younger men. He never dozes on public transportation and always reports for work on time. But a night on the town can leave him exhausted. Often he is content to go home after work, to watch TV and read. He regrets not having developed his mental capacities earlier—wishes he had *studied* in school and not just played.

Beisuke shies away from medical examinations, refuses vitamins, and snorts about friends who are resorting to aphrodisiacs to sustain sexual potency. I am chary about Freudian word games, but am struck by the fact that *seikō* is among Beisuke's favorite words. In spoken Japanese seikō ("success, victory") and seikō ("orgasm") are homonyms; in written form, different graphs obviate confusion between the two, and most of the time in conversation, too, context will make clear which meaning is intended. But there were occasions when, listening to Beisuke, I was not always certain about his referent.

Success in its commercial sense has not been his—at least not yet. Beisuke is obliged to excuse his performance in that domain. Some may not get the breaks, he says, though he refuses to blame the fates in his own case. Life is more complicated than that. He remains in awe of his aggressive eldest brother and father (the latter continued his virile ways even after becoming partially crippled by illness). They seem so different from him that Beisuke wonders if they may not even be of a different personality type than he.

Perhaps there is still time in which to strike it rich. He has connections, he knows the world of finance. He should have sought out experience in the past more energetically, and not been so caught up in the floating world—he warns his children to do just the opposite of what he did. If he really tries, gives it all he has, then he can collapse into old age satisfied—that if he did fail it was not for lack of nerve. And if he should happen to make the Big Money, who knows? With enough money you still can live out the dream of kaishō—and keep a mistress.

And yet—the floating world still beckons. Instead of becoming a financier he could become a host, open a little bar of his own. He could capitalize on his knack for rapport, his fund of songs and stories, his connoisseurship of the pleasures. He could "turn pro" in a way that he was never able to do as an athlete. However vicariously, he would still be a participant in the realm of the sensual. His wife Yoshiko came from that world, and should understand and accept its enduring allure for him.

But there will be no plunge until family obligations are settled. For Beisuke a few close friends have furnished an important line of continuity across the fading years. A good friend, he says, is one who doesn't change, whether you succeed or fail. But more and more the continuity is coming from wife and from family. Of late, Beisuke thinks about gratitude toward the ancestors, and once in a while about how he himself will be remembered after his death. He has provided for his children's schooling and is prepared to pay their wedding expenses at the going rate. On the other hand, he has never achieved great closeness with his son or daughter, any more than he did with his father.

With Yoshiko, however, what started as physical attraction has ripened into an intimacy greater than he had perhaps foreseen. They understand each other, are open with each other. They know the same songs. And they can have deep conversations of a kind that are more and more difficult to engender with other people as one grows older. Now in retrospect Beisuke cannot easily excuse the duplicity he showed when he blatantly womanized during the time he was courting Yoshiko. And he is determined to make amends for having been so tardy about installing her in the home that he had promised her soon after marriage. (Yoshiko described the first years of their marriage, before they moved out of his parental house, as a time of material comfort but emotional desolation, an enforced idleness that came right upon her years of managing a house of pleasure.) But like Nishimura Kōtarō, Beisuke too wishes Yoshiko were not such a dull hausfrau these days.

Perhaps Nishimura is not hero material, because he is the consummate townsman, unable to part with his creature comforts. But his illness forces him to come to terms with bodily decline, and his recuperation is a "regression" with positive results. He emerges from it with a reenergized will to be; he gains resilience and new windows of self-awareness.

Over the years, Nishimura had become artful about manipulating others. He was sensitive to them, but mostly in terms of what he wanted from them, seldom in terms of their needs. During his recuperation he realizes how much he had been "using" the young hostess to satisfy his kaishō ambitions. He realizes, too, the double standard he had applied when he demanded that his daughter follow the pathways of proper marriage, while for himself at the same time he claimed freedom from them. And though he "resists" grandparenthood, there are already hints that his range of empathy toward descendants is expanding in anticipation. Resistance can fail at 48 and still be a vital, if painful, episode in the creation of a new integrity.

Two years later I was able to call on Beisuke and Yoshiko briefly in their newest home. The structure was not pretentious, though it was well appointed, in that blend of traditional and modern that characterizes contemporary Japanese suburban dwellings. But neither was it modest, in containing more rooms than a married couple would ordinarily seem to need.

In the intervening months Beisuke's mother had died, after a lingering illness, tended constantly by Yoshiko and his youngest sister. Beisuke himself had been having bouts of difficulty with stomach complaints. His hair was now streaked with gray, and his face carried incipient lines of slackness.

It was Sunday midday, and Beisuke was disappointed that I could not spend the afternoon drinking with him. We sipped sake and bantered for a while. The tone was gay and teasing, but the undertone was a warning from Beisuke that he wondered if I was enjoying life enough while I was still able.

CHAPTER 5

A Spoiled Daughter

For one thing is certain as we grow older: The few people who
have truly passed through us and us through them, until the
dreams, images, memories are past sorting out, these people become precious links to our continuity.

GAIL SHEEHY, *Passages*

I. THE RHYTHM OF OTHER LIVES

We have already looked in briefly on the Makiokas of Osaka
and Ashiya. They are a fictional family. But most readers find
them thoroughly believable, and no real Japanese family has ever
been described in such detail. Of the four Makioka sisters, the
youngest two remain unmarried, although Yukiko is 30 and
Taeko 25. Their parents have been dead for more than a decade.
And so, responsibility for finding mates for the two sisters has
devolved officially upon Tsuruko, the eldest of the four, and her
adoptee husband. (See Figure 4.)

Yukiko and Taeko have long felt put off by the stuffy Tsuruko
and her husband. Rather than remain with them in the main house
in Osaka, Yukiko and Taeko connive to spend much of their time
in suburban Ashiya with their more sympathetic second sister,
Sachiko. And so it comes about that de facto responsibility for the
two young women is taken over by Sachiko and her husband
Teinosuke. If Sachiko's affection for her younger sisters is deep,
warm, and sororal, her duty toward them has become maternal.
Furthermore, she is bound to them by a lifelong continuity of
shared experiences and interests.

Sachiko has no towering compulsion or supercharged interest by which to plot her course through the coming years. She has no career separable from her family: she is neither artist nor professional. But she finds the root meaning of existence, as Beisuke does, in the Osaka bourgeois lifestyle. In the novel this is symbolized by her appreciation of traditional dance performances done in the Osaka manner. She herself is spectator, not dancer: the dancers in the family are Yukiko and Taeko—destined by the norms of the life cycle to marry and leave. If Sachiko is to sustain the richness of her involvement in the bourgeois lifestyle, she must somehow remain close to her younger sisters while at the same time helping them into life's next stage.

To sustain her engagement with the Osaka lifeways, she must maintain the coherence of her Ashiya ménage, as Beisuke must his. But as a man, Beisuke can be tolerant of himself—if not very pleased—so long as he continues to support his family financially. Certainly he attempts to do more than merely that. But as a woman, Sachiko finds that her first task is to sustain each member of her ménage emotionally in the rhythms of their several courses to maturity. The challenge is not so much to her inner integrity as to her ability to manage the interpersonal integrity of her convoy of consociates. Their failures and successes are hers.

During our younger years we are figuratively in society's foyer; in old age, near the back door. It is during maturity, as never else, that we are most fully inside the house, most fully *persons*, with all that our society attaches to that status. Terms translatable as "householder" or "housewife" are synonyms for maturity in many languages. They refer to a period during which we must manage properties, not only physical ones but also the properties of lives bound to our own. We are engaged with, responsible for, the life cycles of others as well as our own. There may be relatively few times when our sense of being or of aging changes because of anything we ourselves have done, any new identification we claim. But that sense of being may change fairly often because of what another has done, thus bringing on an identification that "happens" to us, as when a child marries and we become parents-

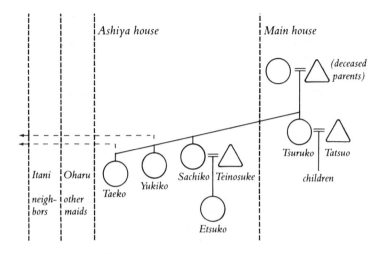

FIGURE 4. A visual representation of Makioka Sachiko's most important consociates during the years of the novel *Sasameyuki*. Solid lines indicate the kinship ties between the main Makioka house in Osaka and the branch house (Sachiko's) in Ashiya. Shown on the peripheries are maids (e.g. Oharu) who live in the Ashiya house, and other persons such as Sachiko's hairdresser Itani, who have secondary roles in the action.

in-law. In adulthood we are life-cycle jugglers spinning several plates simultaneously, grasping at wheels within wheels as three or more generations of our contemporaries orbit around us in the social present.

Of Time and the Household

To focus upon Sachiko is to assault the architecture of symbols that Tanizaki has built into the five years of narrative time and the more than five hundred pages of text in *Sasameyuki*. A delicate sensuality of time permeates the entire book. "It is the interior time that passes within humans that is the central concern of this novel," Tanizaki was to write later.

Symbolically, the author plays the "artificial" time of men's concerns—their rise and fall in commerce and politics and war—against the "natural" tempo of women's lives. Within women's tempo he contrasts the repetitive pulses of menstruation and childbirth, of dance recitals, of annual excursions to Kyoto, with the serial pulses of bodily aging and the stages of the life course. By preserving the pattern of the Osaka lifestyle, Sachiko provides herself and her ménage with a channel of continuity within which the wild currents of natural time can be domesticated, and thereby aesthetically savored. Since the book is neither pornographic nor manifestly unpatriotic, a foreign reader may find it curious that portions of the novel were banned during the Pacific War. Perhaps its very celebration of the voluptuousness latent in the modern townsman lifestyle (a favorite theme of Tanizaki's) was sufficient to arouse the censorial impulse.

More important for our purposes here, Tanizaki conveys this artistry of time in a narrative form that is close to cinema verité. The Makioka women are, in fact, drawn closely from Tanizaki's second wife (who becomes Sachiko in the novel) and her three sisters. Events in the novel replicate events in their actual lives, even to taking place on the same dates in the late 1930's. People confront just the right range and balance of improbabilities to remain credible.

All four sisters are portrayed in depth; and only slightly less attention is accorded Teinosuke, Sachiko's husband, and Etsuko, their pre-teen daughter. But if Tanizaki occasionally takes us into the minds of others in the house, he consistently makes us privy to Sachiko's feelings and reactions. She does not narrate the story, nor do we see events unfold only through her eyes. But the action revolves around her position in this community of fate. Sachiko does not dominate the galaxy, but the others gravitate about her, relying upon her to mediate conflicts and hold the system in balance.

Sachiko is not fully confident that she can meet their needs. Back when the Makioka family had thrived in Osaka merchant glory, she had been her father's pet. She recognizes that even at 35 she retains traces of the spoiled daughter she had been. Her defenses are still wobbly, and she is prey to minor colds and indispositions. Nevertheless, in the dozen years she has been married she and Teinosuke have evolved a stable, compassionate partnership.

Teinosuke is an accountant able to balance his investments to career and to home. He and Sachiko still exchange poems, take second-honeymoon trips, and erupt in little marital tiffs in public without later slipping into bitter recriminations. He is quick to sense her blue moods and to find ways to coax her out of them. And he seems almost as fond of her younger sisters as she herself is.

Daughter Etsuko is more troublesome, a coltish and willful child. At times she acts mildly neurotic, and is more attached to Yukiko than to her mother. Yukiko responds by fussing over her more than would even a devoted nanny.

In addition, the household includes one or two maids, who require correcting and supervising. Nowadays, domestic service has become a commercial trade, but at the time of the story the "helper" more often was a teenage girl sent for training as an apprentice housewife. Her services were rewarded with lessons in household and marital arts and with help in finding a husband.

Problem Performers

Husband, daughter, maids—all require Sachiko's attention. But if it were only a matter of looking after them, she reflects, the Ashiya ménage might be terribly dull. The problem performers who add zest to her challenge are Yukiko and Taeko.

Not that they were a bother to her: she was delighted at the color they gave the life of the family. Sachiko among the four sisters had in largest measure inherited her father's love of excitement. She disliked too quiet a house. Out of deference to her married sister and her brother-in-law she could not purposely lure her younger sisters away. Still she rejoiced in the fact that they preferred her house to the main house, and it seemed natural that they should be where there was more room and where children were less of a problem.

The younger sisters are by no means unsought in the marriage market. Like Sachiko herself, both are cheerful, stunning women who look a decade younger than their years. They take lessons in French conversation as well as in Osaka dance. They combine

East and West, traditional and modern, in appealing blends, though each with her own accents: Taeko being the bold modern woman and Yukiko the demure maiden of old.

If the Makioka fortune is gone, the family name remains known and respected across mercantile Osaka. Kin, friends, and Sachiko's helpful hairdresser Mrs. Itani staff a distant-early-warning line that detects the approach of potential husbands. But Yukiko is in danger of superannuation. During the span of the novel she even enters the "danger year" (*yakudoshi*), traditionally thought to be most inauspicious for a woman: 33. She and her supporters are being pressed by that most scarce of all natural resources, time.

Taeko affirms that she will not marry out of order, not before Yukiko has been married. She holds to that position partly from regard for family honor, partly from personal affection for Yukiko. The difficulty is that Taeko has had a steady boyfriend for some years. He is the pampered son of a merchant family, socially acceptable to the Makiokas but personally crude. And he and the impulsive Taeko are feisty; once they even try to elope. Both families took a hand in suppressing the affair but could not prevent it from being reported in a local scandal sheet—which erroneously gave the name of the wayward Makioka sister as Yukiko.

Taeko is the sort who, having once made up her mind, proceeds "quite without hesitation—sometimes even to the point of making herself a little unpleasant." She is as socially adept as Yukiko is socially inept, so worldly-wise that now and then her more housebound sisters feel she is condescending to them. She develops a following as a maker of Japanese-style dolls and an instructress in the craft. From there she wants to go on to become a modiste, designing and making Western clothes. She demands that the family support her plans to study in Paris and then open a salon in Kobe. But if the Osaka main house will tolerate her doll-making "hobby," it flatly rejects her ambition to become a "working woman" in the pedestrian trade of a "seamstress."

Yukiko, on the other hand, is a fragile snowflake, beautiful but so shy that she sometimes cannot even articulate her feelings and wants to others in the family. Outside the house she almost never speaks, even in situations where common courtesy expects it. She will plead with others to accompany her even when she leaves the house on a trivial errand. One of her suitors loses heart when she can only mumble an incoherent reply to his telephoned invitation to join him for a cup of tea. Sachiko, Teinosuke, and the marital go-betweens must exert themselves to convince prospects that first impressions of Yukiko can be mistaken. Her intimates know that within the protecting walls of home she can be a treasure. "With Yukiko back, the Ashiya house was gay and noisy again. Yukiko, so inarticulate that one hardly knew she was about, added little to the noise, but one could see from the difference she made that something bright was hidden behind that apparent melancholy and reserve."

Physically Yukiko is the toughest of all the Makiokas, never prey to colds or aches. On the other hand, she has a blemish that erupts prominently on her forehead during menstrual periods. Physicians assure them that this is common in young women, and that it will disappear permanently soon after marriage. But it means anxious moments for Sachiko and the go-betweens whenever they must schedule a "viewing" for her. Eventually, Yukiko agrees to submit to a series of inoculations that will, it is thought, erase the spot.

Sustaining and Steering

Sachiko finds herself in a polygon of conflicting interests—between Taeko and Yukiko, between each of them and the main house, between her duty to them (and to her dead parents) to find mates for them and her delight in what they add to the Ashiya ménage. They are her younger sisters, and yet they are more like daughters. They are also her best friends; and not only friends but co-sharers in the Osaka lifeways.

Everything considered, then, her feelings for the two had not been what one usually understands by the affection of sister for sister. She was sometimes startled at the thought that she spent more time worrying about her sisters than about her husband and daughter, but they were like daughters—they were on a level with Etsuko in her affections, and at the same time they were her only friends. Left alone, she was surprised to note that she had no friends worthy of the name. Her relations with other housewives had for the most part been cool and formal. Because of her sisters, she had not needed friends.

When they were girls in the Osaka house the three of them always slept in the same room, down to the night before Sachiko was married. Tsuruko was off in a room of her own. Even now, the three of them freely borrow and wear each other's kimono, obi, undergarments. No one in the Ashiya house can muster any enthusiasm for a suitor who, though otherwise acceptable enough, would take Yukiko away to rusticate with him in a distant country town. And when negotiations turn serious with another man (whom Yukiko eventually marries), Sachiko is chilled because he lives in Tokyo—until he remarks that he plans to move to Osaka. The sisters must marry, Sachiko allows, but if they move far away the Ashiya house will go humdrum. "It was like a spring breeze to have all the sisters under one roof. The mood would be broken if one of them were to go."

Sachiko has heard that people accuse her of holding Yukiko in the Ashiya house as a cheap nanny for Etsuko. That may not be entirely untrue, Sachiko admits, but it is a minor motive. Far more prepotent is her appreciation for Yukiko's rare beauty, beauty that can be achieved, like the beauty of a bonsai, only by careful cultivation along traditional lines. If Yukiko re-embodies the classic appeal of their Kyoto mother, Sachiko is modeled more after their Osaka merchant father. But Sachiko is devoted to the classical forms, at least as a patroness. She could not push Yukiko into marriage to any philistine incapable of appreciating and cherishing such beauty.

Her involvement with the arts inclines Sachiko in favor of Yukiko. Still, Sachiko is also partial to the "Japanese maiden" who emerges in Taeko when she dresses in kimono and performs (as she does with great skill) Osaka dances. After all, Sachiko reasons to herself, Taeko never enjoyed her fair share of parental affection and guidance. Sachiko would like to make amends for that.

There were reasons why Taeko should be different from the rest of them. It was not entirely fair to reprove her. She alone of the four sisters had known almost nothing of their father's prosperous days, and she had but the dimmest memories of her mother, who had died just as the youngest daughter was starting school. Their pleasure-loving father gave the daughters everything they wanted, and yet Taeko had never really known—had never had an immediate sense of—what had been done for her. . . . She remembered chiefly how her father would describe her as the darkest and plainest of all, and indeed she must have been a most untidy girl, with her face quite uncared for and her clothes so shapeless that she could have passed for a boy. She liked to say that some day she too would finish school and dress up and go out as her sisters did. She would buy pretty clothes. But before she had her wish, her father died, and the good days were over for the Makioka family.

Taeko is more complex than Yukiko, is even capable of deceiving her sisters. Rumors of Taeko's misconduct—which she denies—rebound to harm Yukiko's marital prospects, and reflect back upon Sachiko herself for not being more firm about supervising this flamboyant sister. Taeko has an affair with a photographer, then one with a bartender. Sachiko is inclined to blame herself more than Taeko, blame herself for not having judged her sister's character more accurately. But the time has come for Sachiko to act decisively, or else Yukiko and Taeko will be summoned back to live again in the main house.

Crisis Management

Sachiko expels Taeko from the Ashiya house—at least for appearance's sake—and reports to the main house that from now on Taeko will be living alone. Perhaps Sachiko is not deliberately conning the main house, but more and more she is discouraged at Tsuruko's lack of sympathy toward Taeko and Yukiko, by Tsuruko's thralldom to family pride. Tsuruko had been distant from the three younger sisters even when they were in childhood. Her actions now, however, alienate her further; when the Makiokas of Ashiya next call at the main house, it is only to transact official business.

Sachiko's trials reach a climax when Yukiko is at long last betrothed—and Taeko announces that she is pregnant. It is too late to risk an abortion, and her condition soon will be visible. Sachiko now activates the entire Ashiya household. Teinosuke talks to the bartender-lover Miyoshi, who proves to be a decent man more than willing to marry Taeko—once Yukiko safely has been married—if the family will accept him. Taeko is sent to a resort, where she registers as "Mrs. Abe." She is tended, but now also policed, by the maid Oharu. Once a blabbermouth country girl, in her years under Sachiko's tutelage Oharu has grown into a cool-headed young woman who can be trusted to guard the family's reputation, even to the point of bossing Taeko around.

Sachiko purposely called a cab from a stand some distance away, and had her sister change to another cab in Kobe for the trip across the mountains. She gave Oharu detailed instructions: Taeko was to be in Arima for several months, under the name Abe; Oharu was to call her Mrs. Abe and not Koi-san [the family's pet name for her]; for liaison a messenger would be sent from Ashiya, or Oharu herself would come back, and no one was to use the telephone; Oharu was to understand that Miyoshi and Taeko were not to see each other and that Miyoshi was not to be told where Taeko was staying; and Oharu was moreover to watch for strange letters, or telephone calls or visitors.

But when Taeko's labor proves troublesome, a breech presentation, Sachiko herself "breaks cover" and rushes to the hospital. Waving her husband's business card she demands that "Mrs. Abe" be treated with the German pharmaceuticals she is sure the hospital has in reserve for its favored patients. In what seems a rather melodramatic tribute to propriety, however, the child is stillborn.

Perhaps the sisters do not live on happily ever after—for the shadow of war is over the nation—but they will be living not far from Ashiya. Sachiko has held her convoy together, seen them through illness and tragedy, covered their failures and helped salvage their self-respect. Teinosuke offers to pay the expenses of Yukiko's wedding and to repay Taeko's debts to a former boyfriend, even though such obligations should fall to the main house. Etsuko is growing out of her neurotic habits and turning into a sassy but likeable teenager. Even Oharu has become discreet and competent, ready to be sent as a bride herself. Taeko will live with Miyoshi until it is time for them to be married.

Yukiko can finish packing her trousseau, the bride of a man who (Sachiko is confident) will nourish her fragile charm. And yet— "At the thought of how still the house would be, Sachiko felt like a mother who had just seen her daughter married."

II. CONVOYING THE SELF

As each of us owns a unique subjectivity and memory, so each of us owns a unique panel of consociates who are involved in our passage through all the phases of our life course. It is useful to have a label for this co-journeying: let us call it "convoying." I am adapting a notion suggested some years ago by the Indian anthropologist Triloki Madan in his monograph on the pandits of Kashmir. In Madan's more limited use, a convoy was a panel of villagers who became so caught up in the course of his research that they often accompanied him on his journeys of inquiry around their community. Taken more broadly, a convoy is the committee or special-interest group that is charged with the promoting and policing of any one human life. All the Makiokas, for example, have an investment in assuring a suitable marriage for Yukiko.

From society's point of view, a convoy is that group delegated to sponsor one person's maturation and aging. This is easiest to see at turning points where passage is ceremonialized. For example, during her period of exclusion from the family, Taeko falls seriously ill with dysentery. Tsuruko complains worriedly that if Taeko should die, having been expelled, who would there be to hold a funeral for her and where could it be held? Indeed, passage rites are likely to be the only occasions when, if ever, the full membership of a convoy will assemble in one place. In day-to-day existence, one meets his convoyers severally in an array of separate settings.

This is not to say that a convoy is dormant amid the trivia of the everyday, only that its functioning is more difficult to discern. Some of the others in your convoy may meet and interact apart from you—family members at home, colleagues at work. At times they may present you with a united front on some issue. Most of the time, however, it is you who must actively coordinate their relationships, at least so far as they involve your being. You must reconcile their different opinions of you, different demands upon you; your emotional stability and openness to further growth hinge upon being able to manage this diversity. Your ability to sustain convoy coherence rests in turn upon your social skills: you must act appropriately toward each of the others separately, to protect the privacy and intimacy of each relationship, indeed at times to prevent the rest from even knowing of a relationship. Taeko has difficulty concealing her affairs with men. And with each successive exposé the family feels obliged to impose greater sanctions upon her.

From a subjective point of view, on the other hand, your convoy is your primary jury of being. It judges your actions against the cultural norms, it authenticates your performances and your identities. Put another way, your convoy warrants your uniqueness as a person: no other human being has precisely the same social anthology. The convoy assures you of the "capacity to be missed," as Jules Henry phrases it, of your right to improbabilities. These improbabilities, idiosyncrasies, are your most treasured possessions, inalienable indicators that you are an individual. The Makiokas, for example, are adamant that Yukiko not be given as bride to any man incapable of savoring and preserving the peculiar beauty of her shyness. "Only a man who sees her good points is qualified to be her husband," says Teinosuke.

As a unit of society, then, each person is a kind of institution: an embodiment of a web of consociation with its unique history of co-experience. The passage of time adds depth and complexity. Bernice Neugarten puts it this way:

In a sense the aging individual becomes a socio-emotional "institution" with the passage of time. Not only do certain personality processes provide continuity, but the individual has built up around him a network of social relationships that supports and maintains him. The "institutional" quality involves an individuated pattern of strategies for dealing with the changing world within and without, strategies that transcend many of the intra-psychic changes and (social) losses that appear.

Seen thus, a convoy is ego-focused and ego-dependent. It is not a corporate institution in the sense that, say, the Mitsubishi Trading

Company is a corporate institution. It has no abstract table of organization, no origin myth, no functions or justifications apart from its work in the processing of an individual human life. At most it might in limiting cases evolve a formal structure as the retinue surrounding a television personality, for example, or a chief of state.

This means that for purposes of analysis the usual tools of structural sociology are blunted, as are those of personality psychology. There is no "social solidarity" to be explained. Rather there is a "coherence," an ordering of relationships that is contingent upon the wit, social maturity, and efforts of the focal person. Conversely, the focal person's integrity does not reduce to "primal defense mechanisms" but is bound up with the kinds of supports and demands proffered by the others. In short, there is a continuous dynamic of engagement between what happens to the convoy and what happens to the self. To even begin to unravel its components we must consider cultural definitions of life stages as they apply to self *and* others in the convoy; we must consider the personnel of a convoy and their individual patterns of character; and we must consider the co-histories that they share in their courses of mutuality. In this chapter and the next we shall be exploring these linkages, particularly as they manifest themselves in the lives of women.

Women's tempo may be no more "natural" than men's time: both are the product of cultural definitions of experience. In Japan's heritage the pathways and life rhythms of the two estates of gender are plainly demarcated. But decades of modern social change have muted and remodeled the lines of demarcation in complicated ways. Women's tempo now mingles with men's time in arenas of work and politics once reserved for males. Japanese women now face the work-vs.-family dilemmas well-known to the middle and upper ranks in other industrial societies. (The Makiokas don't mind Taeko's hobby as a dollmaker, but object to her ambition to work as a modiste.) We shall take up this dilemma as a major theme for Chapter 6.

Notwithstanding, women's tempo remains bound up with the

home and the rhythm of the generations to a degree approached only by the most homebodyish of men. The safest style of self-realization for a Japanese woman, her most secure pathway to "sincerity," leads to the roles of "good wife and wise mother." In poorer families, or in those that operate a farm or small shop, she may have no choice but to work and work hard all her life, in addition to caring for home and family. Throughout this century Japan has had a high proportion of women in its labor force. But ideally a woman should, at marriage or soon thereafter, concentrate on the full-time occupation of *okusan sen'gyō*, loosely translatable as "specialist homemaker" or "professional wife."

Commonplace as it may seem, this is a human transformation that cannot be achieved without dedication and self-discipline. "I used to be such a spoiled daughter . . ." is a theme in Sachiko's reminiscences. The theme was echoed by most of my Hanshin female interviewees as they examined their own lives.

The majority seem to evolve this new personal configuration adequately, and to maintain it through those self-changes that are imposed during later stages of adulthood. Look again at Figure 2, the age-curves of what it is that most makes life worth living. In youth years the priorities are as variable for women as for men. But before age 30, women's priorities have stabilized, with family and children predominating; they are almost unwavering after that. Men's priorities gradually approach the women's pattern, but continue to alter across the years.

In the rhetoric of female maturity, the pains of marital transformation may become exaggerated. "I worried myself thin in the early years," "I killed my sense of self the day I married" are phrases that come up often in the interviews. No one would claim that the task is undemanding. Tradition dictated that two or three times a year a bride must be sent to visit her parents and allowed a vacation from marital duties. Even today, custom expects a woman to stay in her parental home for the final weeks of pregnancy and first weeks of motherhood.

But a bride does indeed die a symbolic death with respect to her natal family. Her name is erased from its official register. She must never speak of "returning" home, but must use circumlocutions to refer to a visit there. And those who lead her to her wedding must study the curving streets and roads thoroughly so that the procession never turns back in the direction she came from.

A bride is expected to shelve or abandon dreams of a career in any profession other than the homely one. Many corporations pressure female employees to resign at the time of marriage or first pregnancy—though the practice is contrary to postwar law. Furthermore the young bride must accede to the dictates of a sexual double standard. She must prove her fidelity in a culture that has always put more faith in women's self-control than in the physical restraints of purdah, veils, and other devices favored in some parts of the world.

She must prove fidelity during the very years when a woman is popularly considered to be in her flowering of sensual appeal (*onna-zakari*). Tanizaki portrays this subtly but insistently—from a male point of view, perhaps—in his characterizations of Yukiko and Taeko. Taeko is unable to restrain her sexuality. Yukiko, as some critics have put it, is almost a vestal virgin—it is a sacrilege (to Tanizaki, if not to the Makiokas) to send her into the contaminations of mundane marriage.

In a manner of speaking, then, a woman in her early adult years must shift attention from her "natural" pulse of growth as an erotic being to her "cultural" pulse of growth as the chief person in a household: controlling its finances, sustaining its emotional harmony, supporting the others in their "selfish" courses of aging. Sachiko at 35 is still not certain she can meet that challenge.

The conversion process is intensified when a woman marries into an established household line and becomes the wife of its heir. This is the traditional ideal and the stereotype of woman's fate, though in fact the majority of women will wed non-heir junior sons. In the latter situation a woman and her spouse become the founding couple of a new household line. They establish a ménage of their own, apart from his parents. In practice, this is Sachiko's situation in Ashiya. She and Teinosuke are the founders of a new household line, though in this instance Teinosuke took on the Makioka name. Since he is not the heir to the main line, his reasons for taking the name are not clear, nor does Tanizaki offer any explanation for them. Presumably he saw advantages to sharing the Makioka reputation; and the Makiokas in turn could demonstrate their power to make a man give up his own family name.

The woman who marries into an established household becomes its *yome*, its "junior wife." Not only must she transform herself like other brides, adjusting to husband and household tasks and to parenting: she must submit to the tutelage of the "senior wife," her mother-in-law. She becomes a live-in apprentice under 24-hour-a-day surveillance. She will be given practical lessons in her new family's ways of cooking and cleaning, and emotional hazing into the family's ways of maintaining harmony and esprit. In the United States, the caricatured cranky mother-in-law is the wife's mother; in Japan, it is the husband's mother. And in Japanese popular imagery, the senior wife is at best a gloved despot. The stereotype is so powerful that novelists shy away from portraying senior-junior wife relations. Tanizaki, at any rate, makes his, and Sachiko's, task simpler in this regard.

In her early years, then, the junior wife must transform herself while under the added burden of living with her mother-in-law in *her* house. Later the junior wife must demonstrate the strength of her conversion by supporting that mother-in-law through the toils of old age. Here, too, demographic change has brought a drastic shift in co-longevity. In 1920 the statistically average junior wife could anticipate that her mother-in-law would be dead within 10 years after the marriage. Today that figure is 20 years.

The relationship is packed with explosive potential. But through years of co-experience it can also grow bonds of respect and affection and colleagueship. It complicates a woman's tempo and her problems of convoy management. It is also the chief test of her maturity. And this is what we see in the life of Goryōhan.

III. GORYŌHAN

"Goryōhan" is an Osaka localism for "the lady of the house." In conveying a touch of deference, it is most appropriately used by bill collectors

and repairmen; it is too distant for the mouths of neighbors or acquaint-ances. I use it as her name to call attention to the woman's chief adult role and her consciousness of it, though I am not suggesting even ironically that she is only a role-persona. She is a trim, lively woman of 43, talka-tive, whimsical, even teasingly flirtatious—and at the same time the skilled hostess who continues to press her guests with what seems to be an endless supply of coffee, tea, soft drinks, cakes, and homemade puddings and ice creams.

The house is a sprawling two-story structure of prewar vintage, in an older neighborhood in the central part of Amagasaki. Long glassed-in verandas ring its rooms and offer views out into the well-tended gardens in the surround. A wall beyond shuts away the street and the eyes of strangers.

The living room is a dozen mats in size—or about 12 by 18 feet—its central two-thirds covered by a rug. The alcove is always decorated with care: hangings, flowers, art objects according to season. During March it is filled by an elaborate display of Girls' Day dolls, a gift to Goryōhan when she was a child. The other interior wall of the room is dominated by a television console. Atop it is a foot-high golfing trophy inscribed in English, "Hole in One." Behind it is a jumble of HO-gauge electric-train tracks.

The other rooms and the hallways reinforce the impression of good taste. Toward the rear of the first floor is a room constructed especially for performing the aesthetic of Tea, with its special pantry adjoining. These are the domain of Granny, a lifelong devotee of the aesthetic. Granny is the senior wife or shūtome *in this household, though Goryōhan never refers to her by such a distance-putting locution.*

Goryōhan herself might be more at home on an operetta stage than in the Tea chamber. Her histrionics approach the Italian. She speaks rapid-ly, snapping out words, punctuating them with gestures. In her prelude to a topic she may utter the polite or expected attitudes, more or less follow-ing the standard cultural script for a junior wife. But soon she ad-libs. She likes to replay verbal exchanges she has had with family and friends, at times doing so with comical touches. Some of these are pat routines. She obviously has performed them many times. They are mini-dramas that express this family's view of the world and of human existence.

Her narratives drift into byways, then return. After a while you real-

ize that she is constantly attuned to audiences—to the audience of the moment, but also to the audience of those with whom she enacts the dramas of her, and their, maturity and aging.

It's hard to say just what sort of person I am. I wonder how I look to others. Pretty easy-going, I suppose.

I certainly don't consider myself quiet. I blurt out whatever's on my mind. But I am hesitant, sensitive to other people's expectations. That may be true for anybody, but when you are living with a senior wife as I am, then that's absolutely essential if you want to get any satisfaction out of living. My friends from girls' school days say to me, "Golly, you sure have put up with a lot from that woman." I was the only daughter in my family, and people thought I was spoiled. But my mother was strict. She trained me very firmly in how to get along with a mother-in-law: I can do as I'm told, and not get myself into a sweat over it.

On the whole I'm regarded as sunny, maybe because I always try to be. School report cards listed me as cheerful and vivacious. That lively spirit has to be my strong point. But I'm also on the passive side, not stubborn—I'm tractable. That's about it. My weak point, on the other hand—let me see—it doesn't really show on the outside, but I'm a worry wart.

You'd better believe I have changed over the years. I'd say I've matured; as a girl I was much more self-centered. I've had to deal with all kinds of people. That takes away the rough edges and makes you rounded. I give a smile to everybody and try not to make enemies. Not that I will continue to see a person I dislike, or go out of my way to avoid them. But you'd be surprised at the different kinds of people who come to this house. And though I'm not the one who should say so, I treat all of them well.

I couldn't have done that when I was a girl. I remember my Mom saying to me, "Even if it leaves you with a sour taste, you make sure that guests are entertained properly." In other words, don't let your feelings interfere. It's partly because our family was in the restaurant business. I could see my mother stifle her impulses and be nice to nasty customers. It made a big impact on me. Naturally, I have come to take it for granted that everything will sail along smoothly when you're pleasant to people. That's probably why I have many friends. To them I may be a spoiled only daughter, but we get on well with each other.

I don't have any great skills or compulsions. I know that a person needs to develop a skill all her own, one nobody else has, one she can use in her later years. But the real me is the me that says, "You did pretty well, old gal," when we've had a flock of guests and all of them were entertained properly, the atmosphere was congenial, and they all went away saying they really enjoyed it.

I can put up with what I don't like. I have self-confidence about that.

Girlhood

I come from an old samurai line. When I was little, my younger brother and I used to drag out Great-Grandfather's battle helmets from the storeroom and wear them when we had swordfights. The family was originally from Owari but was driven out by a flood or some such disaster, and settled in Wakayama. In the Meiji period, when the feudal system was abolished, the samurai had to find some other line of work, of course, and Great-Grand-dad went into the restaurant trade.

I am more like my Mom than my Dad, although I also resemble Mom's elder sister in some ways. I've always found it easy to talk to my aunt, ever since I was little. She reads a lot for a woman, and makes an effort to understand the younger generation. She's a good one to ask for advice. I can tell her things I wouldn't dare say to my mother. After all, Mom's a realist, Aunt's a romantic. She married for love, and is sympathetic to the idea.

Naturally, you come to see your parents in a different light than you did when you were young. Once you are grown up and an adult yourself, you stand on the same level with them and can see that they are only people after all, human beings. Between the time I graduated from girls' high school and the time I married, I gradually began to see them as just ordinary folks. Now I think of them as my experienced seniors.

It may seem strange, but I admire my Mother, more than anybody I know. I often wish I could be more like her. Never caught up in trivia—how should I put it—not exactly conscious of it, but a person who never makes other people uncomfortable. If you want to be nasty about it, you could say she tells people only what they want to hear. That's not a good posture to take: it slips into fawning. But when anyone asks her what *she* thinks, she doesn't parrot somebody else's opinion, she gives her own then and there.

Old as she is, she seems to have more spunk than I do. She's into all sorts of activities, meeting all sorts of people. I want to be like that when I'm old. My elder brother and his wife live right near the parents, close enough so's the soup doesn't cool off. So Mom and Dad don't expect me to do much for them—still, I wish I could. But I have Granny to look after.

Mom kept that restaurant going even through hard times. Dad became an officer in the prefectural restaurant association and was always away on association business. That left Mom to manage the restaurant. Cooks have fantastic pride, you know, and almost absolute power over the kitchen. Remember that food was often scarce, too, in those days. But Mom did it all: ran a household, raised her kids, took charge of the restaurant. I've often marveled at it.

Our restaurant burned to the ground during an air raid. It had been a beautiful building, in the best location on the main street of the town where I grew up. That area has changed completely since the war. Dad just seemed to lose all heart when the place burned down. After the war he found another one, one that had come through the bombings. But the building was nothing to brag about, and the location was poor. After three years he quit. He tried several trades but never did well at any of them, I suppose because he lacked experience. He ended up having a nervous breakdown, and was not much fun to live with. By then my elder brother was an intern. He went into practice pretty soon after, and he has supported the folks since then.

Anyway, I grew up in a *huge* household. Only an elder and a younger brother, and no sisters, but ten waitresses also lived with us. When we kids would try to get a waitress to do something for us, Mom would say, "The waitresses are here to serve customers.

You take care of what you need done." We were supposed to separate business from family. But one of the older waitresses really acted as housekeeper most of the time, and she would fuss over me, especially when Mom was busy. But don't get the idea I was overprotected!

On the other hand, Mom also urged me to make the most of being young, make the most of every single day or I'd be sorry when I grew up. And I did! I enjoyed myself, and have heaps of happy memories. Despite the war. Despite the troubles after the war. If I could go back in time it would be to those years after the war. Food was scarce, but I don't remember going hungry. We went hiking, went to the movies, went swimming. The best part of it was that my girlfriends and I did what we felt like doing. We'd ride all the way into Osaka just to putter around shopping.

I also went wild making Western clothes for myself. I'm not good at it anymore, but then I could look at an outfit in a foreign movie and design one like it for myself. I made two suits like those Ingrid Bergman wore in *Casablanca*. The dressmaking teacher told me I had potential. But I've lost the knack, don't have confidence anymore. I still enjoy picking out neckties for my husband, though. I can get nostalgic thinking about those years. Life must be awfully empty, it seems to me, if you get old and have nothing to remember.

My younger brother and I are only a year apart, and we've always been so free with each other it's hard to tell which is the senior. When he was little he was sort of effeminate. He'd copy me, carry dolls around, use girls' words. Later on he turned into a regular hellion, and then *I* tagged after *him*. We'd have sword-fights, spin tops, catch dragonflies. After I started school, my girlfriends and I might follow him when he went to the park to climb trees, but we'd pick flowers instead. He and I squabbled all the time, but I was closer to him than to anybody. Nights when we were supposed to be doing homework, we usually horsed around. We were great conspirators, but we drifted apart. Eventually he was adopted into the family of a distant aunt.

But I stayed away from my other brother, even though he's only three years older. He always had a stern look on his face, I suppose because he's the eldest son. I was afraid of him. He was studious and smart, always had the answers to my homework problems. He never played with us, just sat and read.

And my parents always took his side. I'll give you an example, one that was important for me. I had lots and lots of boyfriends; both brothers introduced me to guys they knew. During the war they would write me and I would answer them. I even have some "last letters" from those who were in the Kamikaze Corps. After the war I went to dozens of dance parties. I really was in love with one boy, a friend of my elder brother. But my elder brother was opposed to our getting married, and my parents agreed with him.

I still have the letters that boy wrote me. They're in a funny private code that we cooked up—lovers did that in those days. And I have a doll he bought me at the theater when he took me to see *Aishū*. Now and then I take out the letters and read them and just get to feeling warm all over. Everybody says I'm not much of a romantic, but that's on the surface. I don't see a thing wrong about keeping presents from a boyfriend I had before I was married. I think about him every time I go to visit my folks. He's still living in the home town. Who knows? I might just happen to meet him on the street.

I wonder, though, if the biggest change in my life didn't come when my grade school class got a new teacher. Not much happened when I went to girls' high school: we had classes about half the time, and the rest of the time we worked in war factories. There were lots of adjustments when I came here, of course, but it was a typical arranged marriage, and I knew what was in store for me. And there has never been any major tragedy during my years in this family.

But that teacher—how can I explain about him? He was the sort who insists that you finish whatever you start. Can't tolerate slaggards. He could get us to do things we really hated, like cleaning the toilets, for example. He was insistent as a bulldog. The war was at its worst, and everything was scarce. We didn't even have stockings. Walked the board floors in our bare feet even in winter. When I think about it, kids don't have enough pressure put on them nowadays. They need to be pushed until they have confidence that they will hold up no matter what comes their way.

But that teacher also treated every one of us as an individual. Basically, he was an art teacher, and he'd say, "Every person has bad points, but also at least one good point; you work on expanding that one." It was amazing how he could get us to extend our good points. You don't find teachers like that today. Among my children's teachers, there's not a single one with his kind of dedication. Actually I guess he was rare even in our time, a man full of fight and in love with his work.

He had us spellbound. You hate being cold, you hate working outside when it's hot, you just want to horse around with the other kids. None of that for us! We felt ashamed to neglect our duties, that's how much we were captivated by him. He was a marvel, and I still wonder at his knack for motivating children. We hated him and we loved him. Teacher and pupils were one. We would follow him around, sometimes stay overnight at his house.

You even wanted to go to school on Sunday because you knew he would be there in the classroom drawing pictures and making things. He was very clever that way. Next day when you came in you would find something he had made just for you. He was the Spartan type: we'd cry when he scolded us. But strict as he was, it makes me nostalgic to think of him. He taught us how to hang on.

Marriage

My biggest surprise when I came here was to find out how much Granny asserts herself. Back home my Dad was boss and the women served him. Here Granddad was a real *feminist*—and my husband takes after him. Besides, Granddad took a liking to me. Even before Papa—that's what I call my husband—had a chance to get interested in me Granddad was carrying my photo around. Granddad was wonderful to me after I came here, so I was really lucky. He could be very tough about business matters, but otherwise he had a good sense of humor.

Really, I *have* been lucky. Grandad and Granny are country

folk who don't have extravagant tastes; they go for the plain and simple. And they are basically gentle. I didn't have to take all that much bride-hazing. Sure there were bitter times, times I wanted to run home—but actually I'd never have had the nerve to do it. Mom had taught me that a bride just has to swallow what people dish out to her. So I snuffed out my sense of self, my opinions, tried not to think about what *I* wanted, not have time of my own. If I wanted time to myself I could arrange it, and did. But even then I would be wondering if I shouldn't look in on the senior couple and see if I could do anything for them.

It strains your nerves and your will. I lost a lot of weight. After all, there were six in the house then: myself and Papa, his parents, and his younger sister and brother. I gave up all my hobbies and lessons, became a maidservant. Did all I could to absorb this family's ways. Cut my ties with school friends for more than a year, though we did exchange wedding photographs.

The younger brother is my favorite among my husband's siblings. He's exactly 12 years younger than Papa, both of them born in the Year of the Tiger. He lives close by, and Papa often goes to talk with him. They come over here pretty often, too, with their kids. At the time I moved in he was still in middle school, and he was just a darling. The younger sister was 20, just a little younger than I was. We got along so well that I had pangs of loneliness when she was married. Her daughter is just a year younger than mine, and the two of them get together fairly often.

It's a *very* old family line. I can't remember how many generations are in the family register. No big deal, all of them were peasants until Granddad. He wanted to take up a different line of work, and through family connections he was sent to the Kanamori family in Osaka. A cousin of his had gone there as a bride. He worked for them for many years, and when they offered to set him up in business he decided to manufacture housewares.

Anyway, this family takes good care of its ancestors. We offer them freshly cooked rice every day. Granny says prayers and reads sutras every evening. If people bring us gifts, we first offer them to the ancestors and then receive from them. We also hold memorial services regularly, third and fifth and seventh years and so on.

This family and mine are both originally from the same village in Wakayama and are distantly related. Granddad's cousin, the one who married a Kanamori, was actually *my* mother's mother. She had been a Tabeya—my family line. But her elder brother, the heir to the line, had no children. So her daughter was adopted back into the Tabeya line: that's my mother. Then my father was adopted in to be her husband and heir to the line.

My marriage was arranged through these relatives. But since this is a business family, it was mostly business associates who were invited to the wedding. And the ceremonial go-betweens were from a sort of parent-company to the family's business. Actually, they are also Papa's half-sister and her husband. Granny is Granddad's second wife—the first one died. Papa is Granny's child but the first wife had one daughter. Her husband is on the board of directors of our company.

We've been blessed—no great tragedies have come to us over the years. Maybe I had no real goals for my life, no clear idea of how I wanted it to turn out. I accepted what I was taught, that a junior wife takes the words of her senior wife as gospel. When Granny and I had a difference of opinion I gave in. Even when I was positive I was right, I gave in. Maybe I'm chicken at heart. I can admire a woman who will have it out with her mother-in-law and then just leave. I'm not capable of that, wouldn't even *want* to do it. Nowadays I think, yes, it's been best that I killed myself. Granny and I have come to feel comfortable with one another. You take life as it comes, and you keep the peace. That's the way Japanese women have been. Even if our standard of living drops drastically, we know how to get along.

Bringing up Granny

When people see Granny and me together, they wonder if we are mother and daughter, we talk to each other so freely. But after all, we have known each other for many years, so what's the big surprise if we're not reserved. Basically she is good-hearted, and takes life as it comes. Sure, she can give me what-for, but plenty of mothers-in-law are more petty, much more petty. Granny and I are the kind of people who settle their differences easily. She's gotten used to having people ask if I'm her real daughter; it doesn't upset *her*. But Papa says I upstage him too much. "The neighbors'll think I'm an adopted husband," he says.

Granny's friends say to her, "You have a good yome." That's what I have tried to be. Not that we consciously worked on it to make it turn out this way, but the fact is Granny and I *can* say anything to each other. I even write her letters for her. I kind of enjoy writing, do it all the time. It's a family joke: "Mama, at it again?" Even when a letter comes from her younger sister, I read it and say, "Granny, what do you think?" "She should do such and such!" she'll say, and I put it in her exact words. Or when she's been invited to a Tea and comes home, she says, "Mama, it was delicious. Send them a note of thanks. I'll jot down a list of what they served us." Then I put together a note telling them what she especially enjoyed about it.

She's in her 70's but still very spry. She can do what she pleases, doesn't have to be fussing over a husband anymore. She has her hobbies and her Tea and her gardening. First thing every morning, she putters in the garden, and she is often out there again after breakfast. And she still takes control when we decorate the house for holidays or family celebrations. Then she gets out the pictures and displays from the closet and plans how to arrange them. Times like that I'm just her flunky.

In a sense, I'm not completely grown up yet. Or if so, only recently, because *she* is still in charge around here. I do all the cooking and the housework, that much I had pretty well taken over by the time I had been here a year—you know, buying the groceries and paying the routine bills. But Granny has to be consulted on any major purchases or house repairs or on things like hiring a tree-surgeon.

But the routine cleaning is my department. Like now, when I'm getting the place ready for summer. Papa disappears to the golf course on Sunday mornings; he never lends a hand. The kids are shrewd, "Is it worth a thousand yen to you if I clean the upstairs, Mama?" Look at how *old* this place is. There are times when I feel like I'm a slave to this house. Polish here, clean there. But when the weather's nice, Granny and I can sit in the garden and take our Tea there.

When you're old, it's bad to be stuck at home all the time. You need to get out, be active. Our Granny is away pretty frequently, to meetings and Teas. Sometimes I think she absorbs more new ideas from what she sees and hears than I do. It's a fact that she runs into a lot of younger women. She comes home and says to me, "Don't be so old-fashioned, Mama, wear brighter clothes."

I get away often enough, though I will yield to her if she has an appointment on the same day. Or if I really want to go badly, I arrange for one of the kids to look after the house. This family has an absolute rule that the house must never be left empty. Granddad and Granny have always insisted on it. There isn't much danger from burglars in this part of town, but obviously you can't just lock up a place like this with a single key the way you can an apartment. I like to think that in the future things will be easier, when we aren't tied down to such an old house.

But Granny *has* to have that Tea every day. I wish she'd quit, it's an addiction with her. Every morning after breakfast, 365 danged days a year! I learned how to prepare it when I was a girl, like everybody else, but I've never had a taste for it. It's not very pleasant. Not that Granny fusses about how we prepare and serve it. We follow a simple style. But she has her Tea room, and utensils—not expensive ones, mind you. She used to give lessons, but says it's too much for her to do now. I get along with her by sticking to the policy my Mom taught me: the customer is king.

Granddad was 88 when he died. He was bedridden for some weeks, and went senile after that. He and Granny would go for a walk every day. Then he started to wander off on his own, usually toward Nishinomiya, where he used to live. Then he'd get lost, and we would have to ask the police to look for him. At least he always remembered his name. There were times when the police called us at eleven at night to come pick him up. Maybe he just wore himself out. Seems like he only caught a little cold and then took to bed.

It was a strain on all of us during his last days. Granny put aside her hobbies and activities and waited on him day and night. She says her head's no good, and that's why we don't have to worry about *her* going senile. It's the sharp people like Granddad who go doddering at the end, she says.

But she's free of that now. She keeps telling Papa and me to take over more of the dealings with neighbors and with the relatives in the country. But she still does most of it, going back to the village for weddings and funerals. After all, she's known those people for ages.

Husband

For a year, year and a half after we were married, there weren't any babies, so my husband and I could get out of the house. Just the two of us. His younger brother and sister were still here, so Granddad and Granny would not be left alone. Many of Papa's friends live around this area, and at that time most of them had just been married too. So we'd go out in groups. Rent a bungalow at Suma beach—that was tremendous. Getting up early. I love to watch the sea in the morning. It wasn't polluted the way it is now. Or we'd go on long boat rides. After all, I grew up by the sea.

He used to buy clothes for me, too, when we were first married. Of course, if I didn't like them, I would take them in and exchange them next day. In the beginning I called him Shin'ichi-san, then it got to be Shin'ichi. Once the kids were born it just naturally became Papa. I still call him Shin'ichi once in a while, but the kids laugh if they hear me. And I don't dare call him *anata* ["dear"] in front of them anymore.

I hope that in the future the two of us will have time to go to movies and such more often. It's not easy these days. Especially not evenings. We don't have many chances to eat dinner together. His business brings in buyers from all over the southwest: Kyushu, Shikoku, down the Hokuriku. They check into a hotel and then come over to the office to talk business. For them it's a bore to sit in the hotel room, so they are glad to hang around the office until lord knows when, gabbing. Papa offers them dinner, takes them out to a restaurant or has it delivered to the office. It's bound to be late by the time he gets home.

I don't know anything about business, though Papa tries to educate me. You have to realize that ours is the tiniest of companies, no more than 30 employees in all. And the big plastics corporations are making such inroads that it's a declining industry. So the company is having a building built, as a diversification. The lot where the office is is in a good location downtown. First, they talked about putting in a parking garage. But they decided on a seven-story building: company offices on the first floor, rental offices on the second, apartments above that. Papa consults me about details, about colors for elevators and stairwells and so on; I enjoy that.

It's rare that we fail to agree. We've been growing more and more alike over the years. Our thinking and tastes are pretty much the same. Except golf, I don't care for it. We enjoy the same TV programs. He is your mister ordinary—to the point where I wouldn't mind if he did something weird for a change.

I can tell what he's thinking, what he plans to do. I know what will make him sore. He's more conservative than I am, but he's been that way as long as I've known him. If I say, "Times have changed, people do it this way now," he will mumble, "Hmmm, I wonder. . . ." But he has to consider the family line; he has his obligations as an eldest son. All in all, he's a kindly sort who can overlook my selfishness.

Our most difficult times are when we disagree because of something that comes up between Granny and me. I always report those to him. But we sort of dote on each other. When I see couples being cool to each other, I feel sorry for them. Papa himself says that we're different from other couples our age. I wonder—anyway he isn't afraid to show affection to me in front of Granny or the kids. I mean we walk and sleep holding hands.

It's about fifty-fifty as to who is depending on whom. The family is my department and my responsibility, that has always been so. He gives me his pay envelope to use for family expenses. Grandad did the same when he was still working for the company. Papa also has a small income of his own from stocks he holds, and when I happen to need a little extra money, I can get it from him. He also seems to hold a whole raft of insurance policies. I don't believe in the stuff myself, but one of my friends is in the insurance business, and I let her talk me into taking out a small policy on each of the kids.

Emotionally, I may be the one who is most dependent. But apart from business matters, he does lean on me a lot. He teases me about that: "When I'm not looking, Mama always manages to get her way."

One thing I *don't* need to manage is his health. He gives it enough attention for both of us. Always worried that it's cancer or something. He even invents diseases for himself. One time when he was playing golf he took a tremendous swing and knocked the wind out of himself. They say it does happen. "You've got to get me to a hospital," he said—and he stayed there a whole week.

I do try to feed him a balanced diet. He eats anything, doesn't say a word about it. I also encourage him to get more sleep. "Come to bed, Papa," I'll say. "I'm not the least bit sleepy." "So close your eyes and try." But he won't pay attention. Often as not, he is up 'way beyond midnight poking at the Go board or playing solitaire or letting the TV blat on and on.

But he *is* far and away the younger looking of the two of us. And don't you *dare* tell me I look like an "elder-sister wife"!

Children

The kids have always been my responsibility, of course, and I suppose they are the most important part of my life. Papa has always left matters up to me, though he takes more interest now that our boy is about to finish high school. I was the one who picked their names, though I talked it over with Granddad and with a name specialist.

All my friends tell me that I over-mother my kids, especially Ken'ichi, the boy. He gets cross about it himself. "Lemme alone, you're too eager to do things for me," he'll say. I guess I like to meddle. When they were in primary school I hired a home tutor for them, but we gave it up after a couple of years. They objected to being scolded by a tutor. They wanted to go to the tutoring center down the street, because their friends would be there. I don't know if they learned much, but they were happy there, and it was a lot cheaper.

In the olden days children couldn't help thinking of their parents as powerful people. Now they are more like friends or equals, don't keep any distance. Papa barks at them when they deserve it, but I just can't bring myself to, even though I know I should. When they give me lip, I correct them for it but hold my temper.

On the other hand, in the olden days you couldn't say some things to your parents. For that I prefer the way things are now. I try to create an atmosphere in which the kids feel free to talk. I offer topics, ask leading questions—and when they answer, it often strikes me that they are still children after all. When you live together, you soon learn to anticipate what it is they want to talk about.

I sense some kind of "generation gap" with them. I'll hear one of their friends talking and think to myself what a brat he is. Later the kids will tell me, "Mama you couldn't have it more wrong." Some days I don't understand what they're saying or what they're up to. Maybe it's because I had an old-fashioned upbringing before the war.

Clothes! I think a girl in her late teens looks real cute in red, but my daughter, Makiko, insists on wearing only grays and navy blues. And Ken'ichi looks just like a *hippie* with his long straggly hair. These days he's a rabid SL fan. Knows all the scheduled runs that still have steam locomotives. Trots off and waits for them, to take photos and record the sounds. Sometimes the whole house shakes when he plays those tapes. He'll scoot out in the middle of the night and sleep on a station bench somewhere, just so's he can see a steam locomotive pull through next morning. On a station bench, like a tramp. All sorts of people are doing it lately, even women.

Makiko, on the other hand, goes in for ballet. She's been taking lessons for about ten years, and has a recital about once a year. She can also play the piano—poorly. We bought her a *koto* [Japanese harp], but she complains that it's too difficult. We've also tried to get Ken'ichi to play the *shakuhachi* [flute] and accompany her, but no dice yet.

Do kids ever turn out the way you want them to? Makiko insists that she's going to do research in Africa—no ifs, ands, or buts. She's crazy about animals. Well, maybe she'll get her chance. Ken'ichi doesn't want to follow Papa in the business but wants to become an attorney. Well, if that should pan out, fine by me. I try not to pin too many hopes on them. But if both of them go to college, I'll be pleased: it's an opportunity I never had.

Activities

When the kids were in primary school I was active in the PTA, but I tapered off after they went to middle school. In recent years I've been much more involved in our local branch of the Nada Consumer's Cooperative. I'm on the editorial board of the co-op newsletter and go to the monthly board meetings to put in my two cents' worth. I'm also a member of the executive advisory committee, but I don't attend their meetings as regularly. All in all, I average two or three meetings a month, some months none at all. I'm very irregular when it comes to participating in other Co-op activities.

Most of the women on the executive advisory committee are older than I am. Many have married children, even grandchildren. I'm the youngster there, with my kids not married yet. Really, we need to lower the average age on that committee and hear from the younger mothers, the ones with babies. They're the ones with the most energy, the ones who'll fight hardest for lower prices. By the time you get to middle age you're not so strapped for money. So prices go up a yen or even five yen, so you'll get along all right. By middle age you start to goldbrick. I'm talking about myself. Maybe other people can stay involved, but I can't seem to. I can get pretty outspoken and complain now and then, but I don't keep it up. I've been involved in it for about five years, and it's time I stepped down.

I want to spend more time on crafts and hobbies. Also, there are piles of things needing doing in the house, and I don't always do them. Some days I just feel lazy and dull—that's part of getting older, too. But I don't take naps and don't look at the telly in the daytime except at meals. I found that as the kids went into high school and didn't need so much attention, my own interests began to deepen.

For my age I may be a little old-fashioned. I get to feeling that I've run to seed. According to the kids, I talk like an old fogey. But part of becoming older is finding that history is sort of fascinating after all. It's a shame that young people are so cool toward Japanese traditions, but what can you do about it? You can't force them. I remember that I didn't care much for history when I was in school. School tours to Nara or Kyoto were just picnics to me. Now when I go, I drink in every word the guides say.

My older brother is very well informed about Japanese history, and I suppose that has influenced me. I like watching historical TV series. When I have the time I like reading about the Man'yō period, about Nara and Yoshino. Papa also takes an interest in it. Remember the *Shin Heike Monogatari*, when it ran as a serial in the weekly *Asahi*? We clipped the entire series and pasted them up in two books. Papa made covers for them, and I did the titles.

I've always liked calligraphy, too, and keep wanting to take more lessons. One friend tells me I ought to set myself up as a teacher, but I'm not ready to take that big a step yet.

Also singing. I sing all the time. *Loud!* Belt out songs. You wouldn't think it to look at me. Sing when I'm doing the laundry, working around the house. Noh is this family's performing art, chanting Noh lyrics. Papa was in a Noh group in college. Over the years I've picked up some of it from him and from Granddad and Granny. It's good for your health to get out a loud chant. Papa can also do a few Noh dances. You do them without accompaniment, just with fan and voice. They don't involve much motion, so they're just right for performing when you are called on at a wedding reception or party.

For some months I've been taking lessons in chanting poetry. Just had my qualifying test the other day. I haven't heard how well I did, but I didn't miss a line, hung in there to the end of the piece, so I should have qualified for at least the lowest rank. I still get stage-fright when I have to chant in front of an audience. But

I like the chanting, and since you're chanting old poems you naturally learn more about language and history.

But you have the family to think about. Cooking can be a bore, but it simply has got to be done. No matter what else you do, you have to plan the meals. I suppose a woman would feel empty without that, but *still*! It gets complicated. The rest of them take toast in the morning, and Granny and I eat Japanese style, with bean soup. Lunch is Western style. We have our rice at suppertime. When Granddad was still here, I often had to make three different meals, one for the kids, one for the old folks, and one for Papa and myself. Now it's never more than two. I used to be crazy about greasy foods, fix them for the kids and eat the same thing myself. Lately I would rather eat what I fix for Granny. That's the way it goes as you grow older; you're stuck with it and might as well accept it.

I was watching a TV program on volunteer work today. I still haven't done anything for the good of society and wish I could be useful for a change. I enjoy talking with people, always have. If I could be useful in that way—.

Health and Aging

I am ridiculously healthy. Strong. Don't know what it means to be sick. How should I put it? Until I was in primary school, I was sick all the time. A weakling. "Is this one going to pull through?" they wondered. But in six years in primary school I never so much as missed one day. It was a total turnaround— threw off all my illnesses, and I had had just about every one in the book. Since then, I've always been well. Oh, I catch a cold once in a while, but basically I'm okay. Granny talks about how "Our yome was brought up in the country, and they grow 'em tough out there."

Lately, though, I've felt odd. Nothing to go to a doctor about, just my own diagnosis. I think I may have a touch of low blood pressure. When I've been busy several days in a row I start to feel the strain—not exactly a dizziness but a kind of breathlessness. A queasy sort of sensation. But if I go slow for a day, nothing comes of it.

I don't believe in using a thermometer on myself or on the kids. Take your temperature and soon you're always paying attention to it. Try it next time you feel punk and wonder if it's a fever. Papa, now! The nervous type, always taking his temperature. Always diagnosing himself. "Major cancer." "Major nothing, there's nothing wrong with you," I tell him. "I can tell as well as the doctors," he says. I have to laugh sometimes, he's such a hypochrondriac. I suppose I'm a little insensitive about health. But once he sleeps on it, the problem goes away. Granny tends to be that way, too, even though she knows it's not a good idea, always trotting down the street to the doctor's office.

As I said, my older brother is a physician, so whenever I visit at home they fill my bag with medicines. Cold tablets, vitamins, digestion pills, stomach remedies. I use the digestion pills when I overeat, but I almost never touch the vitamins. Maybe if I'm really feeling bushed, but even then I only use a few, never a whole bottle so's I would have to buy more. Not that I believe they make any big difference. I like to say that I am healthy enough not to need medicines.

About ten years ago when she was here visiting, my Mom mentioned that somebody said you should take the bathtub brush —the stiff one you use for scrubbing out the tub—and use it on your skin. Granddad and Granny picked up the habit right away. Granny pestered me to try it, but I said it would hurt too much, and I didn't try until about five years ago. At first I could only go in one direction, but eventually I could rub both ways. You know it really does make your skin healthier, you don't catch colds as easily. It stings! Sometimes you think you're going to rip your skin open, but no. You have to rub until your whole body is ruddy. Granddad did it every day until just before he died. When he had digestive troubles, he would strip naked and rub hard until he came out with a good healthy belch.

One time I bought brushes for the rest of the family. But the kids quit in three days and Papa on the second day. Only Granny and I are still at it. Ten minutes a day, or maybe only five, depending on the mood I'm in. It makes you bend and stretch, to get at places you can't reach easily, and so it also turns into a kind of exercise.

I keep telling myself to make a point of going to bed earlier. But the kids need to study for exams. They nap in the afternoon, then want me to wake them up so they can study at night. Sometimes they can be inconsiderate. But it means midnight and later by the time I get to bed.

Friends

I keep in touch with about ten women I've known ever since we were in primary school. I see others, of course, at class reunions or when I visit my home town. Some of them live here in the Hanshin, and we have lunch every so often.

Our contacts vary. One will move away, or be tied down at home for a while, or take a job. But you're cut off from each other only for the first year or so of marriage. Two of them are especially close to me. I'd like to have them come to the house more often, but with Granny around they feel sort of constricted. Neither of them has a mother-in-law at home, so we usually go to their places.

Everybody says that my class is unusual for the way we keep in touch with one another. Papa almost never goes to his class reunions. His business takes up most of his time, after all. Also, he says his reunions are too stuffy. "Meet, greet, eat, and move feet," he calls them.

We girls tell each other that when our kids have grown up we don't want to have to depend on them, and that's why friends need each other. "We'll take care of one another," we say, and joke about being widows. It would be horrible to lose your friends. You just *know* they'll always be there. You only have to pick up the phone—no reason to hesitate just because you haven't seen her for a long time. Eventually, we're going to arrange to take craft lessons together, but right now we still have too many family duties.

I'm not sorry that I'm getting on in years. As you gain in experience you build a certain charm into your daily work. A kind of pleasure. I do have the feeling that I am more and more conservative. Not that I can put my finger on anything in particular; it has to do with my way of thinking. Today it's "do your own thing." People used to have more regard for their families, but that is surely changing. It's like there's a split inside me. One part is not the least bit conservative, it leaps to do whatever is new. The other part is less and less willing to do so as the years go by. I don't think I'm stuck in any old rut, but neither can I always move with the changing times. So I end up in the middle, halfway.

It's taken for granted that when anything goes wrong the junior wife is to blame. I like to think that when my son brings home his bride I won't be that way toward her. But when you come right down to it the situation could be tricky. Especially as you begin to get old. What I want most is for Ken'ichi and his wife to be happy together. Papa and I will gladly take care of ourselves; I know he'd be helpless without me. Even so, I expect to die first.

But I don't worry about the future. I let Papa worry about it for me.

IV. THE DILEMMAS OF CARING

The logical opposite of a spoiled and selfish daughter would be a generous and self-giving mother. Hanshin female interviewees were reluctant to claim the latter qualities for themselves. Modesty may account for some of their hesitation, but for many of them the appraisal has a touch of realism. That is, they have progressed along the classic pathway of womanhood, but they have not yet achieved the peak position. Certainly I have matured, says Goryōhan, I have outgrown my spoiled-daughter self. On the other hand I am not fully grown up yet, because *she* is still around. Even if for all practical purposes Goryōhan controls the domestic arena, the senior wife, by her very presence, continues to define Goryōhan's juniority.

For Shōji, for Beisuke, for men in general, the dilemmas of maturity tend to be phrased in terms of pathway options. Family is one of those pathways, to be sure. As the years accumulate, most men find themselves pulled more and more by duty and affection toward wife and children. But men's time calls for bursts of pure action or for marathons of competition with one's peers. Women's tempo is shaped much more by the long-wave cycle of the succeeding generations. For Goryōhan, for Sachiko, for women in general, *which* pathways to follow, and what priorities to assign them, are not major causes for ambiguity. The uncertainties have to do with one's rate of progress. Progress is measured chiefly by the successful passage of others along *their* life's courses. And so the demand upon a woman is not so much for self-focused coping as it is for other-focused caring. You must kill your sense of self symbolically—rhetorically—without doing so literally. You must decide *who* among those you care for is to hold priority.

You must confront this dilemma over a long span of years. And you must continue to handle its tensions amid the welter of bonds that evolve among your consociates. This is true for adult women in general, as is demonstrated by Sachiko's convoluted difficulties in seeing her younger sisters safely married. But it is all the more true for a woman who, like Goryōhan, has the added engagements of serving as a junior wife.

How she masters the role of junior wife in a stem-family household is one of the classic measures for maturity for a Japanese woman. Goryōhan has learned to play the role with gusto. A junior wife needs some of the talents of a career diplomat who is in the service of an alien regime. Over time, she can expect to gain recognition as a member of the house in her own right. But she enters as a stranger, there to carry out the policies of others.

She must begin by proving her loyalty, establishing that she has severed all competing allegiances. Goryōhan describes the early period of her marriage in phrases that crop up in interviews with other women. She "killed her sense of self" and tried to think every minute of what she could do for her parents-in-law. She worried herself thin. She set aside all the hobbies and interests that had given zest to her girlhood. For more than a year she cut off contact with her friends and classmates (except to exchange wedding photos). When she and her husband went out, they went with *his* friends. All of this, after all, says Goryōhan, is just the standard formula for success as a junior wife; this is what her mother taught her. The senior wife's word is gospel; never dispute it. If she scolds you, thank her for caring enough to want to correct you.

In the retrospect of two decades, Goryōhan does not see her self-conversion as a bride as having been such a drastic turning point in her life. She knew what was expected, and did it. The only item not in the standard scenario was Granny's power over the men of the house. They proved to be "feminists" of a sort that Goryōhan had not forecast from extrapolations of her father and older brother.

"Feminism" might imply an opportunity for open assertiveness by the women of the house. For a junior wife, however, it would, if anything, add an edge to her dilemmas of self-expression. Her mastery of the role will be gauged, as it were, by reflex, by how well she helps others in the family progress along *their* stages of life. Acting the social cipher is no solution. To win Oscars, a junior wife must compete as best supporting actress. The only female star is the senior wife.

Supporting a Shūtome

Seconding a senior wife is likely to be the toughest of all career tasks for a Japanese woman. Over the years, the relationship is likely to be transformed, as the partners grow at different rates and enter disparate phases of the life cycle. At first the junior wife must convert from the sheltered freedom of girlhood to the rigors of apprenticeship. Later she must demonstrate the strength of her conversion by sustaining the senior wife through the pains of senility. This is Goryōhan's current "developmental task."

Twenty years later, Goryōhan has become the emotional pivot of the household. When nobody is looking—she quotes her husband as saying—Mama always gets her way. She could openly claim the baton of command if she chose, especially now that her father-in-law is dead and her husband directs the family business. But her strategy is to trust time to move the generations in their appointed orbits. Rather than crudely thrust her senior wife into retirement, Goryōhan continues to thrust her forward as the person nominally in charge. Before long Granny may die, or may retire of her own volition. And Goryōhan has had two decades of co-living in which to form judgments of the woman's character. The strategy requires interim tradeoffs. A rambling house must be maintained, and somebody must always be there to guard it. (Pragmatically, this is explained as a hedge against burglary; symbolically, it is to look after the ancestors and to rescue their tablets from the family altar in case of fire.) Granny must be consulted about any major expenditures. Her outings take precedence over Goryōhan's, and when Granny is at home, Goryōhan's friends feel constrained about visiting. Goryōhan is Granny's social secretary—a useful position for intercepting communiqués—and is fetch-and-carry assistant when Granny periodically changes the art objects on display in the house. And though Goryōhan dislikes the taste of bitter Tea, she prepares a bowl of it for her senior every morning after breakfast—365 danged days a year.

Goryōhan carries out these tasks with little of the self-doubt that assails Shōji as he pours bourbon for his clients. This *is* the self she was meant to be. Nor does she, like Beisuke, labor under guilt for having stinted on the care she previously gave to those in the household. She can draw a relatively uncomplicated feeling of achievement from her progress along her career line.

Goryōhan is stage-managing some of Granny's performances. One day, for example, she described to me how her senior recently had come home beaming from an outing with Tea companions. Goryōhan had, without saying a word, packed a picnic basket full of unusually elaborate and tasty dishes. Granny was genuinely surprised when she opened it and shared the contents with her cronies. They then heaped praise upon *Granny* for having displayed such skill at training her successor.

Again: the Goryōhan that I saw did not always dress in the latest fashion, though she dressed smartly. Nevertheless, she allows Granny to chide her for dressing too plainly, for looking too conservative. By reflex, Granny is made to appear more youthful and up-to-date. The picture reminds me of the classic Confucian tales of the heroes of filial piety, such as the man who put on diapers and crawled like an infant in front of his 70-year-old parents in order to make them feel young again.

Does this mean that Goryōhan's care for her mother-in-law is phony? Goffmanian gaming? I suspect that when the time comes, Goryōhan will shed tears of honest grief for Granny. In the Sheehy phrase, Granny has become, for her junior wife, "one of those people who have truly passed through us and us through them." Years of colleagueship and co-aging have penetrated and softened the official norms of senior-junior conduct. We speak to each other so freely, says Goryōhan, that people mistake us for a real mother and daughter—to the point where her husband protests (if only jokingly) that people will begin to think he is an adoptee.

This complicated personalizing is a feature of most ties with others in one's convoy. And that it commonly occurs in Japan between senior and junior wives is the view of one of Japan's leading family sociologists, Masuda Kōkichi. Were it not so, Masuda argues, then once the junior wife grasps real power over the household she should have no scruples about taking revenge upon the now-aging senior who so long defined her very existence. However, he goes on to say:

I sense that relatively few yome actually take advantage of the opportunity. Now confronting the same household management problems herself, the typical yome is likely to have developed a mature sympathy with the shūtome for having previously shouldered the burden. . . . In one sense this is the final test of her loyalty to her "new" family: helping the shūtome achieve a good death and honestly being able to weep for her. In short, an aging shūtome probably will be given good care not simply because of broad norms of respect for elders. Good care is also encouraged by a yome's personal sympathy for her career predecessor, by her need to further prove that she indeed fully identifies with her family-of-marriage, and by her growing recognition that soon she in turn will become a shūtome.

Goryōhan, for example, longs to move into a modern apartment or townhouse, easy to clean, lockable with one key. But to do so now would put an end to Granny's gardening and to her Tea room; it would probably break her heart.

Goryōhan's ties to Granny have become too multiplex for that —bonds of role duty but also of affection, empathy, shared experience, even of gratitude. Granny is good-natured, not half so petty as some mothers-in-law. Granny has cultivated "feminism" in the men of the house. And I suspect that Goryōhan remains just a little in awe of Granny's strength of character and body-scrubbing toughness.

There are also changes in Goryōhan herself. Consider the matter of meals. Goryōhan has always prepared separate meals to suit the tastes and needs of the three generations in the household. It used to be that she herself would eat a portion of what she prepared for her children, but her appetite is less and less stimulated by a plate of greasy kid stuff. Now she not only takes most of her meals in Granny's company, but she is beginning to prefer the taste of Granny food.

So Tea may be a post-breakfast addiction. But Goryōhan prepares it and shares it every morning—on fine mornings in that garden that Granny has been tending for decades. It has become a daily ritual, resonant with multiple meanings, a personal reassurance of continuing support and respect.

Sachiko's case illustrates, in obverse fashion, the importance of the personalizing of convoy ties. Goryōhan's duties toward her senior wife are defined by their roles and respective phases along the life cycle. But two decades of consociation make it unlikely that the duties will merely be carried out mechanically. For Sachiko it is otherwise: by rights, it is the duty of the main house to see Yukiko and Taeko into marriage, but the two sisters are personally much closer to Sachiko than to Tsuruko. So, out of affection for them, out of three decades of growing up together, Sachiko reluctantly comes to serve them *in loco parentis*. This then obliges her to "stage" Yukiko's marriage arrangements in such a way that the main house still appears to be in command. And it obliges her to "cover"—from the main house and from society in general—Taeko's misdemeanors, affairs, and eventual pregnancy.

In the symbolic logic of the novel, Sachiko is more fully human and compassionate than Tsuruko because she cares about the two youngest sisters as individuals. Sachiko wants to repay Taeko for her relative deprivation of parental affection. And she wants to be certain that Yukiko will be wed to a man who will nourish her delicate beauty. True, Tsuruko has always been somewhat distant from the other three sisters; true, she is understandably constrained by her role-duties as successor to the main house. But as time goes on Tsuruko seems more and more the slave of status-honor. If only *someone* would marry Yukiko, she says one day in exasperation; it hardly matters who anymore, even if it ends in divorce. And when Taeko is stricken with dysentery, Tsuruko interprets it as well-deserved punishment and can scarcely suppress a wish that Taeko will not recover.

Tsuruko, then, has allowed herself to shrink into the dimensions of her role as eldest sister, while Sachiko has preserved her fullness as a person. Goryōhan initially cut back her sense of self to fit the role of junior wife, but having proved her ability to do so she has, for two subsequent decades, been expanding her potential to become more than what the role requires.

For Goryōhan, adult growth has also involved the cultivation of "selfish" interests and of ties with others in her convoy. She voices a phrase I heard from almost every interviewee: you must have something only you can do, some activity or interest that is purely yours, that says, "This is me." As a proper bride she set aside the interests of her girlhood and picked up instead the arts that are the custom of this house: Tea and Noh-chanting, for example. For a decade the interests of her children took priority. But now she can more openly pursue interests that are her own—long-muffled ones such as calligraphy and dressmaking, new-found ones such as Co-op committee work, poetry-chanting, or the study of Japanese history.

Once Granny is out of the picture, Goryōhan's children will be the next in line as problem performers in her convoy. They are cause for some worry and much uncertainty. They have minds of their own, seem to be into a rebellious phase of adolescent identity-testing. Friends tell her she is over-mothering them. Perhaps, but it would be rewarding if they both could go to college, thereby realizing a hope she had had to set aside in her own life.

Her husband, on the other hand, is if anything too steady. The relationship seems not to be going anywhere. Goryōhan would welcome a bit of bizarre behavior from him—and less from her son and daughter. Papa remains affectionate, and will demonstrate his affection in front of his mother, though if the children see it they snigger. Once Granny and the children are less in the picture, perhaps Goryōhan and her husband can rekindle the ardor of their early months of marriage. During one session she hurried from the room to fetch and show me the album of snapshots taken during their period of post-wedding courtship.

Or if not Papa, then—in memory and fantasy, at least—there is the young man she fell in love with and had dreamed of marrying. A closet romantic, Goryōhan tenderly preserves the letters and presents she received from him. With mingled pride and embarrassment she brought them to show me—and quickly snatched them back from my hands. One of these days she could just happen to meet him on the street when she goes to visit her parents in the old home town.

Friendships

Friends are yet another significant source of Goryōhan's identity, well-being, and adult continuity. Friendship ties are valuable precisely because they are not complicated by the role-demands of group membership. With neighbors, with colleagues at work, with Co-op wives, there will always be hidden agendas or residual overtones of social control. You fear it may turn out to be, after all, a *rigai-kankei*, a "profit-and-loss relationship," the phrase most interviewees used. With a true friend you need not be on guard against ulterior motives, the human affection is "pure"—yours as well as theirs. Thus you can be completely frank, and "spill your guts" [*hara watte hanaseru*].

A true friend, says Beisuke, basically doesn't change. With such a friend, each of you can appreciate the other's personal point of view. Such relationships may evolve with persons met during adulthood, with neighbors or acquaintances. But given the role-demands of adulthood, these later contacts are likely to remain shallow or interest-laden. The critical period for establishing friendships is in adolescence.

During her bridal phase, Goryōhan broke contact with her friends from primary school and girls' high school. But before long the relationships were revitalized. She remains confident of them—they are just a phone call away. And now, more free to leave the house, she gets together with them more frequently. Friends offer continuing testimony that she is more than just a wife and mother. At the same time they provide a special kind of testimony that she has become a *good* wife and mother. They knew her even before senior wife, husband, or children did; they knew her back when she was a spoiled daughter.

Here again, Sachiko serves as a contrast case. One day an epiphany comes to her: she realizes she has no friends "worthy of the name." Now past the phase of life when friendships are easiest to cultivate, she understands that she has yet another reason for remaining close to her two youngest sisters. They may be the only friends she will ever have.

Tanizaki takes care to explain how this came about. For it is not a matter of personality but of co-biography. Sachiko has always been gregarious, cheerful, the sort of person who can make friends easily if she wants to. But she did not take the trouble to do so during the seedtime years of girlhood because she was "friends" with her father, sharing his passion for the theater, restaurants, the urban good life. He simply did not mind if his daughters skipped school or were lukewarm about their studies (Goryōhan never missed a day). As often as not, the father himself would entice his daughters away from school to spend the day with him at the theater. Because her father and her sisters were her steady companions during those crucial years, Sachiko simply never became involved with her peers.

Tomoko (Chapter 6) provides further confirmation of the point. She talks with mixed feelings about her "Education Papa." It was not her mother but her father who pushed her to do well academically. One long-range result was being admitted to Osaka National University and later taking up a successful professional career. But friendships were the price. Her father pressured her into enrolling illicitly in a prestigious junior high school outside her official district of residence. As an outsider and commuter into the district, she had few opportunities to become close to girls either in that district or in her own neighborhood. Today she has carried only one friendship forward from adolescence.

In old age, friendships may take on yet another dimension. Goryōhan is explicit about this. Before long, she and her friends will again be companions in hobbies and activities, once their families need less attention. "And when the time comes," they will be each other's insurance against loneliness and feelings of uselessness in those predictable years of widowhood. If friendship is a life-course insurance policy for the self, then the premiums, like all insurance premiums, are cheapest when paid early.

Goryōhan at 43 is at ease with the trending of her life. From her mother she learned how to please others, from her favorite teacher she learned how to hang on. Armed with these two chief virtues of Japanese womanhood, she has pursued the pathway of caring ever since she became an adult. She has not known a sick day since it all began.

She is not yet at her peak position as senior wife. But Granny is shifting into retirement. Goryōhan is more and more free to pursue her own interests. The children are something of a question mark, still a risk. But if all goes well, her son will bring home a junior wife who will look after her, as she has Granny. Perhaps there will be second-honeymoon trips with Papa. And when she becomes a widow, free of having to care for a husband, she can turn again to her friends.

Goryōhan usually scheduled our sessions for afternoons when her senior wife was away from the house. Granny, however, eventually insisted upon meeting the investigator personally and taking his measure for herself. This she did in the way she knew best, by serving me in her Tea chamber. I have no idea whether or not I met with her approval. I am untutored and possibly tone-deaf to the chamber music of the Tea aesthetic. But even my philistine soul could appreciate the poise and the ballerina smoothness of the woman's movements, the charm of her well-modulated voice. If I should ever want to learn the art, I thought to myself, I could do far worse than to take my instruction from Granny.

CHAPTER 6

An Honor Student

For there is no doubt that there does persist the feeling, and it is probably the deepest one we have, that what matters most is that we learn through living.

DORIS LESSING, *The Summer Before the Dark*

I. CARING AND CAREERING

Tachibana Shigezō, 84, has suddenly gone senile. His daughter-in-law Akiko is talking with a social caseworker about putting him into a home for the aged. Akiko explains that being waked several times a night to look after the old man is ruining her effectiveness during the day as a secretary. "You're a working wife, too," she says. "Surely you understand what my job means to me." The social worker replies:

I do understand. But try to think about it from an old person's point of view: the happiest thing of all is to live your twilight years at home among the young folks. I know what it means to you to have a job, but there isn't a thing that can be done about it. When an old person has to be looked after, somebody has to sacrifice. After all, in time you and I are going to be old too.

The scene is from *A Man in Ecstasy*, Japan's best-selling novel of 1972. A million copies of the book were sold within six months after publication, and more than another million since then. By the end of the year a film based on the book was already in first-run theaters. And the phrase "age of ecstasy" was soon a popular euphemism for dotage.

This swift popularity is a tribute to veteran authoress Ariyoshi

Sawako (who, incidentally, donated her royalties from the book for the use of old-age centers). She captures a tragic beauty in the physical and mental decay of senility. She portrays as well the impact that a dodderer can have upon those charged with sustaining him. And in doing so she knits together two issues that throb in Japanese consciousness today. One issue is how to care for an expanding population of seniors. The other is how to legitimize careering in work roles for women—upon whom, as we saw with Goryōhan, the burden of old-age caring was traditionally placed.

For a woman, Japan's heritage opened few pathways for long engagements outside the home. Even those open to her were basically ones that involved nurturing functions. A few women became Shinto priestesses or Buddhist nuns, or free-lanced as shamans. A substantially larger number entered the water trades as maids, masseuses, prostitutes, or entertainers. But in taking up such careers, they generally had to abandon all hopes for the security and self-respect of a proper marriage. Popular stereotypes today still assume that most women in the water trades must be divorcées or widows or runaways.

Throughout the decades of industrialization some 30 to 40 percent of Japan's labor force has in fact been female. But for a married woman to work—short of coping with acute financial crisis —has been, among the symbol-bearing middle and upper classes, a stigma of treason to the norms of gender. Women began moving into professional and executive careers early in the twentieth century in very small numbers, and some of them were married. But the doors of opportunity only began to swing wide after the Pacific War. Women were allowed to vote for the first time. And in the revised law codes of the late 1940's they gained a degree of equality with men that *on paper* is as good as and often better than that obtaining in most Western nations.

But taking advantage of equal-opportunity-by-decree is not easy. As Shōji and his male age-mates had to "die" in 1945 with the end of Empire, so their female companions suddenly faced new options to "live" as never before, in careers away from home. On the practical plane, a working wife must reconcile men's time with women's tempo. She must develop routines for compartmenting her roles and behavior domains, becoming like her husband a commuter between identities as well as between home and shop. She is expected both to control the quality of household life, as does a traditional wife, and to attend to her vocational growth. On the emotional plane, she risks being regarded—or regarding herself—as unfeminine. And caring for the generations adds to the classic female concerns. The working wife must invent a new pathway in the very act of living it.

Decline—and Resistance

Dramatic action in *A Man in Ecstasy* is spurred on, scene after discouraging scene, by Shigezō's relentless senile regression. The central story line traces the curve of his decay against the curve of Akiko's growth as his caretaker. She too engages in a middle-age "resistance"; but unlike Nishimura Kōtarō's campaign, hers is against the aging of another person, whose collapse threatens to bring down her career of 20 years as secretary and girl Friday in a law office.

Shigezō retired almost two decades ago from a position in an up-country bank. Since then he and his wife have been living in Tokyo, in a cottage provided for them by their son Toshikazu (Akiko's husband) on land adjoining the younger couple's modest house. Blithely indifferent to the fact that he and his wife are dependent on the junior couple, Shigezō has continued to rumble on as befits one of the proverbial four terrors of Japan: earthquake, thunder, fire, and father. Though the whole family would be financially strapped without Akiko's income to add to Toshikazu's, Shigezō has continued to mock her for being a working woman.

He seems to have been a sour, humorless hypochrondriac for as long as anyone can remember. For instance, not one of several sets of professionally made dentures ever satisfied him; eventually, he bought tools and materials and produced his own. His wife has always had to prepare greens-soups and Chinese herbal infusions to quiet his complaining about his delicate stomach. His one appeal has been his tall, rugged masculine beauty: his wife had fallen for him at a glance. Even now his hair remains richly black and he looks no older than 70.

If Shigezō has been able to carry the self-centeredness of childhood through life into old age, perhaps it is because he has been overprotected by his wife, who has always treated him as gingerly as one would a swelling. "Maybe I'm so healthy," muses son Toshikazu, "because Mother had her hands full with him and I was able to escape her overprotective impulses." "It's incredible how she took his browbeating all that time and never talked back," comments daughter Atsuko. "She's your old-fashioned Japanese woman. I'd have divorced him in three days."

But to everyone's disbelief, Mother has dropped dead. Everyone took for granted that such a sturdy woman ten years Shigezō's junior would surely outlive him. Or was it that she wore herself out caring for him for so long? Whatever, with her death his behavior has changed overnight. He no longer recognizes his own son or daughter, he responds only to daughter-in-law Akiko and her son Satoshi. Shigezō gorges on foods that once would have brought diarrhea but that now result only in normal defecation. At times he is lost in a rapturous waking dream.

Daughter Atsuko looks after the old man for a few days, but then must return to her husband and children. Akiko, for her part, resents being expected to substitute for her dead mother-in-law. But her son and husband are not much help, and Shigezō has suddenly become partial to her. "Deny it all you want," says Atsuko, "but Father's got a crush on you." The thought that Shigezō is attracted to her, perhaps even sexually, leaves Akiko shuddering. These feelings are doubled when she is obliged to move downstairs and sleep in the same room with him at night—because when he wakes in the night he shouts that a burglar is in the closet, and if Toshikazu appears, *he* is accused of being the burglar.

Toshikazu takes it as self-evident that Akiko as daughter-in-law must abandon her career and remain at home to tend the old man. Akiko takes this as further evidence of her husband's insensitivity toward her work, his lack of appreciation for how her income has made their life more comfortable. Theirs had been an "office marriage" [*shokuba kekkon*]. That is, they found each other and married out of mutual attraction, not by arrangement. But the company had a rule against employing both partners to a marriage, so Akiko resigned and took a position in a legal office. She has had no special training, but taught herself to use the Japanese typewriter, in masterful fashion. And her years of experience have made her almost indispensable to the two attorneys who share the office.

Akiko is aware that when it comes to women's careers there is a "feudal" streak in the thinking of most men of her generation:

They certainly give no recognition to the fact that when a wife has a paid job it makes it easier for the family financially. They've got it in their heads that they are obliged to be patient and forbearing because the wives are only doing it for the fun of it, and to that extent are really skipping out on their wifely duties. The women, for their part, take as an article of faith that they did not go out and get a job because they were unhappy serving their man, and so they feel constrained toward him about holding a job. At times Akiko was furious about the situation, but she had lived with it for 20 years as something fixed and unalterable.

Akiko has never challenged her husband on this issue. In fact, out of wifely pride in preserving autarchy over her home, she has never even pressed him to help with the household chores. The novel begins on a Saturday afternoon, with Akiko shifting efficiently from the tasks of the office to those of the house. The office closes at noon, and on the way home she buys the week's groceries. She takes advantage of packaged and prepared foodstuffs, frozen waffles and pizzas, as well as the more usual Japanese dishes. The afternoon is devoted to housework. Meals are made ready for the coming week, and the place is swept and vacuumed. Sunday can then be enjoyed as a full day of rest and relaxation. "I'm no Christian," muses Akiko, "but resting every Sunday is one of Christianity's better ideas." By adhering firmly to this routine, Akiko has been able to discharge her duties both at home and in the office. If her husband is reluctant to lend a hand now, after 20 years, the problem is partly of her own making.

The Education of a Caretaker

To save her job, Akiko must embark upon a quest. Above all else she needs to predict Shigezō's probable course of senility: Will he die soon? Will he regain normality? Will he be in this condition indefinitely? Akiko is startled to discover how ignorant she is about the details of the spiral of human aging. Until now she really had not *wanted* to know about it, another protective shield she must throw away. She must also discover the resources, the information, the facilities, the helping hands public or private, and anything else that can relieve her of at least part of her caretaking burden.

She goes to a physician, hoping he can help her understand Shigezō's peculiar behavior. But the doctor shrugs it off: What else can you expect from a man that age? He examines the old man, and the results are a mixed blessing. Physically, Shigezō is a sound specimen; his health needs no attention. But this means that his conduct cannot be traced to physical causes or cured by medical treatment. And it means that he may live on in this condition for a long time.

Akiko thinks it pointless to ask for a leave of absence from her job, as she had done when Satoshi was born. Then she could specify a date of return; now she cannot. While she is away, others might assume her duties so effectively that the lawyers would not welcome her back.

At first, Shigezō is left during the day at the neighborhood Golden Age Center. Some days he is taken there by Mrs. Kadotani, a widow who lives nearby. Other days Akiko drops him off at the Center on her way to work, and Satoshi retrieves him en route home from school. Her periodic glimpses into the Center provide Akiko with examples of active, cheerful elders against which to measure her listless father-in-law. Though Shigezō behaves well at the Center, he remains a spectator, taking no part in the folksinging and dancing, the crafts or games. Before long the others lose interest in him, and he in turn complains about being left among old people.

He begins to wander away from the house, until one day the

family cannot find him. For the first time in her life Akiko must phone the police. They turn out to be considerate—but urge her for everyone's convenience to sew a nametag upon the old man as she would upon a footloose child.

Shigezō's conduct becomes more and more difficult to tolerate. After one particularly revolting display, Satoshi turns to his parents and says, "Dad, Mom, *please* don't you live this long." Akiko consults the welfare office caseworker about nursing homes, only to draw scorn for selfishly attempting to evade her obligations as a daughter-in-law. And when the caseworker hears that Shigezō is a wanderer, she asserts flatly that no nursing home will accept him, for none can provide close supervision. If he is given to straying off, she concludes, your only alternative is a mental hospital with a locked ward.

Unofficially but helpfully, neighbors and workmates tutor Akiko and her husband about the nature of senility. Their folk-prognoses about the course of decline may be vague and unreliable, but to Akiko even an elastic measure is better than none.

"Has the old man begun to lose his sense of direction?" asks one of the attorneys.

"Not yet," says Akiko, "It's just that he's come to eat amazing amounts of food. If you don't feed him he cries like a child."

"Oh well, then it won't be long."

"When you say not long, how long's that?"

"Maybe two, three years he can hold out. That's how it was with my old Dad."

Toshikazu brings home similar stories from his office. He and Akiko find that their curiosity has opened out almost explosively in a direction that they never would have anticipated. They devour every scrap of information about aging that they can find.

Neighbors also prove helpful in more tangible ways. The widow Kadotani, lonely, attracted to the handsome Shigezō, courts him at the Center and then begins to spend whole days with him in the cottage, talking, making tea, helping him to the toilet. Akiko is mildly embarrassed by the blossoming of this affair, but at the same time is grateful that someone will look after him during the day. Unreturned affection ebbs, however, and

Mrs. Kadotani drifts away again. Another neighbor asks if the Tachibanas will rent their cottage to a married student couple she knows. The couple agree to look after Shigezō three days a week in return for reduced rent. And with this arrangement Akiko is able to continue working three days a week.

The Rewards of Ecstasy

At first Akiko interprets her responsibility in terms of securing Shigezō's bodily comfort. Then slowly it dawns on her that she must—though she does not verbalize it in this way—manage his entire career of dying, since he is no longer competent to do so. As this awareness grows in her, she even begins to feel guilty about continuing to work, for through inattentiveness she might be permitting him to die prematurely.

For a time he hovers near death from influenza, brought on when he slipped in the bathtub. Innocently enough, Akiko had left him alone for a moment to step to the phone. If he dies now she could be faulted, she tells herself, for bringing on his demise through carelessness. However, the fever subsides, and the physician assures her that the old man's heart is as sturdy as ever. Akiko is relieved that during the past months she has not overtaxed his heart with sleeping pills, trying to keep him dormant merely for her own convenience. And she resolves to keep him alive as long as she can: "Up to now Shigezō's existence has meant one headache after another, until I could hardly stand it any more, but from now on I am going to give my all to make him live. It's something I alone can do, not anybody else."

She is rewarded in a way that may surprise many Western readers. Thanks to the fever, Shigezō has regressed even further. Before, he had been about like Satoshi at the age of six, and now he is more like Satoshi at age three. Totally dependent for bodily care, having lost his hair and his looks, Shigezō can offer only infantile coin of emotional exchange. Moving with maddening slowness, able to say only one word, *moshimoshi* ("hello"), he sits by the hour with a rattle and a music box that Satoshi had bought for him. Or he gazes at the songbird that was Akiko's present to him for his 85th birthday. But this man who was so sour all his life now wears on his face the most lovable La Gioconda smile. He beams if Akiko brings something he had wanted—he no longer can muster the words to ask—but often he smiles for no obvious reason at all.

Akiko remembers Satoshi's face soon after he had been born. The doctor had called it the "radiant smile of the unconscious" [*mushin no egao*]. Her husband quotes Pascal, but Akiko finds sacred imagery more fitting. Though not a religious sort herself, she cannot help thinking that Shigezō has become one of the gods while yet trapped in worldly flesh. There are times, she muses, when I feel as if it is a god that I am serving.

Nevertheless, the old man still is in this world, and in the most noisome physical form. Akiko thanks progress for providing the electric washer and dryer that ease the toil of cleansing his diapers. And she tells herself: "Shigezō is living in a trance, as if he's watching a dream. Is this how the blessings of long life are consummated? Perhaps to him the songbird in its cage is the sweet bird of Paradise and Emi [the student wife] is a veritable angel."

Shigezō has passed beyond the ordinary limits of human variability and has entered a para-human realm. It is a difficult realm to define, and it is likely to evoke deep ambivalence. The Western impulse is to link this realm to the biological—to describe Shigezō as a "living vegetable." But the traditional Japanese impulse is to link it to the sacred. In the Japanese heritage, the human career does not end with the death of the flesh. The personal or "life" cycle includes more than biological existence. To die is to join the departed members of one's household line. Sanctified but not superpotent, these former consociates remain "alive" as significant others to those still in this world. Shigezō is moving across the threshold into that status. His ecstasy is evidence of successful "status passage." To the psychopathologist it may spell regression; in Japanese eyes it validates Akiko's struggle to sustain the old man's human—cultural—progression.

II. LEARNING THROUGH LIVING

Tachibana Akiko is a kind of middle-aged heroine. Her virtue shows in her ability to marshal a complex of resources and relationships over an extended campaign. Like Goryōhan, she has no single overriding goal. She wants to sustain her family. At the same time, she wants to continue her job and the lifestyle that she has evolved around it, a pattern that promises continuing satisfaction to her plus at least a modicum of challenge.

Her weapons are her managerial skill and her emotional maturity. We see these directly in her activeness, and indirectly in reflections of the passiveness of her son and husband. Where they fall immobile, she summons up fresh energy from within. When the old woman dies, they sit stunned by the discovery of her corpse, and Akiko takes over tasks that ought to be performed by the men of the house—calling in a physician and mortician, notifying kin, rousing neighbors to help prepare a wake. Husband and son turn again and again in disgust from Shigezō. Akiko finds him, feeds him, cleans him, puts him to bed. She is no mute martyr, but she continues to cope.

Emotionally, Akiko blends features from both prewar and postwar Japanese ideal-personality types. In name as in self, she is a woman of the era. The first syllable of her name is written with a graph that, when pronounced differently, is the first syllable of Showa, the name of the current Imperial reign. Akiko grew up in the prewar ethos of hierarchy, self-denial, and "moist" human relationships. She has spent her mature years in the postwar ethos of equality, self-development, and "dry" human ties. She is capable of giving care to son, husband, even hopeless father-in-law, without smothering them in overprotection as her mother-in-law did. She is equally capable of sustaining an office career and of raising a son who appears sure to grow into a self-reliant man.

Her victory is a manager's victory, not a star-spangled triumph. She brings deeply conflicting demands into a workable if not ideal reconciliation. Drawing upon her own stability, rejecting the use of a mental hospital, reducing her office work to three days a week, and getting help from the student couple, Akiko ensures that Shigezō will remain at home through his dying days of "ecstasy."

Akiko emerges from the novel somewhat larger than life, the others correspondingly smaller. Hanshin women told me that they can easily identify with her heroics—as men say they can with Mishima Yukio's suicide—but doubt being able to imitate them. From a literary point of view, this no doubt lowers the quality of the novel. It is a work of "social realism" with a didactic coloring. Authoress Ariyoshi has been explicit that one of her purposes in writing the book was to bring home to her countrymen and -women the human dilemmas that have been thrust upon them by the aging of the population.

But Ariyoshi has put together a documentary novel with admirable craft. Through clever plotting she brings out facet after facet of the problem: the underdevelopment of public facilities for the aged, the obstacles posed by traditional definitions of women as caretakers, the learning processes that younger people must go through in order to appreciate the realities of the issues. Hanshin people who had read the book often told me of similar episodes in their own experience: Goryōhan's father-in-law, for example, had been a runaway in his final weeks.

On a more abstract level, Ariyoshi's book is a valuable portrait of what we might call the career-learning process. Akiko is, so to speak, an honor student in practical adult education. Along the course of any lengthy quest, engagement, career, or pathway you pass through successive stages of learning, meet with successive tasks that must be mastered. You come to know better this aspect of life, this institution, this craft. By reflex, new epiphanies of realization alter your sense of self, as well as your understanding of the world. Everett Hughes, writing about careers, puts it this way:

Subjectively, a career is the moving perspective in which the person sees his life as a whole and interprets the meaning of his various attributes, actions, and the things which happen to him. This perspective is not absolutely fixed either as to points of view, direction, or destination. . . . Institutions are but the forms in which the collective behavior and collective action of people go on. In the course of a career the person finds his place within these forms, carries on his active life with reference to other people, and interprets the meaning of the one life he has to live.

We can watch Akiko being transformed in this way as she moves across an array of different types of thresholds. One such series involves learning about public resources—about old-age welfare systems, about the role of the police in retrieving wandering elders, about the fact (which she had not known before) that pharmacies stock diapers for old people as well as for infants.

Another series of developmental tasks has to do with Akiko's response to Shigezō's needs for bodily attention. At first she is reluctant even to undress him and lead him to the bath. In memory, she contrasts this with bathing her infant son. But having steeled herself to lead Shigezō to the bath, the most she can do in addition is to order him to scrub himself. In time, she begins to wash all of him except his genitals, and eventually she washes even those. Finally, after he dies, she willingly gives his corpse a meticulous and thorough washing and dressing in every pore and fold of flesh.

Akiko also revises her understanding of a domain of Japanese tradition. She had "known" about customary ways for dressing a corpse, conducting a wake, holding a funeral. Had an anthropologist interviewed her, she would have been a useful informant on these matters, able to relate the standard wisdom about them. But hers would have been information divorced from experience. Until the death of her mother-in-law, Akiko had never been the person *responsible* for performing such customary actions. Suddenly she realizes she is ignorant of details, and must call in neighbors and her brother's wife to instruct her. What had been "custom" now becomes steeped with personal as well as collective "meaning."

As she looks at the old people she must now deal with, Akiko also undergoes a rapid widening of consciousness with regard to the nature of human aging and the long-run uncertainties of one's fate. An identity future-shock comes to her as she contemplates the widow Kadotani courting Shigezō:

Toshikazu had said that he could see Shigezō on the extension of his own lifeline, and when Akiko saw the figure of this old woman on the extension of her own lifeline she was petrified. Lord Ō-oka of Echizen is said to have asked his mother if women have sex hunger all their lives . . . but for a widow past 70 to close in on a doddering man past 80 as if she'd just been waiting for his spouse to die—was such conduct decent?

Akiko had thought of herself as being a fairly bland sort in that regard, but as she heard the gay voice and saw the rejuvenated figure of this old woman in front of her, she lost the ability to predict what would happen to her when she got old. Here was an old man whom she could not have imagined from the Shigezō she used to know. As for herself, Akiko could not be confident about what her condition would be 30 or 40 years in the future. She had realized that mankind is mortal, but when she was younger it had never even occurred to her that at the end of the life she was leading, and well before death, this kind of—what has to be called a fiendish snare—would be there waiting for her.

In a similar vein, Akiko tries to project futures for her son and her husband. Will Satoshi care for her in her dotage? Tend her grave? What would it feel like to have Satoshi take out and clean her dentures as she must do for Shigezō? And with regard to her husband, how is their affection for each other being transformed by their confrontation with senility? One night in bed, after conjugation, she tells Toshikazu that once their son has married, if Toshikazu dies she will kill herself.

Akiko vaguely remembered that the two of them had said things like that to each other more than 20 years ago. But then both of them were young, fired up by love; their words were fragrant with romance and disconnected from reality. Even so, that in the future they would be saying the same sorts of things to each other—"If you die, I'll die too"—and would mean them seriously, even with all the romantic aroma dispelled, was something she could never have envisioned then.

This kind of moving perspective, this continuing reappraisal of the world, of others, of oneself, this succession of added comprehensions, is built up through changes in many domains of thought and conduct across the years of a long engagement. In Akiko we see it dramatized with a focus upon caretaking and the problems of senility. In Tomoko we meet a woman who has no such specific problem performer, unless it be she herself in her determination to continue her career as a television producer.

III. TOMOKO

She prefers not to be interviewed at home, though sometimes she is there when her husband is being interviewed. Not that she suspects that her husband or his parents would actually eavesdrop, but their presence in

*the house would be constraining. So we borrow offices, go to a coffee
shop, or meet in my house. What began as interviews end as discussions
that continue long after the tape recorder has been turned off. She is eager
to exchange views on a variety of topics, particularly ones having to do
with women's lives, women's liberation, with issues in social policy. Her
professional curiosity is also active. She is intrigued by the reversal of
roles, by being on the receiving end of an interview for a change. At times,
she is as interested in the way a question has been phrased as she is in
its content.*

*A thoughtful sort of person, Tomoko has formulated a position for
herself on many issues. Her opinions come into words easily, though she
does not appear opinionated. She states her views firmly but not argu-
mentatively. She shows little reserve about answering any question asked
about herself, her work, her marriage. But she does like to emphasize
the contrast she sees between herself and most Japanese women. The
voice flows evenly, controlled and mellifluous. The vocabulary is edu-
cated to the point of being highbrow, more intellectual than Shōji's, rich
in foreign words and phrases.*

*Tomoko sits in the way she speaks, with composure. She is a profes-
sional at this sort of thing. Her movements are definite, deliberate but
not affected. She accepts a highball or a glass of wine without the usual
show of Japanese feminine modesty.*

*A confident woman of 38, dressed well but without flair, Tomoko is
in dubious battle with middle-age spread. The only hints that the talk
may be verging upon a sensitive area must be drawn from hesitation
pauses, verbal gropings, from a slight shrinking down into her chair,
a knitting of fingers, or slow twistings of a handkerchief.*

People tell me that I'm unusually quiet, particularly if they've
only just met me. When I first went into middle school, and again
when I entered high school, they said I was a quiet one. I have to
admit that the same thing happened when I joined the network.
First impressions are powerful ones, and people don't get to know
the real me until they've been with me for rather a long time. I'm
certainly not always taciturn; I speak up when I need to. Then
they're surprised: "You seemed to be such a quiet sort . . ."

To me it's distasteful to be considered the Honor Student Type.

That is positively untrue: I have my unconventional side. When I ask myself why people should think that of me, I wonder if it is because my handwriting is so precise—actually I don't think of it as all that neat—and because I control my feelings so that they don't show on the outside. I couldn't stand it to have anyone see through me.

At the studio they say, "Just once we want to see you working with your hair all mussed up." But I can't be that way. Even when I'm at the end of my tether, you won't know it to look at me. It was true, too, during the time I was studying for university entrance examinations. I don't let the turmoil inside appear on the outside. There are people who go along at an even pace, and then they take a drink and their emotions come surging through. I'm not like that, either. People tell me I'm difficult to get close to, and I admit that that is a problem for me. I get the idea that they think because I am quiet and reserved, therefore I'm secretly sticking my tongue out at them.

Anyway, not many people know my true nature. My parents do, of course. And people who live with me: my husband, my brothers when we were little, they know that I'm not so reserved. My friends and long-time acquaintances ought to know it. The same goes for the women I work with.

As a girl, I was an introvert. My mother was a pain to live with, so I would just yes-yes whatever she said and not offer my own opinion. But over the years I seem to be becoming gradually more of an extravert. I first noticed the change beginning when I was in middle school. There's a phase when you start sassing adults and being bratty. I was not all that verbal, but very crabby. And once I started working, I was thrown together with people from all walks of life, and had to get across to them what I wanted them to do. It was training in how to speak.

I'm told that I'm not like other women. I don't go on crying jags, though most women can get worked up in a hurry. I often think it would be good if I *could* be more emotional. But that's the way I am—a cool customer.

Girlhood

My father's father was killed when he was 23, in the Russo-Japanese war. Dad never saw his own father's face. But the family owned land in the home village in Hiroshima Prefecture, and by renting out land and lending money, by one thing and another, they got along all right. Dad's mother was a mere 18 years old at the time her husband was killed, but she never remarried. Made her son her life. Since he was the only child and the heir to the family line, she naturally looked after him like a precious jewel. And that was a glorious failure of policy because he turned into a playboy. She doted on him, did anything he asked; sent him to college in Tokyo—where he just goofed off. However, he did pick up a fine sense of taste, learned how to enjoy life.

Grandma lived to be 88. She was with us all the time I was growing up—she died two years ago—and meant the world to me after my Mom died. That woman had marvelous dexterity; she was a master at knitting and embroidering. *She* was the one who taught me, Mom was all thumbs. I felt a lot of sympathy for her: losing her husband so early, her son not turning out as she had hoped despite all her efforts. She had had her share of misfortune. But at least she had a long life. First Grandma said she would stay alive until she could see me enter the university. Next it was until I was married. After that it was until my younger brother found a job. And so on until her first great-grandchild—my son—was born. I like to think she died contented, having lived to see all of those things.

My mother came from a similar sort of village-elite family, though from an area that is now a suburb of Kobe. She had a half-dozen brothers and sisters, all living in the Hanshin area when I was little, so I often interacted with the uncles and aunts and cousins. One male cousin about five years older than me often played with me and helped me with homework; made me wish I had an older brother. But I was antagonistic toward the female cousins most of the time. They seemed too docile, too eager to practice their kotos or take cooking lessons. I thought they were drab.

None of the senior relatives ever doted on me, though. Nobody ever said I was cute, or called me by pet names. I suppose it was because to them I was the Honor Student Type.

Dad had a variety of jobs after he left college, and eventually started a small flour-milling company in Niigata. He was there half the time, not at home, when we kids were small. Which meant that when he did come home he would fall all over us being nice, giving us spending money. By and large, he wasn't strict with us. My brothers tell me they used to be afraid of him, but I wasn't at all. He thought girls were special. Mom was the household terror if anybody was; Dad would always put in a good word for us.

But he was an Education Papa, always thinking about how to get me into a good university. He made me go to middle school in a district outside our own, and I suspect that it hurt me, because I had so much more trouble striking up friendships. He registered me as officially living with relatives in that school district. I sometimes wondered why I didn't go to school in my own district but —how should I put it—in those days I didn't often let my parents know what I was really thinking. Kids today would blat it right out, maybe refuse to comply. I was more obedient, docile.

I was in fifth grade when we were bombed out, on June 15th, 1945. We had to move out to the village, to live among Mom's kin. We were there for more than a year, living in a house they owned as rental property. At least we had no trouble finding enough food to eat. I was sent to school there, but about all we did was hold air-raid drills or go out and help the adults in the fields. On the one hand, the social turmoil around us brought the whole family closer together. But on the other hand, I was not given much discipline: the adults were too busy scratching together a living to have any time for putting the eagle-eye on us kids.

When we moved back into town the next year, I wasn't able to resume school until fall. We had to move several times, and the schools weren't always in regular operation anyway. By then I was in my first year of middle school, and for that first year our classes were held in the afternoon in a primary school building. At first we didn't even have desks or chairs; we sat on the floor.

But we didn't care, not really. Because we no longer had to be afraid of bombings, and we could sing Western songs again.

Our teachers did their best to promote co-education and our senses of independence: didn't push bookwork so much as they do now. We did study, of course, studied hard but also played hard, and we were honestly happy. And, once I discovered that most of the time I was as good a student as the boys, I suppose that gave me the idea that I have a right to speak up.

But when I was in school nobody ever gave me a nickname. That made me kind of sad, or should I call it lonely? As though I had no individuality.

I am still friends with one woman who was a classmate in middle school and high school. We became close while both of us were getting ready for college. She's taken a different path in life than I have. I often suspect that her horizons are shrinking as she grows to be more and more a specialist in the wifely arts. Not that we see each other so frequently, about twice a year. But we have known each other for so long, watched each other change, that I want to preserve the relationship.

Aside from her, most of my friends date from my college years. Several were in the same music club that my husband and I joined. I didn't make friends in high school because I was too busy cramming for the university entrance examinations.

I knew I had to have a career. In high school I became a celibatarian. I was not going to marry; I would dedicate myself to my profession. Then I began to think about what I would lose by going through life as an old maid. When I was even younger than that, I had wanted to become a concert pianist. I had been taking lessons ever since primary school. When it came time for high school, I asked people if I should go to a music academy. After all, you have to have the talent. I wasn't sure I did. The piano teacher said, well, as a music student your horizons would become very narrow, that after all I had taken up the piano as a hobby originally. So I dropped the idea of a career in it, and went to an academic high school.

After that I began to think about a career in the mass media—in publishing, newspapers, radio, it didn't much matter. I really knew little or nothing about how the media function, had only a few foggy notions. What I'm saying is that my ambitions were not well focused then, but I knew that as a celibatarian I was going to have to earn my own living.

My Education Papa had been warning me not to pin any hopes on becoming a pianist. He wanted me to concentrate on getting into a good university. So in high school I quit taking lessons and used the time instead to study for exams. I didn't touch the keyboard very often. Dad and I even argued over whether to lock it up. The first time around, I failed the exams magnificently. So I had to cram for them for another year, and that time got accepted into Osaka National University.

That was one of the most important watersheds in my life. It gave me the confidence that I can accomplish what I'm determined to do. Remember that in those days in a national university there might be three or four women to a hundred men. And it wasn't exactly easy for us to find jobs, either, after graduation. In the late '50's, good jobs still were scarce. Of 45 women in my graduating class, only ten of us found work, and the other nine were hired as schoolteachers. Hundreds of people applied to the network that year. When they picked me, I felt as if I had won a lottery.

Working

The network has a training institute in Tokyo now, and new employees go there first. But when I joined the Osaka studio, TV was still a new idea. There were not many hours of broadcasting, and relatively few people had sets. You just trailed after an experienced producer and learned by imitating him.

I've changed since I first began working, and the change has its good and bad sides. In my student days I had been uncritical. I thought my professors were brilliant. I majored in German and took little else, nothing broadening, just narrow specialty courses. But my kind of work is broad-ranging and I find myself asking, "What makes society tick?" and "Is an enemy obstructing our way of life?"

Most men seem to be going in the opposite direction. Maybe

it's just that work and family are too heavy a burden for them, but whatever the reason they tend to withdraw, it seems to me. Possibly I'm too harsh on those who do that, but I get to feeling pity for them. And when a man is in a crunch, his wife not only fails to comfort him, she pokes him in the posterior. "Why aren't you being promoted faster?" Wives have got to become more independent.

People had told me that the private networks are more liberal than the public one. But along about the fourth year here, I began to be aware of what a feudalistic place ours is. They don't do a thing to help a woman develop her abilities. Some programs are utterly routine; on others you can take your time, spend money freely, do it the way you want it done. The men angle to be assigned to the good programs. And though I'm itching to take a shot at one, in more than a dozen years in the studio I've never once been given the chance. Women are stuck with the ordinary little daily programs, the ones the men don't want. And the promotions somehow come your way just a little more slowly.

Not that we stiff-upper-lip it all the time. I am no great admirer of the women in the studio, but it's a fact that they are better at their work than most of the men are. So when I see a man promoted early, even though he has just been mumbling around and not paying any attention to the world outside, I get sore. We complain, but there are so few of us we can be ignored. The administrators are transferred in and out so often that we can't get results by complaining. Three years and there's a complete turnover in the station administrative staff. No continuity.

I've avoided taking administrative positions though they might give me more influence over policy than I have as a producer. As an administrator, you never know where you might be transferred next. You're a tool. You have to change your personality, and the tensions mount. All the men seem eager to go that route. But soon they look so awfully haggard and worn. Administrative work is sheer mental agony. You have no time to learn anything new. You die soon after you retire, or end up as another old dodderer.

Only about 10 percent of the professional staff are female now.

There were more in the past, but they quit for various reasons and were replaced by men. The Fukuoka station is the worst: not even one woman on their staff anymore on the broadcast side. Like it or not, the men there have to handle the Tea-and-flowers programs.

If I could start over again, I would take it from high school. I might not have been able to pass the exams for the college of science, but it may have been a mistake to have gone to the college of literature as I did. I wonder if I've gone into the wrong line of work? What I'm doing now probably could be done by just about anyone. Maybe I should have become a doctor or a judge.

Not that my work is uninteresting, but I find myself in something of a dilemma. I've begun to have doubts about the network. Lately I've begun to wonder whether the very existence of such vast organizations is contrary to the well-being of society, because of the authoritarianism (or whatever you want to call it) built into the very structure of such an institution. And yet here I am working in such a place. I'd been with the network for ten years before I began to think about it all.

Nothing would be solved by my quitting and going elsewhere. And the pay is not the point. I honestly did not expect a white collar professional to be so hedged in by restrictions, but there is an invisible framework that you can't budge. For example, broadcasters are not to comment on the behavior of members of the Imperial Household. Senior men in the studio take that for granted, and if you try to insert anything about the Imperial Household into a program script, they clamp down on you without thinking. The three great taboos are the Emperor, the new religions, and sex. And for sure the network will not offer air time to a leftist or to anybody they think would have the nerve to denounce the very existence of the network itself.

When I'm putting together a program, if I think they might clamp down on me, I make a pitch at the planning conference and try for their approval. But I'm often left with the feeling that the people I pick for my programs are just barely acceptable. The network's rule is to not air anybody who is known to be strongly biased in any direction, which is why you end up with nothing but dullards. What I'm saying is that I'm beginning to reconsider the role of the networks in society. The union pays attention only to the positive side of the role: the cultural and informational functions. That's no threat.

Ours is a closed shop; we're obligated to join the union. I took no interest in it when I first joined the network. The union itself was feeble then, though it has gained a little strength since. But in this line of work, you don't ordinarily think of yourself as a laborer, so most people are smugly indifferent to the union. Nobody wants to run for office, not even the men. I suspect that it's because as an officer you have to do battle with the establishment, and most men don't like to do that.

I was shop vice-chairperson for one term. Part of the reason why I agreed to do it was that I knew rather little about the union and wanted to learn, and part of the reason is that I apparently don't have the high professional pride the others have. While they're working they gripe and gripe. Then the minute an administrator turns up, they button lip. I hoped I could help make the atmosphere more open, that we wouldn't be so afraid to stand up for our point of view as workers. Well, I tried.

The union's main activity is our annual "struggle" for an increase in base pay. During "struggle," the officers are incredibly busy organizing strikes. When a shop is told to strike on the following day, we go to the studio after midnight and activate a telephone network to notify the members. But it amounts to a hollow gesture, since we don't interrupt live broadcasting. There is no law that forbids you to shut down live broadcasts, but the advertisers would bring enormous pressure against the network if that happened, and everybody seems afraid of it.

I don't see that it would inconvenience anybody. You always have a store of videotapes you can broadcast instead. As it is, there will be times during any struggle when a scheduled show has to be replaced anyway—but the transmitters never shut down. Whether or not it's a deliberate strike-breaking tactic, the studio will be full of supervisory personnel who can run movies or tapes or something. That leaves the union members frustrated, unable to work up much enthusiasm for struggles. Not to mention all the factional bickering that goes on within the union itself.

If they ever fired me, I would go right out and get another job. I'd prefer one in the media, though in Japan it is just about impossible to find a position with any large organization once you are in mid-career. So it might mean I would have to free-lance. For the present, however, I'm doing my work for the studio peacefully and don't really want to leave it, for better or worse. I know I could get along as a free-lance commentator on women's affairs; offers come in frequently. Though I'm not certain I'd be really good at it. . . .

Marriage and Partnership

My life has gone along pretty much as I had hoped. I'm the stubborn kind: when a roadblock looms up in front of me, I blast my way through it. Not that adults didn't try to change my mind, when I was younger. When I was taking exams for the university, they said I should consider a woman's college instead. When I wanted to get married, both my parents were absolutely dead set against it. Dad warned me that the man I wanted to marry was the same age as me, that we were both in college, and it's a mistake to marry a man until you know for sure how he'll turn out. It's best to be five years younger than your husband, he said. Because when a woman marries a man her age she starts looking older sooner, and eventually he'll leave her.

Ours is far and away a better marriage than my parents'. But then, they were pressured into marrying each other. I don't regard that as marriage in the true sense of the word. That's where the fault lies, for Mom and Dad did not have a very happy relationship. I used to blame them for it, but over the years I've come to find a little sympathy for them. Otherwise, I suspect I would never have been willing to get married myself.

But from high school onward, I warned them that I had no intention of going into an arranged marriage. Mom was adamantly opposed to the idea of marrying for love, absolutely against it until the day she died. She had a fantastic sense of family pride.

For that reason her death was a blessing—she died of cancer at 42. She'd have exploded if I had so much as ever hinted that I was fond of any particular man.

And she was uncompromising about ideas of liberation. She could very well accept the idea of a woman wanting a career. But as for marriage, she told me, if I would not agree to an arranged marriage, then I would have to stay single.

Your first year in college, suddenly you have much more freedom than you did in high school, and we hung around with boys pretty often. That made my mother furious. Called me a slut. If I would quit seeing boys, she said, I could trust her to find me a good man. But I told her that no matter how hard she searched, if he didn't appeal to me I would never marry him, so why not forget the whole thing. At times like that she would—how should I put it—become *very* worked up. "There you go, playing around the opposite sex just like your father!" she'd bellow. We'd battle. And it would leave me feeling victimized.

After all, I had been attending coed schools from the beginning. I was only being friendly with boys in the usual ways. But Mom could not understand that, our idea of friendship. We often sent letters to each other, and when Mom found out about it, she would get all emotional.

My first impressions of my husband were not exactly favorable, at that. Takeo seemed, oh, call it fragile, womanish. I had this feeling of Hmmmm—so there are men like this in the world, too? By fragile I mean delicate and slender, willowy, weak-looking. Not masculine. This is not the type for me, I said to myself.

We were in the same German class in college. Takeo was a science major. Now he's a research chemist for a pharmaceutical company. Little by little, I began to see his good points. He was kind to everybody, not blunt the way I am. I admired the way he had of always doing the right thing. He was nothing like my brothers, who are hardboiled types. It occurred to me that he and I could help each other, that we might get along very well indeed. And I found that I was intrigued by a man who would be continuing his studies even after he left college.

We were married two years after graduation. By then I was

working, of course, but Takeo was still in graduate school. Most of our friends also married somebody they met in college, and in many of the couples both parties have careers. Among them, our dual-career marriage is nothing out of the ordinary. For that matter, I'm not sure that Takeo and I are so very different from any married couple except that we play the piano together. He's a great talker, and we don't fight very often. Not that we have so much time together, anyway. When we do fight, he's the one who apologizes.

In college we played concertos together, and we're trying to get that going again. There are two pieces that both of us know well; that part of the problem is solved. But we can seldom arrange to be free at the same time to practice together. It's been a year now, and we haven't made much progress. Probably we would get it going if we were to hold a recital. We've talked about giving a performance to celebrate our fifteenth anniversary. Invite friends. With a clear goal to work toward, we'd both really try hard. I'd be delighted if we could perfect just one piece now.

My feelings for him have not particularly changed over the years. But you make discoveries, for better or worse. For example, I knew ahead of time what a sourpuss he can be when he wakes up, but I had no idea how completely absorbed he can be in his work. I had to make all the arrangements for our honeymoon.

By now I can be pretty sure how he will respond. You know *that* much by the time you've been married five years, don't you? But I couldn't say that I fully understand him yet. He could be secretly having an affair.

And he still surprises me. The network has a male–female talk show, and one night the topic was sex discrimination at retirement age. The two of us were watching. I got peeved because it was such a cheap imitation of a broadcast, but he was guffawing and getting a kick out of it. As far as I was concerned, they were not really facing up to the discrimination issue, they had turned it into a question of women's abilities. Somebody had stacked the panel, and the men were getting away with heaping scorn on women in biological terms. It made my blood boil, but Takeo said, "So what, it's a fun show." He believes that men and women are unquestionably different. Intellectually he can accept the idea that it is a result of different life experiences, but he can't accept it emotionally. Men must protect women, in his view.

He thought his woman would clean the house for him every day, but I'm not that type. I've never cared for housework. "Do it right next time!" he used to tell me, again and again, but I didn't follow orders. Little by little, he began doing it himself. Gradually he got the idea that he ought to do his share of the housework too. Now he gets the place spotless. You'd be amazed. I never bother to organize a spring housecleaning, but he'll hire student help and take care of it.

However, he has a fantastic pride in his handiwork, and I have to be careful to praise him for it properly. Like when a child says "Look at this, look at this!" You have to say, "Yes, it's just beautiful." He'll change the furniture around. "I moved the sofa. It's better over here, isn't it?" "Yes, it really is." If you give an equivocal answer he sulks. He was the one who prepared all the baby food when we were weaning our son—since then he's been teaching his friends how to do it. He can't sew, but he's superb at cleaning.

I want to say something more about love and marriage. I'm fumbling for the right words. Well, ordinarily you assume that love leads to marriage. The two of you want to be together forever; then you won't have to write those letters saying how much it hurts to be apart. Love ends in marriage, and a different kind of feeling begins. I don't know how to explain that difference. If you don't see each other for a few days, you want to be together once more: that part of it does not change. And it isn't quite the same as friendship—my husband and I were friends long before we married. "Roommates" is the word some people use these days if they're just living together. But that makes it sound like a random assortment of people in a boarding house.

This may not be the right way to put it, but a kind of "love" can happen again after marriage, with another person. However, you retain your respect for your spouse. Not that I've had much experience in this. I have not yet met a man I wanted so much to live with that I would think of dissolving my marriage, so I won't pretend to be saying anything very original on the subject.

But I do have friends among male colleagues at the station. I see eye to eye with a couple of them and enjoy talking to them. I like the way one of them thinks—he has such a fresh point of view on so many topics. And he's one of those rare individuals who doesn't brown-nose the bosses. He's a good drinker, and I enjoy drinking with him when we're out on trips to gather material for a program. We've taken care not to become involved with each other—though of course the gossips in the studio say we are. I expect they're jealous. I see nothing wrong with that kind of friendship; a man and a woman can be good friends without its having to be an affair. I know that there are young women in the lab where Takeo works, and that they work on projects together. That doesn't upset me. But I've learned not to say anything about my friendships to him. He can't accept the idea.

In a sense, my husband is my best friend. We're trying to sustain a mutual understanding. Others tell me he is a very simpatico guy. And there is no question that I owe him a great deal. Without him I would not be able to have both a family and a career.

I would not protest if he accepted a position elsewhere, but it doesn't seem likely to happen. He isn't interested in the idea. If he did, however, I would not just give up my career to move with him. I believe that we could continue as a married couple even though we were living apart, but he detests the very thought of it. "What kind of life would that be?" he says. I sure don't go for the idea either. Sometimes I wonder if I'm not acting too much as if I don't need my family. He's even been going out and buying his breakfast on his way to work.

Mothering

We very much wanted a child and were thrilled when Tsuneo was born. I try not to think of him as "mine," instead that my circle includes a young friend. We intended to have another, but I became too tied down at work. When Tsuneo was four, he himself asked if he could have a younger brother or sister to play with.

My youngest brother was in fifth grade when my mother died, and I took care of him after that. So my feelings toward my son are a lot like those I had for my youngest brother. I don't dote on him. Sometimes when I compare myself with other Japanese mothers, I wonder if I'm doing the right thing. The touchy part is that Tsuneo has got the idea, from seeing other families, that a wife is supposed to serve her lord and master. When he's a little older, I'll try to explain to him why it is that I'm working.

Anyway, whatever it is that he senses toward me, I'm sure it must be different from the concept of "mother" that I had as a child. Until he went to primary school, he called me *Mama*. Now sometimes it's *Okāchan* ("mother"). Or he'll tease me and say "Tomo-chan" the way his father does. I suppose it may be poor policy for my husband and me to use first names in front of him.

Lately Tsuneo is exhibiting the defects of being an only child. Knows he has a good head, and so he thinks he doesn't need to hit the books. I suppose there's nothing wrong with that. His current ambition is to become a professional baseball player. If he really should turn out to have the needed talent for it, I wouldn't stand in his way. I have no intention of pushing him into a college-prep course.

When he was in first grade, he took piano lessons, but he refused to continue. Kids are more likely to put up a fight these days, when they don't want to do something. "You can have a full human life without playing the piano"—they bring up rationalizations like that. "Besides," Tsuneo said, "it's a girls' instrument anyway."

I've never tried to teach him much of anything, piano or otherwise. I want him to develop the ability to think for himself, decide for himself. And I suppose I want him to end up married to a complete woman. I'm not sure if that means she should have a career of her own or not. And I wonder how he will turn out. Will he become a radical? I couldn't stop him if he wanted to. If it came out of a mature understanding of issues, I could respect him for it. Or what if war comes, and he's drafted? I'm not thinking about myself, but about him. There would be nothing I could do about it.

Lifestyle

Ours was the first generation that came of age under postwar democracy, and many of us women wanted to work. The present generation seems to be moving backwards, with fewer and fewer women pursuing careers. My husband says that if a woman must work, then she needs a special skill so that she doesn't end up just pouring tea for the men. If it's a flunky job that anybody could do, then she is better off staying home and taking care of her family. Most men seem to feel that it's all right for a woman to work if she has talent, but that if it's only for the money it's a loss of face for her husband. Japanese are peculiar that way, not wanting to admit that they're doing anything for the money.

We estimate what we'll need for the month for household expenses, and both of us contribute from our salaries to the family account. I pay the bills from that account—though if necessary I will dip into my own money or ask him for more if I'm short. Most of my own money goes to buy books. But I also buy my clothes, my son's clothes, and his school supplies, from my money. I honestly don't know just what Takeo does with his money. What he doesn't spend goes into his "bureau-drawer account." Or to be precise about it, his piano account; that's where he hides it.

We don't have a savings account. I'm afraid we could get into hot water some time if we don't have a kitty set aside. But Takeo says that considering the rate of inflation these days, you're better off spending everything, even borrowing if necessary. Logically, I guess he's right. We have not even put away money for college for Tsuneo. I tend to feel that he should earn his own way through, if he wants to go badly enough.

So my only "savings," if you want to call them that, are the 1,000 yen a month that every union member is obliged to put into a savings plan in the Labor Bank. With interest, at the end of the year you have about 13,000 yen. You keep your mouth shut about it and blow it on something for yourself.

Takeo has no use for insurance policies other than fire insurance on the house. I have a small policy on myself, but I only took it out because of a friend who sells the stuff. She pressured me into it.

Takeo's whole family are worriers. "Soon there will be no more petroleum, and then we can't use the oil stoves." They're worrying about it already. "When I was a kid we didn't have any heaters, we were lucky when we had a brazier," I say to them, and it riles them. "Be serious. There's no charcoal in the cities anymore, or firewood either." But I saw my whole house go up in flames, in the war, saw my piano burn up. I can't get all that worried about material things. Takeo's family never had a fire, or the experience of having to begin again with everything new. I lost everything I owned—clothes, books—all that was left was a bag of odds and ends that I carried out. Our house was gone, my parents were dazed by it all, and I took it calmly. Like any young girl, my main lament was over the fact that I had lost the whole collection of envelopes and stationery that I had been so much at pains to assemble. That was in 1945, in the bombing raids in Kobe, when I was ten.

Takeo even refuses to buy new furniture. That house is filled with old stuff, and the family is attached to it. He grew up there and likes it the way it is. We moved in with his parents a few years ago. It saves us from paying rent, and he can look after his parents more easily. His father is quite feeble now. When I just can't stand it, I'll go buy new curtains or a few cushions to change the look of a room. Then his mother seems delighted. But on her own she won't do a blessed thing about fixing up the place.

I do the main grocery shopping on Sundays. If we need anything else during the week, I pick it up on my way home from work, or else I ask Takeo to get it. I have Sundays off plus every other Monday. Sundays are for "family service"—I make all three meals that day. Mondays, because Tsuneo is in school all day, I do pretty much what I want to do. Likewise, if I happen to have a day off on another weekday, or if I use my physiological leave. Women get two days a month for that; it seems to be unique to Japan. The network tends to discourage you from actually using those days, unofficially of course. The union has been urging women to take advantage of what's due them, and it seems as if more of them are doing so.

"Family service" on Sunday includes looking in on my own father. My youngest brother still lives with him, unmarried at 28. I try not to become estranged from either side of the family.

If the day is my own, the first thing I do is look for a new film worth seeing. Otherwise, I may go for a walk, or just stay in the house and read or listen to records. I know it's utterly commonplace, but it gives me such a magnificent feeling to listen to classical music by myself, to drown myself in it for a couple of hours. I don't do anything else then. There are chores I can do while listening to FM or watching TV—clipping newspapers or ironing. But when I listen to classics, I give myself to them.

I don't go to movies all that often, only to good ones. For example, a couple of weeks ago there was a film festival in the Asahi Festival Hall. I went to that three days in a row. Takeo is almost never free at the same time I am, so we rarely see a movie together, but I take my son once in a while. The other day he pestered me until I took him to see *Godzilla vs. Megalon*. We took along two boys from his class. It amazed me to see that place just jammed with kids.

The three of us try to take short vacation trips together during Tsuneo's school vacations. But places a kid prefers and places adults find interesting rarely coincide, and that can make for tension. Last year for the first time I went without them—I mean on a trip other than to collect material for a program. A friend was on her way to Hawaii and she asked me to join her. I said "Sure" without thinking twice. But when I got home that night, it was "I object!" And that made the whole thing awkward.

I'm afraid my reading habits have degenerated. Aside from books related to my work I mostly read Itsuki Hiroshi's novels or Matsumoto Seichō's detective stories. I monitor the book reviews and commentaries in the weekly magazines, and I watch the book ads in the newspapers. I buy any book that promises to be interesting. At this point I no longer even know how I should organize my book collection; something has to be done with it. I just go on and on buying books connected with work. I wonder if that's a mistake? The network would pay for some of them for me, but the paperwork is so cumbersome and takes so long that when I see a book I want in the store, I'd just as soon pay for it out of my own pocket.

I don't read them often, I just buy them often. They are piled up all over the place. My husband says that with professional books you can run into a problem by not having a book at your fingertips when you need it, so you have to keep buying them by the pile. They are not on hand for reading but for referring to, is his policy.

Naturally, I watch the tube a great deal. On an average day I am home by 7:30—we start at 10 a.m.—and the set is on until midnight. I'm likely to be doing chores until at least midnight, well past midnight if I have a rush job. Tsuneo stays up until 9, and he is lord of the set until then. "You watch that show every night, let's look at something else for a change," I'll say, but you won't catch him yielding his power. There is an older small set in my mother-in-law's room, and if the grownups want to see a program badly enough, they use *it*.

After 9 o'clock I have the set to myself. Takeo rarely watches; he studies. Most of the time I watch documentaries, and the news, of course. Not family dramas, they turn me off. Movies, often. I'm rarely in bed before 2. Five hours' sleep a night seems to be enough for me. I sleep very soundly. I know that that varies from person to person, but I can go to sleep in an instant. Everybody says it's an asset. Most people have trouble sleeping when they travel. I drop off almost the moment I sit down on a train or bus. I doze in meetings. I dozed on the train on my honeymoon.

But I'm very careful not to overeat. Blows me up like a balloon right away. Metabolism or whatever, I just don't seem to consume much energy. I really only eat dabs of food, but I still have more strength than I need, and sometimes wonder what to do with it. It annoys other people; they say I should eat what I can while I can still enjoy it. But if I eat much I soon feel it, for example when we are out on location and I am lugging equipment around. So I try to eat good food but in small portions. A little toast for breakfast. A light lunch with people from the studio. If

I come straight home from work, I have a few bites of whatever supper my mother-in-law has fixed that day. If we go drinking after work, I don't eat supper, just the snacks you have with your drinks.

My Dad liked his booze, and when I was young he often gave me a glass of beer or wine. I learned the taste of it early. Afterwards—in college—I discovered that I could guzzle all night and not get drunk. I never really have tested my capacity. I drink anything but prefer whiskey, because it doesn't go to fat. With beer you soon sprout a spare tire.

Takeo is a smoker, not a drinker. I've never so much as even wanted to try a cigarette. He gets uncontrollable if he runs out of cigarettes in the middle of the night. So I always have a pack hidden somewhere in the house. I hold him up for a good price for it. "Name it and I'll pay it," he'll say. Because otherwise he has to scrounge butts, and he finds that degrading.

I'm confident of my health and have never wanted to exercise. As a girl I played catch and badminton, but I just ain't the athletic type. When I play catch with my son, he snorts at me for being such a butterfingers. At first I was a little better than him, but he soon passed me by. I was sickly as a child and must have missed about a third of my classes in first grade. I didn't fully recover until third grade. But by middle school I was winning awards for perfect attendance.

My husband has always been weak and willowy. If anything, he frets about his health more than he needs to. But he's never been ill in the years we've been married, and I'm grateful for that. However, he is starting to harp about my needing a thorough examination. My mother died of uterine cancer in her early 40's, and I'm 38 now. I'll soon be in the "cancer age." The whole family has begun talking about it. My Dad won't say anything to me directly but he says to Takeo, "Tell her it's time she went for a checkup."

Futures

To be honest about it, I haven't given much thought to old age yet. I expect to go on working until 55, since age makes no difference in the kind of work I do. After that I'll do as I please—travel, whatever. A while ago I was talking about it with one of the women in the studio, and she said, "That's all very well for you, sweetie, you have a family. I'd have to take another job, because I couldn't live on the retirement pay." She's single. That set me to ruminating. They say you are old at 55, but if the lifespan is over 70, then 55 is still young. So maybe I *would* take up another line of work. But I'd want it to be more creative. Maybe I could study mass communications theory and teach it in college.

It occurs to me that the media are at their most stagnant now. That they have hit a plateau, technologically as well as otherwise. Therefore the search for new ideas is the most important challenge we face. But bureaucratization is holding everybody back. Nobody volunteers new ideas. Suggestions are always being solicited, and seldom offered. Sometimes it seems hopeless. They all seem to have dried up. When you have so little time for study or for self-cultivation, you don't come up sparkling with new thoughts. You go on doing what you did before, or worse yet you do what your predecessor used to do.

Think about the "Overseas Report" programs. A team is put together for a quickie trip, goes out and looks around, and rushes home on a tight schedule. Instead, I'd really like to take a team for two or three years, not just point the camera at the superficial things a tourist can see, but make a long study of how people in that country really live, how they raise their kids. But in the first place, the administrators never even have women in mind when they're drawing up the roster for an overseas assignment. And in the second place, what I have in mind could not be done alone. You need a team. And there is just no way to organize an all-woman team; we don't have enough women who are qualified to handle the cameras and equipment.

That means the team would have to include men. And you know how Japanese are about that, fretting about peculiar questions. "It would be uneconomical, because you would need separate hotel rooms." A male team will all jam themselves into one hotel room. I don't think that my idea is totally out of the ball-park, but it has to wait. I'll be bringing it up again and again.

I've never gotten involved in politics or in movements, only in the union. I've been helping circulate petitions for more public day-care centers, but that campaign hasn't been a signal success so far. Naturally, the network doesn't want its people embroiled in anything very political. They never say outright that you can't do it, but they do make it clear that you must not "engage in conduct unbecoming an employee of the corporation." We have had reporters arrested while covering a demonstration, and the network has furloughed them just for being booked by the police. Not convicted, mind you, merely written up on suspicion of wrongdoing.

I always draw laughs when I say it, but I want to focus my energies on something that will help liberate women. I'm willing to try just about anything that makes good sense. But I can't seem to decide what that might be. Will I maybe know better when I'm a few years older?

I buy just about every book published that has anything to do with women's issues, and I've read most of them. I'm not trying to claim that women are somehow better, but I *am* saying that I would be very bitter to have had to give up on them. To want to be like a man is incredibly irresponsible, as far as I'm concerned. To remain a woman, and still be able to raise the quality of life for the rest—this is what I want to do.

IV. DILEMMAS OF LEARNING AND ACTION

It is a human commonplace that in our adult years we tend to become more conservative. Most Hanshin interviewees acknowledged this to be so in their own experience. As we become engaged in roles of responsibility in the wider society, embedded in a convoy of our own making, we find ourselves both checked and balanced by those around us. Drastic change becomes difficult. Tomoko is the rule-proving exception. In the course of her adult years, she has come to hold increasingly liberal and reformist views about society, and to be increasingly disturbed by the gap between what she has learned and the changes she would like to see enacted.

This gap was not forced open suddenly by ideological conversion. Tomoko does hold a broad-gauge commitment to the cause of women's liberation, but she had already been inclined in that direction by the democratic tenor of her schooling in the early postwar years. It coincided with and mutually reinforced her Honor Student determination to follow a professional or artistic career at whatever cost to her personal life.

Feminist writers of the past decade have helped her sharpen her understanding of the issues. But her growing impulse to *act* has been brought on by her own real-world learning. Bias and discrimination have curbed her career development—though she recognizes that few women in Japan have had her opportunities. (It was like winning a lottery to be hired by a commercial radio and television network.) Tomoko has had 15 years of postgraduate "adult education" in women's issues, just as Akiko had a two-year crash course in practical gerontology. These things have become part of her, *mi ni tsukete iru*, which translates literally as "attached to one's being."

In *A Man in Ecstasy*, the authoress accounts for Akiko's need to work in social or economic terms. Raised by a widowed mother, Akiko could not hope to go to college but had to earn a living as soon as possible. Tomoko, on the other hand, was under no such pressure. Her parents could support her through college and until marriage. But as she herself is well aware in retrospect, her childhood convoy impelled her toward a working career for reasons of self-identity and emotional stability.

Restriction and Reaction

The offspring of embattled parents, she reacted by being sickly, introverted, secretive. Adults and peers became standoffish; uncles and aunts never made a pet of her; schoolmates never gave her a nickname. All the while, she devoted herself to schoolwork and to piano practice, and by middle school she was gaining confidence. Scholastically, she could perform as well as any of the boys, and she attended classes religiously. She struck up a friendship that she has retained to this day. And though her mother pushed her to prepare to become a normal woman, her father pushed equally hard for her to cultivate her intellect. By high school, Tomoko could stand against her mother and vow that she would marry for love or not at all.

The first time she took college entrance examinations she failed, but she forced herself to cram for another year and succeeded on the second try. Her confidence and determination had been confirmed.

Tomoko was a serious student in college—perhaps too narrowly so, she now wonders. But she was competing directly in a men's game. At the same time, she was becoming more outgoing, sociable. Her daring and her determination were what first attracted the young man whom she eventually married, he told me, and added, "They still do." And perhaps the network executives were also responding to these characteristics when they ordered her to train to become a program producer.

Her expectations about the mass media may have been unrealistic. She had hoped for encouragement in developing her creative talents—she already had buried the idea of becoming a musician. She trusted the judgment of others who said that the commercial networks would be likely to support talent. But after three years she began to harbor doubts. Nonetheless, the work is far from boring: Tomoko continues to read widely in topics related to the programs she produces, and to deal with people from many sectors of society. She sends 300 New Year's cards each year to her roster of professional contacts. And as a producer she has developed a "command posture."

But restrictions increasingly grate upon her. Why are some topics so unthinkingly tabooed? Why is the network so skittish about airing controversy? As the organization has expanded, bureaucratization has set in. Executives are transferred routinely every two or three years, to the detriment of continuity in the Osaka studios. And in order to be reimbursed for the cost of professional books, one has to fill out absurdly complicated forms.

Women in particular labor under disadvantages that are not easy to explain or justify. They are expected to be happy with the arts-and-crafts and cooking shows, and are not allowed to bid for responsibility for the more challenging programs. Almost never are they given consideration for overseas assignments. And though the network has many female employees, the majority are secretarial staff or are yes-yes girls who stand alongside male announcers and emcees. The production staff today includes even fewer women than it did ten years ago, those who quit having been replaced by men.

Tomoko has become more active in the employees union. But that too can be frustrating. The union is sapped by factionalism. Members band together only on economic issues, and only then in safely ritualized "struggle" campaigns that disrupt the studio but never actually shut down broadcasting. And the union never disputes the network's stand on political or social issues.

The network discourages political action on the part of its employees, and Tomoko has not been willing to jeopardize her job by becoming openly involved with campaigns or with feminist groups—though she has helped circulate petitions for more daycare centers. Even these small tokens of action, however, are unsettling to her husband, he told me. Open assertiveness could compromise the femininity that Tomoko has so far taken pains to preserve.

She is not ready to risk being fired, though she is confident that she could open a practice as a freelance commentator. That, however, would cut her off from access to the production facilities of a major network. But neither is she ready to accept an administrative position within the network. That would bring pressure on her to soften or even abandon her hard-won political consciousness; she might end up being just another tool of the establishment —like most of the men. She might have power as an executive, but would probably, she fears, become overladen with worries, worn into an early collapse of creative vitality. To become like a man is irresponsible.

And executives cannot refuse being transferred to other stations. As a producer, she has been allowed to remain in Osaka. Takeo will not even discuss the idea of living apart for career reasons. But it is easier for him, because he probably never would be tempted to move from the research laboratory that employs him. Stepping onto the administrative ladder would almost surely mean stepping out of her marriage. And that is a price Tomoko is not willing to pay.

Partnership

A woman who wants to combine family and working careers must be as careful about partners as about pathways. Tomoko herself commented one day that had she married a typical salary man, subject to frequent transfer, their joint careering might not have survived. It also matters a great deal how effectively the two careers are joined in the rub of daily living. As Rhona and Robert Rappaport conclude in their study of dual-career marriage in England, "The way the couple integrate their work situations is as important as the characteristics of their jobs *per se*."

Both Tomoko and Takeo speak of the tension—mingled with excitement—that goes with evolving a lifestyle out of the ordinary. Like Tachibana Akiko, Tomoko must set aside part of the weekend for "family service," for shopping and meal preparation. But Akiko is the superwoman, managing the house single-handedly. Tomoko has trained Takeo to share the chores in cleaning, child care, and some of the cooking. (Nonetheless, he said to me, doing housework is a "psychological burden" on Japanese males.) She will act the role of the servile wife when he entertains guests at home—as she did when I was there to interview him. He in turn silences parental grumbling about the fact that she is not around the house constantly, as a "junior wife" should be.

Tomoko would prefer to live in a modern apartment that she could decorate to her taste. But that would mean paying rent, and forcing their son to become a "key child"; i.e., he would have to carry a key and come home from school to empty rooms instead of to his grandmother. So they live in the grandparental house, defining the arrangement as one of mutual convenience. Takeo's elder brother, now living in Yokohama, is officially heir to the household line. It's a *give-and-take* situation, Takeo said to me, using the English phrase.

Takeo's emotional support is also crucial to Tomoko. Aside

from her father, people in her convoy still do not seem to have fully accepted her life choices, preferring to invoke the conventional wisdom. Her son wonders why she cannot be at home, as are the mothers of all his playmates. Distant kin ask—indirectly —if Takeo is in a poorly paid line of work (so that she has to supplement his income). When classmates meet her, they say, "Are you still with that TV studio?" in a tone implying that she should have settled down as a housewife long ego.

Tomoko and Takeo have evolved an enriching companionship. They share tastes and talents in classical music, and a general compatibility in lifestyles—aside from the issue of getting new furniture. They enjoy arguing social policy with each other. They share a history of having reacted against parental marriages that they perceived as loveless contracts. Tomoko set her life course against a mother who wanted her to follow the traditional woman's route. Takeo struck out on a research career contrary to paternal demands that he become a financier. Though Tomoko is attracted to male colleagues in the network, guilt tugs at her when she sees her man of a dozen married years going off to buy his breakfast on his way to the laboratory.

She gropes for words to classify her family situation. She is not satisfied with trendy phrases for cohabitation; theirs is a regular marriage. Nor is she comfortable with older and slightly pejorative terms such as *tomo-kasegi* ("making a living together") or *tomo-bataraki* ("working together"). Perhaps the vocabulary of friendship (*tomo-dachi*) comes closest. Tsuneo is a "junior" friend and Takeo her "best" one.

Tomoko at 38 is a self-assured professional who has sustained a family and retained her femininity. Like Goryōhan, she can look back over a strong line of continuity extending across her years since she was a schoolgirl, though the two women have moved in different directions.

Doubts and dilemmas arise not because of the course Tomoko has taken, nor because she has succeeded in it, but because that very success has brought with it an acute awareness of contradictions in Japanese social policy, in gender roles, in large-scale institutions. Because of her new knowledge, she feels pressed to act. And because of her attachments to family *and* to her profession, she counsels herself to study the situation a little longer.

I called on her briefly some months later at home. The decor and furniture were as I had remembered them, although a new stereo set of massive proportions had invaded what had once been a wall of bookshelves. Tomoko looked the same, and was friendly but not very talkative. In the intervening months she had been in Eastern Europe for ten days with a film crew—though the network still balked at the idea of allowing her to organize a long-term expedition. She had turned down an offer of an executive position in Tokyo because it would have meant moving from Osaka for at least two years—though she would have been in the network's head office. And she and Takeo had been go-betweens for the marriage of one of the junior men in his laboratory.

CHAPTER 7

Rescuing Maturity

I was reminded of a remark of Willa Cather's, that you can't paint sunlight, you can only paint what it does with shadows on a wall. If you examine a life, as Socrates has been tediously advising us to do for so many centuries, do you really examine the life, or do you examine the shadows it casts on other lives? Entity or relationships?

WALLACE STEGNER, *The Spectator Bird*

Victimage and Growth

The image of the victim of history is fashionable in our day. It is an image that must be cast with caution. Pressed by a Japanese reporter to say something newsworthy about the prewar generation—whose representatives I had interviewed—I remarked offhand that they are perhaps victims of history. That Japan's defeat in the Pacific War had robbed them of their primary pathways to pure action. That the defeat forced men to wonder what to do with their impulses toward dying for the sake of the Emperor—as it did for Shōji. And women what to do with their impulses toward "dying" for the sake of the family—as it did for Tomoko.

The remark was duly printed. Some of my interviewees read it —and at once rejected the thought. To accept the pity of victimage, they were reminding me, would be to demean the effort they had put into overcoming history's dislocations. Yes, they were indicating, we have had to abandon some pathways. We have been tossed around by society. But we accept responsibility for our lives; we own up to what we have become, and we have outgrown earlier formulations as honor students, spoiled daughters, playboys, suicide cadets. Biographical growth, for all its pains and failures and dilemmas, has been a counterfoil to historical atrophy.

Seduced by media attention, I had forgotten the first rule of fieldwork: your informants know their own lives better than you can ever hope to. Worse, I had momentarily lost sight of the very process I was attempting to understand: the mysteries of mastery, the long engagements in the "real" world that are so essential to the maturing of human sensibilities. As often happens, others had to show me my error.

It is true that none of Japan's postwar pathways to mastery has been elevated to national orthodoxy, or polished to the luster of the pathways the prewar generation were taught in their early years. But I have tried to show, through life histories, how men and women have come to have greater confidence in their actions, greater capacity for self-direction, greater ability to nurture those around them. Healthy people in their middle years, they no longer need to cling tightly to early models of growth. They have become journeymen, if not masters, in the craft of fabricating their own biographies. And perhaps it is this, more than historical pity—or even historical glory—that is the greatest strength one can draw from the long years of adult engagement in the real world.

The craftsman in me wants to end the story there, on an encouraging note. The fieldworker in me, having presented four autobiographies set amid the tensions of their time and place, wants to rest. The poet in me, having set these autobiographies off against symbolic homologues in literature, wants to celebrate the mystery of maturity. The scholar in me, however, recognizes another duty: to attempt to rescue maturity from the stereotyping impulses (as reflected in my remark to the reporter) that would explain maturity only by reducing it to something else. There is always risk in probing into mysteries, but we must take that risk if we want to make better sense of long-term human growth, of rhetorics of maturity as cultural and existential phenomena. The reward may be that we will come to know better how to cope with the issues of mass longevity—which is to say mass potential for long engagements—in our world of alienating institutions and superstates.

The Individual and the Personal

My case materials are from Japan, since that is the non-Western corner of the world I happen to know best. Naturally, I hope that these cases have brought home a new appreciation of post-industrial humanity as it appears in its Japanese guise. I will have failed, though, if you conclude by seeing in these autobiographies only what is "Japanese." For I have tried to present not only the cultural but also the existential dimensions of their long engagements. Through the format of ethnography, I have been arguing by example that we need to reconsider our root ideas about the time-warped nature of adult human growth and mastery, particularly as regards our ideas about the self and about intimate relationships.

"There may be wide differences in what is conceived as possible," writes Helen Merrill Lynd in *On Shame and the Search for Identity*, "according to whether one starts with the assumption of separate individuals and then considers how they may be linked together, or starts with the assumption of related persons and then considers how they may develop individuality within the group."

Both dimensions, the individual and the personal, are part of the human condition everywhere. We are born individual: separate organisms each biologically unique. We grow jointly: each in the company of others mutually tending the wild genetic pulse, as we domesticate ourselves along pathways marked out for us by the vision of our group's heritage. In a manner of speaking, we grow as *persons* by feeding upon nourishing symbols (ethnology's "life-giving myths") and upon nurturing others (the "significant others" of social psychology and psychiatry). Any explanation of maturity will be skewed to the extent that it is based upon the idea of the monad individual to the neglect of the social person. But the heritages of thinking in the East and West have started from these contrasting assumptions, and this contrast makes for difficulties in any East–West dialogue about maturity. Each side tends to misperceive the other's archetype of growth, and we end by talking past one another.

I am not referring here to the tumble of everyday conduct, to the moment-to-moment ad hoc situations of being. There, East or West, we have no option but to deal simultaneously with our existence as individuals and our existence as social persons. I refer rather to trunklines of thinking abstracted from the moment, crystallized into common sense, concretized into philosophical postulates and folk archetypes. Let me sharply overstate the differences in order to make my point plain.

In the Western view, individuality is God-given ("endowed by their Creator . . ."). The seeds of its manifestation are already present at the moment of impregnation. We are "born free." We enter society out of concession to animal weakness and practical need. But social participation can only diminish us; our highest self is realized in peak experiences that take us out of the ruck of society. Our cultural nightmare is that the individual throb of growth will be sucked dry in slavish social conformity. All life long, our central struggle is to defend the individual from the collective.

Viewed through this lens, Japan appears deficient. Failing to find many cues of "individualism" in the Japanese milieu, we project its opposite. We see a "collectivism," variously characterized by different observers as anti-individual, sociocentric, sociotaxic, or sociocultic. Japanese as individuals are said to have "weak and permeable ego boundaries," or a "submerged" sense of self, or not even any "real" sense of self at all. Put in historical perspective, Japan is conceded to be modern in technology and in democratic institutions, but is said to be, still, in an "incomplete transition," since Japanese as individuals are not "psychologically modern."

To the extent that they alert us to differences, clichés about the submerged self and its sociocentrism should not be seen as simply wrong. But they block the way to a positive understanding of the differences. If we content ourselves with the clichés, we understand only that the Japanese view does not give all the attention we think it should to the growth of humans as individuals. We fail to understand that our own inherited view may not give all the attention it should (many Japanese would say it should) to the growth of humans as social persons. Downplaying others, we diminish ourselves as well.

Stated positively, the Japanese archetype of growth looks more to "personality"—I use the word here not in its psychological meaning but in the sense of a capacity for human relationships. Perhaps this could be called a people-centered worldview; it is not "sociocentric" in the sense of being primarily attuned to society as an abstract structure of roles. In the Japanese view, we enter into relations with others not from animal weakness but for human strength. What is special about homo sapiens is its capacity for sentience and spontaneity, for tears and laughter. What is special about an individual is not that he uniquely "has" these capacities but what he "does" with them. The lifelong struggle is to carry out one's responsibilities to others without diminishing one's playful responsiveness toward them. The Japanese cultural nightmare is to be excluded from others, for this renders one unable to do anything with his "personality."

Exclusion is depersonalization. One can no longer give or receive the nourishment of personal attention. This need for "personality" transcends mere physical death. In the Japanese heritage (as in many parts of the world outside the West), death does not dispatch us to a distant universe. The departed remain here spiritually, able to continue their daily rapport with family and friends. Exclusion, in a manner of speaking, is a fate worse than death. For without a circle of intimates to attend to it, one's human integrity is in peril, here and beyond.

These cultural differences in archetypes of growth can be shown to result in measurable differences in conduct. Consider two examples, both from recent studies contrasting Americans and Japanese. The first of these studies asked about reasons that are given, in Japan and the United States, for involuntarily placing a person in a mental hospital. What types of behavior proved so threatening to others? The array of reasons is broadly similar in the two societies. But Americans will cite, much more often than Japanese, "bizarre ideas" or "cognitive disorientation" as cause enough for hospitalization. Japanese, on the other hand, will more often report that "aggressive action" proved too upsetting, particularly aggression toward family members.

In the second study, men in Japan and in the United States were asked to rank 18 values items (e.g. equality, pleasure, wisdom) in order of importance to them. Again, the cross-cultural similarities were many: for example, "a world at peace," "family security," and "freedom" were among the top choices East and West. However, American men gave much higher priority than did Japanese men to "sense of accomplishment," "wisdom," "salvation," "national security." Japanese men, by contrast, gave higher rankings to "an exciting life," "mature love," "pleasure," and "true friendship."

The American archetype, in short, seems more attuned to cultivating a self that knows it is unique in the cosmos, the Japanese archetype to a self that can feel human in the company of others.

Why the West continues to selectively misperceive this Japanese archetype is a matter I can only guess at. Careful inquiry into the social sources of knowledge would be needed to settle the question. Our Enlightenment heritage, the ideology of individualism; our Judeo-Christian heritage, the theology of an immortal soul known only to God—these provide part of the bias. Fashions in scholarly theory may be another element. For more than a generation now, the concept of social structure, with its oversocialized view of the human "actor," has held sway. And perhaps the international political climate of the postwar years has added a fillip: Japan has been taking the role of the humbled loser, full of dependency and nonassertiveness toward the victors. How comforting, perhaps, to see the Japanese as deficient in individuality, or by our standards characterologically weak.

In the retrospect of a quarter-century, I find only one book that stands against the current: Ruth Benedict's *The Chrysanthemum and the Sword*. The book is most often categorized as a study of national character. And Benedict has been especially praised for coining the concepts of guilt-culture (the West) and shame-culture (Japan). However, her discussion of guilt and shame covers a total of four pages in a 300-page volume. And I am struck by how seldom she speaks of national character. Rather, her eye is upon character in the older sense of the word, as an outgrowth of long-term cultivation. Cultural idioms such as guilt or shame are crucial for understanding the particulars of the process in any human locale. And Benedict devotes whole chapters to an exposition of Japanese forms of self-discipline, self-respect, and the dilemmas of virtue brought on by an endless need to reconcile the claims of different circles of human attachment.

She gives social structure its due. She begins the book by calling attention to the importance in Japan of "taking one's station" and of "Japan's faith in hierarchy." But social-structuralism stops there. Hierarchy matters because it establishes the initial bargaining positions for human sociability. But the rest of the book is about the drama of sociability and how it shapes character along lines suggested by Japanese pathways—or what she calls "assumptions about the conduct of life." The end product is not the flabby ego of structuralism but a personal character strong enough to stand against society's ineluctable dilemmas of growth.

The trouble with the postwar image of Japanese conformism and the "submerged self" is that it can only explain how Japanese become more acculturated, more like one another. It is no help in explaining how, as they become more adept in their heritage, Japanese adults also become more individuated—which is what I have been at pains to show in these chapters. The conformity thesis confuses "personality" with individuality, and individuality with individualism. It tells more, I suspect, about Western nervous concern over the fate of individualism in a bureaucratic world than it does about Japanese concepts of the person.

Maturity as Cultivation

Can we step around this individualist bias and move toward a vision of maturity as the long-term product of mutual human cultivation? I have been trying to show that it may be possible to do so, and trying to suggest that in the course of doing so we shall be obliged to create a new approach in our human sciences, a new vocabulary of explanation. Such a vocabulary must hold in full view, must express effectively, the growth-giving tensions between a person and his heritage of pathways, and between a person and his life-defining convoy of others. The vocabularies we now have on hand do not do this half well enough. Rather, they operate as conceptual transformers, stepping down the voltage of the tension and sending it out instead into different circuits of human motion and emotion.

The vocabularies of psychology and psychiatry transfer the tensions to the circuits of inner mental integrity. There, adult integrity is reduced to a residue of infantile defensive battles. Time moves through persons, but only in a disguised reenactment of primal wars. A person has little hope of ever recovering from these early wounds of parent-image introjection. We grow chiefly in our capacity to deceive ourselves, and so to make our disguised motivations acceptable to our inner custodians of self-identity.

The vocabularies of anthropology and sociology, for their part, transfer the tensions to the circuits of outer collective integration. There, adult integrity is reduced to a property of role-performance. Role swallows biography, emptying persons of all inner substance but the knack for abiding by social norms. Experience, memory, awareness of being a self with a unique past: these vanish in the comic operas of a human barnyard. Persons move through time, but only in the masks of social conformity. We grow chiefly in the capacity to deceive others, and so to make our disguised conduct more acceptable to the outer custodians of social order.

Anthropology's concept of culture carries an embryonic view of cultivation, culture being the peculiarly human way to grow. But across this century my colleagues in anthropology have tended to push the dynamic of personal growth out to the peripheries of their field of vision. The British scholar E. B. Tylor first put the word "culture" into anthropology's lexicon a hundred years ago. Hoping to de-parochialize the Western world view, Tylor sought a term that would suggest that all codes of human life, even the most seemingly "savage" (as the nineteenth century liked to call them) are worthy of respect. Tylor borrowed a word that was then in high fashion in European humanism: culture, the learning and nurturing of those arts that liberate the best in the human potential. Out of its root meaning of a "tending of natural growth"—a meaning preserved today in words such as agriculture—the word had come, in the minds of men such as Matthew Arnold, to indicate a tending of *human* natural growth. Tylor used the word to suggest, by extension, that all codes of life carry a liberating, humanizing function.

Once taken into anthropological usage, however, the word was soon made plural. The new field of cultural anthropology was to be the study of cultures, of traditional ways of custom, of how growth is made standard in different societies. The humanizing functions, the vital tensions between a code and those who guide their lives by it, were set aside as improper topics for the value-free type of inquiry that was coming to be honored with the label of Science.

By the 1920's, a reaction set in against this stance among anthropologists in the United States. A line of inquiry, eventually to be known as the study of culture-and-personality, opened again the issue of the dynamic of human growth and maturity. In the writings of pioneers in the field, such as Ruth Benedict, Margaret Mead, and Edward Sapir, one reads a fresh awareness of the tensions between person and code—or, as Sapir once phrased it, of "the useful tyranny of the normal."

In the years that followed, however, the topic of long-term personal growth was pushed once more into the penumbras of anthropological curiosity. For students of culture-and-personality, the master problem was not biography but history: to explain historical continuity in the patterns of the normal code. How is it (they asked themselves) that a cultural code can remain much the same from generation to generation despite turnover in the personnel who "carry" it? In the Anthony Wallace phrase, at issue was the "replication of uniformity" across generations. That individuals are anything but uniform at birth, that persons become more unique as they age—this was never denied, but neither was it regarded as problematic.

The explanation for code continuity, put simply, was along the following lines. The early training of infants in any society was

assumed to be virtually uniform. Standardized treatment of infantile traumata, such as weaning and toilet training, would thus
transmit the baton of tradition to all infants in a standard way.
Thus all persons born and reared in that society would come to
share a modal personality, a basic pattern of inner traits. This
modal personality, like the Freudian unconscious, was assumed
to be timeless. So, as each generation would come into maturity,
it would duplicate the habits of its parents, and in turn would
instill the same habits in its offspring.

The study of culture-and-personality began with a lifespan perspective on human growth. This shrank in time to a near-obses-
sion with the study of child training. Growth after puberty was
dismissed as being superficial, not relevant Scientifically. Pushed
to extremes by enthusiasts, the line of argument lapsed into a
destiny-in-the-nursery philosophy that by the 1950's had brought
the whole subject into disrepute.

The idea of modal personality had become another in a long line
of isolating assumptions. Like Adam Smith's economic man, like
Marshall McLuhan's media man, like most concepts of "the individual," modal personality became a conceptual ballistic missile
launched across the human life course. Such a personality, once
launched, was never engaged with its culture's pathways; it already contained them within itself.

Maturity as Discourse

Under the banner of "lifespan development," recent thinking
in the human sciences has conspicuously dropped the ballistic-
missile image of maturation. Individuals are seen as reengaging
the cultural code again and again, in different ways and at different
stages of ontogeny. But lifespan-development studies continue
the earlier focus upon the modal. They follow the individual as an
entity through a linear sequence of stages and transitions, roles
and crises. By contrast, the view I am advocating calls for a focus
upon the *nodal*: upon human character as it evolves through the
long engagements of a web of intimate consociates.

In such an approach, we watch the play of experience and the
play of discourse about the meaning of that experience; and we

follow these across extended encounters and episodes. We see images of self being identified and ratified ("a selfish daughter"); and we follow these images as they are transformed, outgrown in favor of larger integrations ("a self-giving mother"). We try to discover order and pattern as they emerge from within the process, not as given by the fixities of a sequence of average or typical stages of growth.

Perhaps every personal identification, however trivial, has its developmental trajectory. Probably all of us have closets of selfhood we never open to others. The aim here is not to try to account for all such aspects of the person, but to deal with those core images of self that hold together a person's portfolio of identities. For it is these core images that we negotiate with our convoy across the years. Intimates may advance or retard our spark of life. They help us sustain hope for the uncertain promise of growth against the certain promise of change, loss, and death. They help us realize the meaning of life not just in the abstract and modal symbols of common sense, but in the concrete and nodal forms of authoritative biography.

It was George Herbert Mead who gave twentieth-century human science a vision of society as the product of collective discourse. Related currents of thinking appear in the more recent work of Clifford Geertz, Victor Turner, and others of a symbolist persuasion in cultural anthropology. However, it is from the social-rhetoric ideas of Kenneth Burke and Hugh Duncan that I derive most directly my notions of long engagements of maturity.

For Burke and Duncan, all of human life is a grand cosmos of discourse. To live is to engage in a never-ending courtship, an appeal to others and to oneself to act or think or feel in certain ways. We continually address audiences in order to motivate them, not merely to comment on how the world happens to look to us today. And as reflexive beings, able to receive the messages we are sending, we groom ourselves for action by the very acts with which we attempt to groom others.

This conception of rhetoric draws attention to praxis, to the forensic side of human togethering. It calls our attention to language *in use*, rather than to the semantics of meaning or the logics of classification. We utter identifications in order to persuade, because of the results we hope will flow therefrom (e.g. *Brother, can you spare a dime?*). Courtship thus, in the Burke-Duncan view, is partisan—we want it to lead to something. The literal truth of a statement may matter less than the results it can bring (I know you're not my brother, but I need the money).

Not that we always seek a specific reward (e.g. dimes). Often enough, the reward we want is acceptance, recognition of being. And this is particularly so in the rhetoric of maturity. We want other people very literally to come to terms with us over who we are and what we have become. For example, as a girl Goryōhan may not actually have been a spoiled daughter. Massive inquiry would be needed to verify the "objective" truth of the matter. What counts for her and her friends is that the "spoiled daughter" of her childhood serves them as an idiom of consensus. Goryō-han and her friends agree that she has matured over the last 20 years, and one way to express that agreement is to identify her as having once been a spoiled daughter.

Such identifications are properties, always open to dispute. We claim them, others struggle for them. People lie, cheat, bluff, collude. But claims become real only when validated mutually, and here arises the agony of long engagements. "Since we feel real to the extent that a significant other confirms or ratifies our self-image," writes a trio of psychiatrists, "and since this ratification will serve its purpose only when it is spontaneous, only an ideal case of human relatedness could be free from paradox." The future is always open. Our purposes in it must be identified. Thus the rhetorical courtship of maturity can never cease.

Convoys

We can fake identifications easily enough, at times even fake quite complicated role performances. The lives of great impostors show how this can be done by anyone with chutzpah. But as complex persons we crave confirmation that goes beyond particular identifications or roles. We want to be reassured about our whole portfolio of identities, about our core senses of being. For this, we especially need the life-confirming feedback that only consociates can provide. (A number of the most admired modern Japanese novels, such as Sōseki's *Kokoro* and Dazai's *No Longer Human*, portray what happens to men unable to elicit this kind of feedback.)

We can gain some sense of personal change or stability from all the small contacts that arise across the leading edge of our daily movement. Even the casual glances of strangers help us know where we are along life's trajectory. "You know you're getting on in years," Beisuke said to me one day, "when the girls start looking at you as if you're safe." But the most telling responses come from those who know us best.

The idea is scarcely new. A number of terms in modern circulation point up aspects of the phenomenon. Charles H. Cooley's "primary group" is perhaps the earliest and most widely known of these, followed by Harry Stack Sullivan's "significant others." Less familiar are Jules Henry's "personal community" or Helen Perlman's "vital role others." All such concepts emphasize the elements of closeness and interpenetration in core human relationships, the ways in which we literally build parts of our own identity into the lives of others. But these concepts finesse the elements of duration and cumulation, the time-depth needed for relationships of this quality to evolve. And it is these elements that I have tried to underline in these chapters by using the label "convoys," as a reminder of the long mutual engagements that maturity requires.

With a casual stranger, you may share only one idiom of identification, e.g. as buyer and seller. With a convoy member, you come to share many. The ability to switch, often rapidly, from one idiom to another in the relationship is what makes the bond so rich, allows it to incorporate duty, respect, affection, comradeship, a history of shared experience. Makioka Sachiko comments that her younger sisters are more like daughters to her, and at the same time are also her only true friends. Goryōhan comments that although it was not planned, she and Granny have become more like mother and daughter to each other than like in-laws. Convoy bonds, then, are multivocal: we can address each other in various idioms. We are not limited to the "givens" of a single role. We create whole batteries of roles together—cultivate each other as persons.

A convoy, furthermore, is not just audience for a Goffman-esque "encounter," witnesses to a "presentation of self." It has an investment in the longer-run "preservations" of that self. Our successes and failures echo in the lives of our convoy others. When Shōji lost the election for city council, for example, it unquestionably marked a turning point in his inner life and outer career. It was also a blow to his former pupils' idealism about politics. And it seems to have precipitated, or at least aggravated, his wife's somatic complaints. There are important senses in which our convoy creates us.

In dealing with long engagements, then, we must look not just at the change in an individual across life stages, but at the evolution of persons in whole clusters of relationships. Every member of our convoy embodies a mutual history of shared identifications and a stake in shared futures. If one partner is to make a marked change, the others must change in tune. Small wonder that such "conversions" may take periods of many years.

To each new meeting, intimates bring remembered selves. This double encounter with past and present identities is what can make reunions so poignant. We evoke multiple meanings in each other. And as we bundle along the symbols that carry these meanings, and use them repeatedly in varied settings and times, we further deepen their evocative powers. Here we realize our potential for meaning *more* to each other. In this way a convoy not only cultivates persons; it simultaneously cultivates meanings. And this is the lesson of Proust's madeleine—or Goryōhan's and Granny's humble morning Tea.

I have explicated a view of maturity as a rhetoric of long engagements among intimates. I have tried to show some of the dynamics of these engagements as they appear in four real and four fictional lives in modern Japan. And I have suggested a number of concepts—of cultural pathways, of convoys, of perduring self-images—that if given further articulation offer hope for a new vocabulary for the analysis of human aging. With better case records, with more imaginative testing of the concepts, we should, I believe, be able to extend the perspective to the whole time-warped course of human life. For the same rhetorical processes, in still larger orderings of orders of relationships, spread over all of our days and years.

A century ago, in defining the concept of "intelligent love" found in Jane Austen's novels, an anonymous critic called it "the Platonic idea that the giving and receiving of knowledge, the active formation of another's character, or the more passive growth under another's guidance, is the truest and strongest foundation of love." Mass longevity in our era would seem to make possible longer and longer engagements for the mutual expression of "intelligent love." Mass superstates and multinational enterprises, on the other hand, seem unwilling to rest until they have succeeded in depersonalizing our every human relationship. Here is the nub of our dilemma as persons who inhabit the planet in the twentieth and twenty-first centuries. And it is here that a consocial view of human maturity may have practical, and not merely academic, purpose. For such a view goes to the heart of our hopes for finding, for sustaining, in a graying world, ways by which we can continue to grow on one another.

Notes

Notes

The number that precedes each note is the page in text where the relevant material is to be found; there are no corresponding note numbers within the text itself.

Chapter One

1   The chapter motto comes from p. 253 of Edward Whitmont, *The Symbolic Quest*. New York: Harper Colophon Books, 1969.

3   On rhetoric as the art of identification, see Kenneth Burke, *A Rhetoric of Motives*. New York: Prentice-Hall, 1950.

5   I am using James Ware's translation of the famous life-cycle lines from the Confucian *Analects*. See p. 25 of Ware's study, *The Sayings of Confucius*. New York: Mentor Books, 1955.

5   For Erikson's concepts of generativity and integrity, see his *Childhood and Society*. New York: W. W. Norton, 1955.

5   For Robert White, see especially the concluding chapter of his *Lives in Progress*. New York: Holt, Rinehart and Winston, 1966.

5   Bernice Neugarten speaks of executive processes of personality on p. 98 of her essay "The Awareness of Middle Age," which appears as Chapter 10 of a collection of papers she edited under the title *Middle Age and Aging*. Chicago: University of Chicago Press, 1968. Her remark about conscious self-utilization occurs on p. 78 of her "Dynamics of Transition from Middle Age to Old Age: Adaptation and the Life-Cycle," *Journal of Geriatric Psychiatry* 4 (1970), 71–81.

7   The Robert Redfield phrase is from p. 56 of his *The Little Community*. Chicago: University of Chicago Press, 1955.

10 I have taken the episode from pp. 18–19 of Tanizaki Jun'ichirō, *The Makioka Sisters* (tr. Edward Seidensticker). New York: Alfred Knopf, 1957.

12 On zodiacal years and the recording of female births, see Koya Azumi, "The Mysterious Drop in Japan's Birth-Rate," *Trans/Action* 5 (May 1968), 46–68.

13 The passage from James Baldwin is quoted by Theodore Lidz on p. 458 of his *The Person: His Development Throughout the Life Cycle*. New York: Basic Books, 1968.

14 See Glen Elder, Jr., *Children of the Great Depression*. Chicago: University of Chicago Press, 1974.

Chapter Two

18   I have taken the chapter motto from p. 15 of Wright Morris, *The Territory Ahead*. New York: Harbrace Atheneum Books #37, 1963.

27   For Gail Sheehy's comments on her interviewees, see especially pp. 18–19 of her *Passages: Predictable Crises of Adult Life*. New York: E. P. Dutton, 1976.

34   For Oscar Lewis's books built around life histories, see *Five Families: Mexican Case Studies in the Culture of Poverty*. New York: Basic Books, 1959. *The Children of Sanchez*. New York: Random House, 1961. *Pedro Martinez: A Mexican Peasant and His Family*. New York: Random House, 1964. *La Vida: A Puerto Rican Family in the Culture of Poverty—San Juan and New York*. New York: Random House, 1966.

Chapter Three

38   Saigō's saying, used as the chapter motto, comes from p. 243 of Ivan Morris, *The Nobility of Failure: Tragic Heroes in the History of Japan*. New York: Meridian, 1976.

38   Sōshū's self-description appears on pp. 45–46 of Niwa Fumio, *The Buddha Tree* (tr. Kenneth Strong). Tokyo: Charles E. Tuttle, 1966.

43   The quotation on Sōshū's cowardice is from p. 90, and that on Mineyo's habits is from p. 33, of *The Buddha Tree*.

44   The quotation on despair and salvation is from p. 155, *The Buddha Tree*.

45   The passage on lack of courage is from p. 154, *The Buddha Tree*.

46   The lines on salvation and the self appear on pp. 249–50, *The Buddha Tree*.

47   Kurt Singer's phrase is from p. 108 of his *Mirror, Sword and Jewel: A Study of Japanese Characteristics*. New York: George Braziller, 1973.

48   I have taken the statement from p. 289 of Takie S. Lebra, "Compensative Justice and Moral Investment among Japanese, Chinese and Koreans," *Journal of Nervous and Mental Disease* 157, 4 (1973), 278–91.

49   Rohlen's remarks appear on p. 52 of his *For Harmony and Strength: Japanese White-Collar Organization in Anthropological Perspective*. Berkeley and Los Angeles: University of California Press, 1973.

50   On the difference between skill and "expertness," Ruth Benedict's discussion remains the most succinct and thoughtful. See Chapter 11 of her *The Chrysanthemum and the Sword: Patterns of Japanese Culture*. Boston: Houghton Mifflin, 1946.

51   For a discussion of how womanpower was utilized in Japan during World War II, see Thomas H. H. Havens, "Women and War in

Japan, 1937–45," *American Historical Review* 80, 4 (1975), 913–34.

52 Mishima's remark on the green snake is quoted by Harry Scott Stokes on p. 23 of his biographical study, *The Life and Death of Yukio Mishima*. Tokyo: Charles E. Tuttle, 1975.

70 Quoted from pp. 136 and 138 of Thomas Rohlen, "The Promise of Adulthood in Japanese Spiritualism," pp. 121–48 in Erik H. Erikson (ed.), *Adulthood*. New York: W. W. Norton, 1978.

75 From p. 7 of Everett Hughes, *Men and Their Work*. Glencoe, Illinois: Free Press, 1968.

Chapter Four

77 The chapter motto is taken from p. 87 of Sōseki's *The Three-Cornered World* (tr. Alan Turney). Tokyo: Charles E. Tuttle, 1968.

77 The only available English translation of Ishikawa's novel is a rather pedestrian one by Nakayama Kazuma. See Ishikawa Tatsuzō, *Resistance at Forty-eight*. Tokyo: Hokuseido, 1960. The sections I quote are my own translations from *Yonjū-Hassai no Teikō*. Tokyo: Shinchōsha, 1958.

79 The quotation from Mark Twain is taken from p. 204 of Evan Esar (ed.), *Dictionary of Humorous Quotations*. New York: Bramhall House, 1949.

80 The comment on weariness comes from pp. 173–74, and that on baldness from p. 13, of Ishikawa, *Yonjū-Hassai no Teikō*.

80 The ideas about saliva are from p. 63, and the remark on warped minds is from p. 44, of *Yonjū-Hassai no Teikō*.

81 The remarks on parenthood are from p. 137, and those on Faust's freedom are from p. 38, of *Yonjū-Hassai no Teikō*.

82 The quotation about age and options is from p. 118 of *Yonjū-Hassai no Teikō*.

84 The attitudes toward grandfatherhood are from p. 315 of *Yonjū-Hassai no Teikō*.

85 Saikaku's catalog is taken from pp. 59–60 of G. W. Sargent, *The Japanese Family Storehouse*. Cambridge, England: Cambridge University Press, 1959.

91 Figure 2 is redrawn from p. 43 of Mita Munesuke, *Gendai no Ikigai: Kawaru Nihonjin no Jinseikan*. Tokyo: Nikkei Shinsho #128, 1970.

92 The Asahi surveys underlying Figure 3 were reported in the daily *Asahi Shimbun* for November 21, 1972.

93 The survey on Kobe executives' habits was reported by the Kobe Shimbun Sha in its monthly research journal 55, issue #102, 1973.

102 For a full translation of the Imperial Rescript for Servicemen, see p. 706 of Theodore W. de Bary (ed.), *Sources of the Japanese Tradition*. New York: Columbia University Press, 1958.

117 Mita's study of attitudes toward history appears on pp. 125–29 of his *Gendai Nihon no Seishin Kōzō*. Tokyo: Kōbundō, 1965.

118 The phrase "homo tasteless" occurs in an unsigned article, "Tokaku

Mukiyō na Shōwa Hitoketa Otoko no Ikikata," *Gendai no Esupurii* 69 (1973), 153–61.

120 On the concept of terminal culture, see Katō Hidetoshi, "The Growth and Development of 'Terminal Culture,'" *The Japan Interpreter* 7, 3–4 (1972), 376–82.

Chapter Five

127 I have taken the chapter motto from p. 302 of Gail Sheehy's *Passages: Predictable Crises of Adult Life*. New York: E. P. Dutton, 1976.

128 The Tanizaki quotation is given on p. 6 of Noguchi Takehiko, "Time in the World of *Sasameyuki*," *Journal of Japanese Studies* 3, 1 (1977), 1–36.

130 The quotation is from p. 256 of Tanizaki Jun'ichirō, *The Makioka Sisters* (tr. Edward Seidensticker). New York: Alfred Knopf, 1957.

131 The passage on Taeko's mannerisms is from p. 189 of *The Makioka Sisters*.

132 The comments on Yukiko are from p. 288, *The Makioka Sisters*.

132 The section on friendship is from p. 256, and that on the sisters is from p. 288, of *The Makioka Sisters*.

134 Sachiko's explanation of what makes Taeko different is from p. 266 of *The Makioka Sisters*.

135 The quotation appears on p. 504, *The Makioka Sisters*.

136 The quotation is from p. 530, *The Makioka Sisters*.

136 Triloki Madan discusses the notion of "convoy" on pp. 243–46 of his *Family and Kinship: A Study of the Pandits of Rural Kashmir*. Bombay: Asia Publishing House, 1965.

137 For Jules Henry's concepts of idiosyncrasy and personality, see his "Personality and Aging, with Special Reference to Hospitals for the Aged Poor," Chapter 2 of his *On Sham, Vulnerability and Other Forms of Self-Destruction*. New York: Vintage, 1973.

137 Neugarten's remarks come from p. 16 of her "Personality Changes in the Aged," *Catholic Psychological Review* 3 (1965), 9–17.

166 Masuda's statement appears on p. 17 of his "Bride's Progress: How a *Yome* Becomes a *Shūtome*," *Journal of Asian and African Studies* 10, 1–2 (1975), 1–19.

Chapter Six

172 The chapter motto comes from p. 7 of Doris Lessing, *The Summer Before the Dark*. New York: Alfred Knopf, 1973.

172 This and other quotations are my rendering from Ariyoshi Sawako, *Kōkotsu no Hito* [A man in ecstasy]. Tokyo: Shinchōsha, 1972. This one is from p. 225.

175 The quotations on overprotectiveness are from p. 43 of *Kōkotsu no Hito*.

176 The quotation about attitudes toward women who work is from p. 94, *Kōkotsu no Hito*.

178 The exchange between Akiko and the attorney occurs on p. 70, *Kōkotsu no Hito*.

179 Akiko's reflections of what Shigezō's life means to her appear on p. 268, *Kōkotsu no Hito*.

180 Akiko's thoughts about long life occur on p. 202, *Kōkotsu no Hito*.

182 Everett Hughes's remarks on careers are taken from pp. 63 and 67 of his *Men and Their Work*. Glencoe, Illinois: Free Press, 1958.

183 The quotation on old age as a trap is translated from pp. 128–29 of *Kōkotsu no Hito*.

184 Akiko's reflections on conjugal aging are from p. 107 of *Kōkotsu no Hito*.

210 The comment on integrating conjugal work situations is from p. 280 of Rhona and Robert Rappaport, *Dual-Career Families*. Middlesex, England: Penguin, 1971.

Chapter Seven

213 I have taken the chapter motto from p. 162 of Wallace Stegner, *The Spectator Bird*. New York: Doubleday, 1976.

215 The Lynd quotation is from p. 159 of Helen Merrill Lynd, *On Shame and the Search for Identity*. New York: Harcourt, Brace, 1958.

217 The study of reasons for mental hospitalization is reported in William Caudill and Carmi Schooler, "Symptom Patterns and Background Characteristics of Japanese Psychiatric Patients," in W. Caudill and T. Lin, eds., *Mental Health Research in Asia and the Pacific*. Honolulu: East-West Center Press, 1969.

218 The study of rankings of values was carried out by Kusatsu Osamu, and is described on p. 105 of Part II of his "Ego Development and Sociocultural Process in Japan," [in English] *Keizaigaku Kiyō* 3 (1977), Part I, pp. 47–109, and Part II, pp. 74–128.

218 Ruth Benedict, *The Chrysanthemum and the Sword: Patterns of Japanese Culture*. Boston: Houghton Mifflin, 1946.

224 Quoted from p. 72 of Paul Watzlawick, John H. Weakland, and Richard Fisch, *Change: Principles of Problem Formation and Problem Resolution*. New York: Norton, 1974.

225 Sōseki Natsume, *Kokoro* (tr. Edwin McClellan). Chicago: Henry Regnery, 1957. Osamu Dazai, *No Longer Human* (tr. Donald Keene). New York: New Directions, 1958.

227 The anonymous critic was writing for *The North British Review* 72 (April 1870), pp. 129–52; the statement on intelligent love is given by Lionel Trilling on pp. 53–54 of his *Beyond Culture*. New York: Viking Press, 1965.